The 100 Most Influential
Writers
of All Time

The Britannica Guide to the World's Most Influential People

The 100 Most Influential Writers of All Time

Edited by J. E. Luebering, Manager and Senior Editor, Literature

Britannica Educational Publishing in association with Rosen Educational Services

Published in 2010 by Britannica Educational Publishing
(a trademark of Encyclopædia Britannica, Inc.)
in association with Rosen Educational Services, LLC
29 East 21st Street, New York, NY 10010.

Distributed exclusively by Rosen Educational Services.
For a listing of additional Britannica Educational Publishing titles, call toll free (800) 237-9932.

First Edition

Britannica Educational Publishing
Michael I. Levy: Executive Editor
Marilyn L. Barton: Senior Coordinator, Production Control
Steven Bosco: Director, Editorial Technologies
Lisa S. Braucher: Senior Producer and Data Editor
Yvette Charboneau: Senior Copy Editor
Kathy Nakamura: Manager, Media Acquisition
J. E. Luebering: Manager and Senior Editor, Literature

Rosen Educational Services
Jeanne Nagle: Senior Editor
Nelson Sá: Art Director
Matthew Cauli: Designer
Introduction by Chris Hayhurst

Library of Congress Cataloging-in-Publication Data

The 100 most influential writers of all time / edited by J. E. Luebering.—1st ed.
p. cm.—(The Britannica guide to the world's most influential people)
ISBN 978-1-61530-005-1 (library binding)
1. Authors—Biography. 2. Literature—Bio-bibliography. I. Luebering, J. E. II. Title: One hundred most influential writers of all time.
PN451.A15 2010
809—dc22
[B]

2009029207

Manufactured in the United States of America

On the cover: The influence of William Shakespeare, considered the greatest dramatist of all time, has spread far and wide and transcends the ages. *Getty Images*

Photo credits: p. 8 © www.istockphoto.com/Nick Schlax; p. 16 © www.istockphoto.com/Vetta Collection.

CONTENTS

Introduction	8
Homer	17
Aeschylus	22
Sophocles	26
Aristophanes	29
Gaius Valerius Catullus	31
Virgil	33
Imru' al-Qays	38
Du Fu	39
al-Mutanabbī	41
Ferdowsī	42
Murasaki Shikibu	45
Rūmī	46
Dante	51
Petrarch	55
Geoffrey Chaucer	58
Luís de Camões	62
Michel de Montaigne	64
Miguel de Cervantes	67
Edmund Spenser	73
Lope de Vega	76
Christopher Marlowe	78
William Shakespeare	80
John Donne	89
John Milton	93
Jean Racine	96
Aphra Behn	99
Bashō	100
Sor Juana Inés de la Cruz	103
Daniel Defoe	105
Jonathan Swift	108
Voltaire	111
Henry Fielding	114
Samuel Johnson	116

Johann Wolfgang von Goethe 119
Robert Burns 125
William Wordsworth 129
Sir Walter Scott, 1st Baronet 132
Samuel Taylor Coleridge 135
Jane Austen 138
George Gordon Byron, 6th Baron Byron 142
Percy Bysshe Shelley 145
John Keats 148
Aleksandr Pushkin 151
Victor Hugo 154
Nathaniel Hawthorne 158
Edgar Allan Poe 160
Charles Dickens 164
Robert Browning 168
Charlotte Brontë 171
Henry David Thoreau 175
Emily Brontë 177
Walt Whitman 179
Herman Melville 183
George Eliot 188
Charles Baudelaire 192
Fyodor Dostoyevsky 196
Gustave Flaubert 199
Henrik Ibsen 200
Leo Tolstoy 203
Emily Dickinson 206
Lewis Carroll 212
Mark Twain 215
Émile Zola 222
Henry James 224
August Strindberg 226
Oscar Wilde 229
Arthur Rimbaud 233

George Bernard Shaw 235
Anton Chekhov 238
Rabindranath Tagore 240
William Butler Yeats 243
Luigi Pirandello 246
Marcel Proust 249
Robert Frost 251
Thomas Mann 253
Lu Xun 256
Virginia Woolf 260
James Joyce 267
Franz Kafka 271
T. S. Eliot 275
Eugene O'Neill 278
Anna Akhmatova 280
William Faulkner 283
Vladimir Nabokov 286
Ernest Hemingway 289
John Steinbeck 293
George Orwell 295
Pablo Neruda 297
Samuel Beckett 300
Richard Wright 303
Eudora Welty 306
Naguib Mahfouz 308
Albert Camus 310
Aleksandr Solzhenitsyn 312
Jack Kerouac 316
Flannery O'Connor 319
Toni Morrison 321
Wole Soyinka 323
Sir Salman Rushdie 325
J. K. Rowling 327
Glossary 330
For Further Reading 332
Index 334

290

307

321

Introduction

Open a book—any book. In it you'll find words, of course, but look closely and you'll also find art, crafted, in detail, by a writer proud enough to sign his or her name to the work. In a book, or in any piece of writing, words are joined together at the whim of the author. Sentences are created, paragraphs and stanzas formatted, chapters built, and stories told. In a book or a poem, a play or a short story, everything is there, on the page, for a reason: To show, to tell, to convey a message. Most works of writing, quite simply, are meant for reading. The great ones, however, by the most talented and ingenious authors, are for study. In such works—*The Old Man and the Sea*, by Ernest Hemingway, *Moby Dick*, by Herman Melville, *Hamlet*, by William Shakespeare—it's the art one finds within that sets them apart from the rest.

So how is it possible to whittle down a list of influential writers—artists of the written word—to just 100 people? That's the challenge—making choices, based on the evidence, and to ultimately compile a reference that does its best to envelop world history and disparate cultures, varying values, and regional tastes. Many individuals included in this compilation, including the three mentioned above, are paradigms of English literature. Others, such as Sophocles, Aeschylus, and Aristophanes, hail from ancient Greece. Aleksandr Sergeyevich Pushkin, a Russian writer of the early 1800s, is a founder of modern literature in that country. Leo Tolstoy, also of Russia, was a novelist, essayist, and dramatist, and is most famous for his novel *War and Peace*, considered by many to be one of the greatest books ever put into print. The 13th-century Sufi poet Rūmī is known today as a musically influenced master on subjects like mysticism, love, and spirituality.

The sheer panoply of nationalities represented in this book, as well as variances in style and theme, brings up an interesting question. Can Lu Xun, the founder of modern Chinese literature and a huge influence on Communism in that country, rightfully be compared to someone like Emily Brontë, the English novelist who is remembered for writing one great masterwork, *Wuthering Heights*? Perhaps, but their spheres of influence are so different—Brontë's in the English-speaking world, Lu Xun's, for the most part, in China and the East—that a direct comparison would certainly be difficult. Writers are influenced by the places in which they live and the cultures in which they are steeped. They are all "greats," and they all have had influence on their respective readerships.

As the title of this book indicates, all those featured in this collection are influential. Through their work, they've reached out to the masses, touched the hearts and souls of millions, and left their mark on the world. But how exactly is influence defined in this case? Perhaps it's the ability of one person, through his or her writing, to change the way the world thinks. Jack Kerouac is a prime example. Kerouac, an American writer and the literary leader of the so-called Beat Generation, achieved instant fame when his second novel, *On the Road*, was published in 1957. Kerouac typed the book on one long scroll of paper. Written like a jazz piece, it seems spontaneous and improvised, a fluid and furious work of art that could almost be read in one long breath, cover to cover.

On the Road captures readers' imaginations, takes them for a ride, spins them around, and makes them dizzy. It paints a picture of America like no other novel before it. What's more, the book has dared countless readers to explore the world themselves, to take to "the road," either literally or in their imaginations, just like Sal Paradise, the book's narrator.

Perhaps a writer's influence is determined by timeless prominence, the ability to remain relevant hundreds of years after initial publication. Several of the authors in this book fit that bill, particularly Jane Austen. Her penned explorations of everyday life in middle-class England are timeless classics primarily because her characters have many of the same foibles, and become embroiled in many of the same situations, as contemporary citizens the world over in the present day.

Not only are Austen's books required reading in many school curriculums, but the author's works have permeated modern culture in a way she never could have predicted. Movies and television miniseries based on her novels have proved quite successful, and groups dedicated to the reading and discussion of Austen's work are virtually everywhere; national and regional chapters of the Jane Austen Society dot the globe. Several authors have paid homage to Austen by writing fictionalized accounts of her life or using the themes and style of her novels as the inspiration for their own narratives. This ability to sway audiences so deeply, and in so many ways, a century or more after the fact is arguably the very definition of influential.

Prize-winning authors, whose mastery of language and storytelling is acknowledged by prestigious literary organizations, may be considered highly influential as well. Toni Morrison is the author of the books *Song of Solomon*, (1977) which won the National Book Critics Circle Award for Fiction, and *Beloved* (1987), which won the Pulitzer Prize for Fiction. In 1993, Morrison became the first black woman to win the Nobel Prize in Literature.

But Morrison's influence extends well beyond awards and honours. In addition to her status as a best-selling author, she is also a teacher, lecturer, and activist. Her work in these arenas cannot help but inform her writing. Throughout her career, Morrison has delved into black culture and the black female experience in America. Through her novels, she has reached and influenced millions on a much more personal, socially conscious level. She's made readers think about issues facing society, about the implications of racism in America and the struggle that blacks and women—and black women in particular—continue to go through to secure their place in an often hostile world.

The same holds for Richard Wright, who brought protest fiction to the fore as an American literary movement. Protest fiction is that which tackles social injustice; in this case, racism. At a time when many publishing houses were reluctant to distribute books by or about blacks, Wright succeeded in getting first *Native Son* (1940), then *Black Boy* (1945), onto shelves and into readers' hands. Wright's success paved the way for future generations of black writers, which, in turn, helped strengthen the resolve of those in the civil rights movement.

With carefully crafted prose or a verse, a writer can influence individual allegiances, support or defame a political regime, or effect change by shedding light on an untenable situation. The Chilean poet Pablo Neruda is a case in point. In the beginning of his career, Neruda spoke of love and heartbreak, drawing heavily on his own romantic adventures and disappointments. After being named an honorary consul and being posted in Spain during that country's civil war, however, he denounced his early work and began to tackle more serious issues. The war in Spain polarized Neruda's political beliefs, which began to infiltrate his work. His poems soon took on the tenor of propaganda; he hoped to stir the masses into a patriotic fervour with simple yet lyric passages and sombre, sometimes anguished, imagery. Through his writing he became, in large part, the voice of the Chilean people.

Neruda's activist tendencies eventually got him into trouble, and he wound up fleeing his native country in 1948 to avoid prosecution for openly criticizing Chile's right-leaning president. He returned years later and is now considered by many to be among the most significant Latin American writers of the 20th century.

The outspoken and rebellious nature of Aleksandr Solzhenitsyn's writings brought the wrath of his country's government down on him as well. A soldier for the Soviet Union during World War II, Solzhenitsyn spent eight years in a prison camp for criticizing Joseph Stalin. He later turned his prison experience into his first novel, *One Day in the Life of Ivan Denisovich*, which was an immediate success. Buoyed by the reception that book received, he continued to write works of fiction that were thinly veiled criticisms of the Soviet way of life. The government tried to suppress his masterwork, *The Gulag Archipelago*, a historical narrative of the Soviet prison system that blends fiction with firsthand accounts by the author and other former prisoners. That book resulted in him and his family being expelled from the country.

Political climates change, however, and Solzhenitsyn returned to his homeland after the fall of the Soviet Union some 20 years after he was exiled. At that time he was welcomed as a hero and credited with foretelling the collapse of the Communist government.

When all is said and done, perhaps what makes a writer influential is simply the ability to entertain, to keep readers up at night, turning page after page, just so they can learn what happens next. After all, the books of J. K. Rowling do not masquerade as political commentary or allegory, nor do they have pretensions of winning the Nobel Prize in Literature—although several ardent fans have petitioned the Nobel committee on Rowling's behalf. No, instead Rowling's Harry Potter series is simply a tale well told, with a truly magical setting and characters that capture the reader's attention and affection. The one way in which Rowling's books wield strong influence is in getting children interested in reading again.

The truth is, influence can mean so many things and can be measured in so many ways. Those who read the works of any of the writers profiled in this book may very well discover an experience they've perhaps never had before. They might have their imagination sparked and be transported, however briefly, from the travails of the life they're living. An author's writing might, with its insight, highlight an injustice, leading readers to speak out themselves and demand an equitable resolution. Whatever the case, one can't read a work by authors such as those detailed here without being influenced in some way. That's the power of great writing. And that's the real reason we read.

HOMER

(flourished 9th or 8th century BCE?, Ionia? [now in Turkey])

Homer is the presumed author of the *Iliad* and the *Odyssey*. Although these two great epic poems of ancient Greece have always been attributed to the shadowy figure of Homer, little is known of him beyond the fact that his was the name attached in antiquity by the Greeks themselves to the poems. That there was an epic poet called Homer and that he played the primary part in shaping the *Iliad* and the *Odyssey*—so much may be said to be probable. If this assumption is accepted, then Homer must assuredly be one of the greatest of the world's literary artists.

He is also one of the most influential authors in the widest sense, for the two epics provided the basis of Greek education and culture throughout the Classical age and formed the backbone of humane education down to the time of the Roman Empire and the spread of Christianity. Indirectly through the medium of Virgil's *Aeneid* (loosely molded after the patterns of the *Iliad* and the *Odyssey*), directly through their revival under Byzantine culture from the late 8th century CE onward, and subsequently through their passage into Italy with the Greek scholars who fled westward from the Ottomans, the Homeric epics had a profound impact on the Renaissance culture of Italy. Since then the proliferation of translations has helped to make them the most important poems of the classical European tradition.

Early References

Implicit references to Homer and quotations from the poems date to the middle of the 7th century BCE. Archilochus, Alcman, Tyrtaeus, and Callinus in the 7th century and Sappho and others in the early 6th adapted

Homeric phraseology and metre to their own purposes and rhythms. At the same time scenes from the epics became popular in works of art. The pseudo-Homeric "Hymn to Apollo of Delos," probably of late 7th-century composition, claimed to be the work of "a blind man who dwells in rugged Chios," a reference to a tradition about Homer himself. The idea that Homer had descendants known as "Homeridae," and that they had taken over the preservation and propagation of his poetry, goes back at least to the early 6th century BCE.

It was not long before a kind of Homeric scholarship began: Theagenes of Rhegium in southern Italy toward the end of the same century wrote the first of many allegorizing interpretations. By the 5th century biographical fictions were well under way. The Pre-Socratic philosopher Heracleitus of Ephesus made use of a trivial legend of Homer's death—that it was caused by chagrin at not being able to solve some boys' riddle about catching lice—and the concept of a contest of quotations between Homer and Hesiod (after Homer, the most ancient of Greek poets) may have been initiated in the Sophistic tradition. The historian Herodotus assigned the formulation of Greek theology to Homer and Hesiod, and claimed that they could have lived no more than 400 years before his own time, the 5th century BCE. This should be contrasted with the superficial assumption, popular in many circles throughout antiquity, that Homer must have lived not much later than the Trojan War about which he sang.

The general belief that Homer was a native of Ionia (the central part of the western seaboard of Asia Minor) seems a reasonable conjecture for the poems themselves are in predominantly Ionic dialect. Although Smyrna and Chios early began competing for the honour (the poet Pindar, early in the 5th century BCE, associated Homer with both), and others joined in, no authenticated local

memory survived anywhere of someone who, oral poet or not, must have been remarkable in his time.

Modern Inferences

Modern scholars agree with the ancient sources only about Homer's general place of activity. The most concrete piece of ancient evidence is that his descendants, the Homeridae, lived on the Ionic island of Chios.

Admittedly, there is some doubt over whether the *Iliad* and the *Odyssey* were even composed by the same main author. Such doubts began in antiquity itself and depended mainly on the difference of genre (the *Iliad* being martial and heroic, the *Odyssey* picaresque and often fantastic), but they may be reinforced by subtle differences of vocabulary even apart from those imposed by different subjects. The similarities of the two poems are partly due to the coherence of the heroic poetical tradition that lay behind both.

Partly on the basis of the internal evidence of the poems, which is of some use in determining when Homer lived, it seems plausible to conclude that the period of composition of the large-scale epics (as distinct from their much shorter predecessors) was the 9th or 8th century, with several features pointing more clearly to the 8th. The *Odyssey* may belong near the end of this century, the *Iliad* closer to its middle. It may be no coincidence that cults of Homeric heroes tended to spring up toward the end of the 8th century, and that scenes from the epic begin to appear on pots at just about the same time.

Homer as an Oral Poet

But even if his name is known and his date and region can be inferred, Homer remains primarily a projection of the great poems themselves. Their qualities are significant of his taste and his view of the world, but they also reveal something more specific about his technique and the kind of poet he was. Homeric tradition was an oral one: this was a kind of poetry made and passed down by word of mouth and without the intervention of writing. Indeed Homer's own term for a poet is *aoidos*, "singer." Ordinary *aoidoi*, whether resident at a royal court or performing at the invitation of a town's aristocracy, worked with relatively short poems that could be given completely on a single occasion. These poems must have provided the backbone of the tradition inherited by Homer. What Homer himself seems to have done is to introduce the concept of a quite different style of poetry, in the shape of a monumental poem that required more than a single hour or evening to sing and could achieve new and far more complex effects, in literary and psychological terms, than those attainable in the more anecdotal and episodic songs of his predecessors.

The Poems

Even apart from the possibilities of medium-scale elaboration, the *Iliad* and the *Odyssey* exemplify certain of the minor inconsistencies of all oral poetry, and occasionally the composer's amalgamation of traditional material into a large-scale structure shows through. Yet the overriding impression is one of powerful unity.

The *Iliad*—consisting of more than 16,000 verses, which would have taken four or five long evenings, and perhaps more, to perform—is not merely a distillation of the whole protracted war against Troy. It is simultaneously an exploration of the heroic ideal in all its self-contradictoriness—its insane and grasping pride, its magnificent but animal strength, its ultimate if obtuse humanity. The poem is, in truth, the story of the wrath of Achilles, the greatest warrior on the Greek side, that is announced in its very first words. Yet for thousands of verses on end Achilles is an unseen presence. Much of the poetry between the first book, in which the quarrel flares up, and the 16th, in which Achilles makes the crucial concession of allowing his friend Patroclus to fight on his behalf, consists of long scenes of battle, in which individual encounters alternate with mass movements of the opposing armies. The battle poetry is based on typical and frequently recurring elements and motifs, but it is also subtly varied by highly individualized episodes and set pieces: the catalog of troop contingents, the formal duels between Paris and Menelaus and Ajax and Hector, Helen's identifying of the Achaean princes, and so on. Patroclus's death two-thirds of the way through the poem brings Achilles back into the fight. In book 22 he kills the deluded Hector. Next he restores his heroic status by means of the funeral games for Patroclus, and in the concluding book, Achilles is compelled by the gods to restore civilized values and his own magnanimity by surrendering Hector's body to King Priam.

The *Odyssey* tends to be blander in expression and sometimes more diffuse in the progress of its action, but it presents an even more complex and harmonious structure than the *Iliad*. The main elements include the situation in Ithaca, where Penelope, Odysseus's wife, and their young son, Telemachus, are powerless before her arrogant suitors as they despair of Odysseus's return from the siege of Troy, as well as Telemachus's secret journey to the Peloponnese for news of his father, and his encounters there with Nestor, Menelaus, and Helen. Odysseus's dangerous passage, opposed by the sea-god Poseidon himself, from Calypso's island to that of the Phaeacians, and his narrative of his fantastic adventures after leaving Troy, including his escape from the cave of the Cyclops, Polyphemus, follows. His arrival back in Ithaca, solitary and by night, at the poem's halfway point, is followed by his meeting with his protector-goddess Athena, his elaborate disguises, his self-revelation to the faithful swineherd Eumaeus and then to Telemachus, their complicated plan for disposing of the suitors, and its gory fulfillment. Finally comes the recognition by his faithful Penelope, his recounting to her of his adventures, his meeting with his aged father, Laertes, and the restitution, with Athena's help, of stability in his island kingdom of Ithaca.

Homer's influence seems to have been strongest in some of the most conspicuous formal components of the poems. The participation of the gods can both dignify human events and make them seem trivial—or tragic. It must for long have been part of the heroic tradition, but the frequency and the richness of the divine assemblies in the *Iliad*, or the peculiarly personal and ambivalent relationship between Odysseus and Athena in the *Odyssey*, probably reflect the taste and capacity of the main composer. The *Iliad* and the *Odyssey* owe their unique status to the creative confluence of tradition and design, the crystalline fixity of a formulaic style, and the mobile spontaneity of a brilliant personal vision. The result is an impressive amalgam of literary power and refinement. The *Iliad* and the *Odyssey*, however, owe their preeminence not so much to their antiquity and to their place in Greek culture as a whole but to their timeless success in expressing, on a massive scale, so much of the triumph and the frustration of human life.

AESCHYLUS

(b. 525/524 BCE—d. 456/455 BCE, Gela, Sicily)

Aeschylus, the first of classical Athens's great dramatists, raised the emerging art of tragedy to great heights of poetry and theatrical power. He grew up in the turbulent period when the Athenian democracy, having thrown off its tyranny (the absolute rule of one man), had to prove itself against both self-seeking politicians at home and invaders from abroad. Aeschylus himself took part in his city's first struggles against the invading Persians. Later Greek chroniclers believed that Aeschylus was 35 years old in 490 BCE when he participated in the Battle of Marathon, in which the Athenians first repelled the Persians. If this is true, it would place his birth in 525 BCE. Aeschylus's father's name was Euphorion, and the family probably lived at Eleusis (west of Athens).

Aeschylus was a notable participant in Athens's major dramatic competition, the Great Dionysia, which was a part of the festival of Dionysus. He is recorded as having participated in this competition, probably for the first time, in 499 BCE. He won his first victory in the theatre in the spring of 484 BCE. In the meantime, he had fought and possibly been wounded at Marathon, and Aeschylus singled out his participation in this battle years later for mention on the verse epitaph he wrote for himself. His brother was killed in this battle. In 480 BCE the Persians again invaded Greece, and once again Aeschylus saw service, fighting at the battles

Aeschylus, marble bust.

of Artemisium and Salamis. His responses to the Persian invasion found expression in his play *Persians*, the earliest of his works to survive. This play was produced in the competition of the spring of 472 BCE and won first prize.

Around this time Aeschylus is said to have visited Sicily to present *Persians* again at the tyrant Hieron I's court in Syracuse. Aeschylus's later career is a record of sustained dramatic success, though he is said to have suffered one memorable defeat, at the hands of the novice Sophocles, whose entry at the Dionysian festival of 468 BCE was victorious over the older poet's entry. Aeschylus recouped the loss with victory in the next year, 467, with his Oedipus trilogy (of which the third play, *Seven Against Thebes*, survives). After producing the masterpiece among his extant works, the *Oresteia* trilogy, in 458, Aeschylus went to Sicily again.

Aeschylus wrote approximately 90 plays, including satyr plays as well as tragedies; of these, about 80 titles are known. Only seven tragedies have survived entire. One account, perhaps based on the official lists, assigns Aeschylus 13 first prizes, or victories. This would mean that well over half of his plays won, since sets of four plays rather than separate ones were judged. According to the philosopher Flavius Philostratus, Aeschylus was known as the "Father of Tragedy."

Aeschylus's influence on the development of tragedy was fundamental. Previous to him, Greek drama was limited to one actor and a chorus engaged in a largely static recitation. (The chorus was a group of actors who responded to and commented on the main action of a play with song, dance, and recitation.) The actor could assume different roles by changing masks and costumes, but he was limited to engaging in dialogue only with the chorus. By adding a second actor with whom the first could converse, Aeschylus vastly increased the drama's possibilities for dialogue and dramatic tension and allowed more variety and freedom in plot construction. Although the dominance of the chorus in early tragedy is ultimately only hypothesis, it is probably true that, as Aristotle says in his *Poetics*, Aeschylus "reduced the chorus' role and made the plot the leading actor."

Aeschylus was an innovator in other ways as well. He made good use of stage settings and stage machinery, and some of his works were noted for their spectacular scenic effects. He also designed costumes, trained his choruses in their songs and dances, and probably acted in most of his own plays, this being the usual practice among Greek dramatists. But his formal innovations account for only part of his achievement. His plays are of lasting literary value in their majestic and compelling lyrical language, in the intricate architecture of their plots, and in the universal themes which they explore so honestly. Aeschylus's language in both dialogue and choral lyric is marked by force, majesty, and emotional intensity. He makes bold use of compound epithets, metaphors, and figurative turns of speech, but this rich language is firmly harnessed to the dramatic action rather than used as mere decoration.

Aeschylus is almost unequaled in writing tragedy that, for all its power of depicting evil and the fear and consequences of evil, ends, as in the *Oresteia*, in joy and reconciliation. Living at a time when the Greek people still truly felt themselves surrounded by the gods, Aeschylus nevertheless had a capacity for detached and general thought, which enabled him to treat the fundamental problem of evil with singular honesty and success.

The chronographers recorded Aeschylus's death at Gela (on Sicily's south coast) in 456/455, at age 69. A ludicrous story that he was killed when an eagle dropped a tortoise on his bald pate was presumably fabricated by a later comic writer. At Gela he was accorded a public funeral, with sacrifices and dramatic performances held at his grave, which subsequently became a place of pilgrimage for writers.

SOPHOCLES

(b. *c.* 496 BCE, Colonus, near Athens [Greece]—d. 406 BCE, Athens)

Sophocles, one of classical Athens's great tragic playwrights, was born in a village outside the walls of Athens, where his father, Sophillus, was a wealthy manufacturer of armour. Sophocles was wealthy from birth, highly educated, noted for his grace and charm, on easy terms with the leading families, and a personal friend of prominent statesmen. Because of his beauty of physique, his athletic prowess, and his skill in music, he was chosen in 480, when he was 16, to lead the paean (choral chant to a god) celebrating the decisive Greek sea victory over the Persians at the Battle of Salamis.

Marble portrait bust said to be of Sophocles. © Photos.com/ Jupiterimages

The relatively meagre information about Sophocles' civic life suggests that he was a popular favourite who participated actively in his community and exercised outstanding artistic talents. In 442 he served as one of the treasurers responsible for receiving and managing tribute money from Athens's subject-allies in the Delian League. In 440 he was elected one of the 10 *stratēgoi* (high executive officials who commanded the armed forces) as a junior colleague of Pericles. Sophocles later served as *stratēgos* perhaps twice again. In 413, then aged about 83, Sophocles was a *proboulos*, one of 10 advisory commissioners who were granted special powers and were entrusted with organizing Athens's financial and domestic recovery after its terrible defeat at Syracuse in Sicily. These few facts, which are about all that is known of Sophocles' life, imply steady and distinguished attachment to Athens, its government, religion, and social forms.

Sophocles won his first victory at the Dionysian dramatic festival in 468, however, defeating the great Aeschylus in the process. This began a career of unparalleled success and longevity. In total, Sophocles wrote 123 dramas for the festivals. Since each author who was chosen to enter the competition usually presented four plays, this means he must have competed about 30 times. Sophocles won perhaps as many as 24 victories, compared to 13 for Aeschylus, and indeed he may have never received lower than second place in the competitions he entered.

Ancient authorities credit Sophocles with several major and minor dramatic innovations. Among the latter is his invention of some type of "scene paintings" or other pictorial prop to establish locale or atmosphere. He also may have increased the size of the chorus from 12 to 15 members. Sophocles' major innovation was his introduction of a third actor into the dramatic performance. It had previously been permissible for two actors to "double" (i.e., assume other roles during a play), but the addition of a third actor onstage enabled the dramatist both to increase the number of his characters and widen the variety of their interactions. The scope of the dramatic conflict was thereby extended, plots could be more fluid, and situations could be more complex.

The typical Sophoclean drama presents a few characters, impressive in their determination and power, and possessing a few strongly drawn qualities or faults that combine with a particular set of circumstances to lead them inevitably to a tragic fate. Sophocles develops his characters' rush to tragedy with great economy, concentration, and dramatic effectiveness, creating a coherent, suspenseful situation whose sustained and inexorable onrush came to epitomize the tragic form to the classical world. Sophocles emphasizes that most people lack wisdom, and he presents truth in collision with ignorance, delusion, and folly. Many scenes dramatize flaws or failure in thinking (deceptive reports and rumours, false optimism, hasty judgment, madness). The chief character does something involving grave error; this affects others, each of whom reacts in his own way, thereby causing the chief agent to take another step toward ruin—his own and that of others as well. Equally important, those who are to suffer from the tragic error usually are present at the time or belong to the same generation. It was this more complex type of tragedy that demanded a third actor. Sophocles thus abandoned the spacious Aeschylean framework of the connected trilogy and instead comprised the entire action in a single play.

Sophocles' language responds flexibly to the dramatic needs of the moment. It can be ponderously weighty or swift-moving, emotionally intense or easygoing, highly decorative or perfectly plain and simple. His mastery of form and diction was highly respected by his contemporaries. Sophocles has also been admired for the sympathy and vividness with which he delineates his characters; especially notable are his tragic women, such as Electra and Antigone. Few dramatists have been able to handle situation and plot with more power and certainty; the frequent references in the *Poetics* to Sophocles' *Oedipus the King* show that Aristotle regarded this play as a masterpiece of construction, and few later critics have dissented.

Sophocles is also unsurpassed in his moments of high dramatic tension and in his revealing use of tragic irony.

In one of his last plays, *Oedipus at Colonus*, he still affectionately praises both his own birthplace and the great city itself. Sophocles' last recorded act was to lead a chorus in public mourning for his deceased rival, Euripides, before the festival of 406. He died that same year.

ARISTOPHANES

(b. *c.* 450 BCE–d. *c.* 388 BCE)

Aristophanes is the greatest representative of ancient Greek comedy, and the one whose works have been preserved in greatest quantity. He is the only extant representative of the Old Comedy, that is, of the phase of comic dramaturgy in which chorus, mime, and burlesque still played a considerable part and which was characterized by bold fantasy, merciless invective and outrageous satire, unabashedly licentious humour, and a marked freedom of political criticism. But Aristophanes belongs to the end of this phase, and, indeed, his last extant play, which has no choric element at all, may well be regarded as the only extant specimen of the short-lived Middle Comedy, which, before the end of the 4th century BCE, was to be superseded in turn by the milder and more realistic social satire of the New Comedy.

Little is known about the life of Aristophanes, and most of the known facts are derived from references in his own plays. He was an Athenian citizen belonging to the *deme*, or clan, named Pandionis, but his actual birthplace is uncertain. (The fact that he or his father, Philippus, owned property on the island of Aegina may have been the cause of an accusation by his fellow citizens that he was not of Athenian birth.) He began his dramatic career in 427 BCE with a play, the *Daitaleis* (*The Banqueters*), which appears, from surviving fragments, to have been a satire on his contemporaries' educational and moral theories. He is thought to have written about 40 plays in all.

A large part of his work is concerned with the social, literary, and philosophical life of Athens itself and with themes provoked by the great Peloponnesian War (431–404 BCE). This war was essentially a conflict between imperialist Athens and conservative Sparta, and so was long the dominant issue in Athenian politics. Aristophanes was naturally an opponent of the more or less bellicose statesmen who controlled the government of Athens throughout the better part of his maturity. Aristophanes lived to see the revival of Athens after its defeat by Sparta.

Aristophanes' reputation has stood the test of time. His plays have been frequently produced on the 20th- and 21st-century stage in numerous translations, which manage with varying degrees of success to convey the flavour of Aristophanes' puns, witticisms, and topical allusions. But it is not easy to say why his comedies still appeal to an audience more than two millennia after they were written. In the matter of plot construction, Aristophanes' comedies are often loosely put together, are full of inconsequential episodes, and often degenerate at their end into a series of disconnected and boisterous episodes. Aristophanes' greatness lies in the wittiness of his dialogue; his generally good-humoured though occasionally malevolent satire; the brilliance of his parody, especially when he mocks the controversial tragedian Euripides; the ingenuity and inventiveness, not to say the laughable absurdity, of his comic scenes born of imaginative fantasy; the peculiar charm of his choric songs, whose freshness can still be conveyed in languages other than Greek; and, at least for audiences of a permissive age, the licentious frankness of many scenes and allusions in his comedies. Among his plays are *Wasps* (422 BCE), which satirized the litigiousness of the Athenians in the person of a mean and waspish old man who has a passion for serving on juries, and *Lysistrata* (411 BCE), in which the women of Athens seize the Acropolis and the city's treasury and declare a sex strike until such time as the men will make peace. *Lysistrata* achieves a mixture of humour, indecency, gravity, and farce that marks many of Aristophanes' plays.

GAIUS VALERIUS CATULLUS

(b. *c.* 84 BCE, Verona, Cisalpine Gaul—d. *c.* 54 BCE, Rome)

Gaius Valerius Catullus was a Roman poet whose expressions of love and hatred are generally considered the finest lyric poetry of ancient Rome.

No ancient biography of Catullus survives. A few facts can be pieced together from external sources and in the works of his contemporaries or of later writers, supplemented by inferences drawn from his poems, some of which are certain, some only possible. Catullus was alive 55–54 BCE on the evidence of four of his poems, and died young, according to the poet Ovid—at the age of 30 as stated by St. Jerome (writing about the end of the 4th century), who nevertheless dated his life erroneously 87–57 BCE. Catullus was thus a contemporary of the statesmen Cicero, Pompey, and Julius Caesar, who are variously addressed by him in his poems. He preceded the poets of the immediately succeeding age of the emperor Augustus, among whom Horace, Sextus Propertius, Tibullus, and Ovid name him as a poet whose work is familiar to them. Catullus owned property at Sirmio, the modern Sirmione, on Lake Garda, though he preferred to live in Rome and owned a villa near the Roman suburb of Tibur, in an unfashionable neighbourhood.

In a poem externally datable to *c.* 57–56 BCE, Catullus reports one event, a journey to Bithynia in Asia Minor in the retinue of Gaius Memmius, the Roman governor of the province, from which he returned to Sirmio. His poetry also records two emotional crises, the death of a brother whose grave he visited in the Troad, also in Asia Minor, and an intense and unhappy love affair, portrayed variously in 25 poems, with a woman who was married and whom he names Lesbia, a pseudonym (Ovid states) for Clodia, according to the 2nd-century writer Apuleius. (She may have been a patrician, one of the three Clodia sisters of Cicero's foe Publius Clodius Pulcher. All three were the subject of scandalous rumour, according to Plutarch.) His poems also record, directly or indirectly, a homosexual affair with a youth named Juventius.

Among his longer poems are two marriage hymns; one romantic narrative in hexameters (lines of six feet) on the marriage of Peleus with the sea goddess Thetis; and four elegiac pieces, consisting of an epistle introducing a translation of an elegant conceit by the Alexandrian poet Callimachus, followed by a pasquinade, or scurrilous conversation, between the poet and a door, and lastly a soliloquy addressed to a friend and cast in the form of an encomium, or poem of praise.

In his lifetime, Catullus was a poet's poet, addressing himself to fellow craftsmen (*docti*, or scholarly poets), especially to his friend Licinius Calvus, who is often posthumously commemorated along with him. The conversational rhythms of his poetry, as he managed them for lyric purposes, achieved an immediacy that no other classic poet can rival. For the general reader, the 25 Lesbia poems are likely to remain the most memorable, recording as they do a love that could register ecstasy and despair and all the divided emotions that intervene. Two of them with unusual metre recall Sappho, the poet of the Aegean island of Lesbos, as also does his use of the pseudonym Lesbia. The quality of his poems of invective, which spare neither Caesar nor otherwise unknown personalities, is uneven, ranging from the high-spirited to the tedious, from the lapidary to the laboured. But their satiric humour is often effective, and their obscenity reflects a serious literary convention that the poet himself defends.

VIRGIL

(b. Oct. 15, 70 BCE, Andes, near Mantua [Italy]—d. Sept. 21, 19 BCE, Brundisium)

The Roman poet Virgil, best known for his national epic, the *Aeneid* (from *c.* 30 BCE), was regarded by the Romans as their greatest poet, an estimation that subsequent generations have upheld. His fame rests chiefly upon the *Aeneid*, which tells the story of Rome's legendary founder and proclaims the Roman mission to civilize the world under divine guidance.

Early Life

Virgil, whose Latin name was Publius Vergilius Maro, was born of peasant stock. He was educated at Cremona, at Milan, and finally at Rome, acquiring a thorough knowledge of Greek and Roman authors, especially of the poets, and receiving a detailed training in rhetoric and philosophy.

During Virgil's youth, as the Roman Republic neared its end, the political and military situation in Italy was confused and often calamitous. The civil war between Marius and Sulla had been succeeded by conflict between Pompey and Julius Caesar for supreme power. When Virgil was 20, Caesar with his armies swooped south from Gaul, crossed the Rubicon, and began the series of civil wars that were not to end until Augustus's victory at Actium in 31 BCE. Hatred and fear of civil war is powerfully expressed by both Virgil and his contemporary Horace.

Virgil's life was devoted entirely to his poetry and studies connected with it. His health was never robust, and he played no part in military or political life. It is said that he spoke once in the law courts without distinction and that his shy and retiring nature caused him to give up any ideas he might have had of taking part in the world of affairs. He never married, and the first half of his life was that of a scholar and near recluse. But, as his poetry won him fame, he gradually won the friendship of many important men in the Roman world.

Literary Career

Virgil's earliest certain work is the *Eclogues*, a collection of 10 pastoral poems composed between 42 and 37 BCE. Some of them are escapist, literary excursions to the idyllic pastoral world of Arcadia based on the Greek poet Theocritus (fl. *c.* 280 BCE) but more unreal and stylized. One eclogue in particular stands out as having relevance to the contemporary situation, and this is the fourth (sometimes called the Messianic, because it was later regarded as prophetic of Christianity). It is an elevated poem, prophesying in sonorous and mystic terms the birth of a child who will bring back the Golden Age, banish sin, and restore peace. It was clearly written at a time when the clouds of civil war seemed to be lifting; it can be dated firmly to 41–40 BCE. It seems most likely that Virgil refers to an expected child of the triumvir Antony and his wife Octavia, sister of Octavian. But, though a specific occasion may be allocated to the poem, it goes beyond the particular and, in symbolic terms, presents a vision of world harmony, which was, to some extent, destined to be realized under Augustus.

One of the most disastrous effects of the civil wars—and one of which Virgil, as a countryman, would be most intensely aware—was the depopulation of rural Italy. The farmers had been obliged to go to war, and their farms fell into neglect and ruin as a result. The *Georgics*, composed between 37 and 30 BCE (the final period of the civil wars), is a plea for the restoration of the traditional agricultural life of Italy. It is dedicated to Maecenas, one of the chief of Augustus's ministers, who was also the leading patron of the arts. By this time Virgil was a member of what might be called the court circle, and his desire to see his beloved Italy restored to its former glories coincided with the national requirement of resettling the land and diminishing the pressure on the cities. It would be wrong to think of Virgil as writing political propaganda; but equally it would be wrong to regard his poetry as unconnected with the major currents of political and social needs of the time. Virgil was personally committed to the same ideals as the government.

In the year 31 BCE, when Virgil was 38, Augustus (still known as Octavian) won the final battle of the civil wars at Actium against the forces of Antony and Cleopatra. Virgil, like many of his contemporaries, felt a great sense of relief that the civil strife was at last over and was deeply grateful to the man who had made it possible. Augustus was anxious to preserve the traditions of the republic and its constitutional forms, but he was in fact sole ruler of the Roman world. He used his power to establish a period of peace and stability and endeavoured to reawaken in the Romans a sense of national pride and a new enthusiasm for their ancestral religion and their traditional moral values (bravery, parsimony, duty, responsibility, and family devotion). Virgil, too, felt a deep attachment to the simple virtues and religious traditions of the Italian people. All his life he had been preparing himself to write an epic poem (regarded then as the highest form of poetic achievement), and he now set out to embody his ideal Rome in the *Aeneid*, the story of the foundation of the first settlement in Italy, from which Rome was to spring, by an exiled Trojan prince after the destruction of Troy by the Greeks in the 12th century BCE.

The theme he chose gave him two great advantages. One was that its date and subject were very close to those of Homer's *Iliad* and *Odyssey*, so that Virgil could remodel episodes and characters from his great Greek predecessor. The other was that it could be brought into relationship with his contemporary Augustan world by presenting Aeneas as the prototype of the Roman way of life (the last of the Trojans and the first of the Romans). Moreover, by the use of prophecies and visions and devices such as the description of the pictures on Aeneas's shield or of the origins of contemporary customs and institutions, it could foreshadow the real events of Roman history.

The real greatness of the *Aeneid* is due to Virgil's awareness of the private, as well as the public, aspects of human life. The *Aeneid* is no panegyric; it sets the achievements and aspirations of the giant organization of Roman governmental rule in tension with the frustrated hopes and sufferings of individuals. The most memorable figure in the poem—and, it has been said, the only character to be created by a Roman poet that has passed into world literature—is Dido, Queen of Carthage, opponent of the Roman way of life. In a mere panegyric of Rome, she could have been presented in such a way that Aeneas's rejection of her would have been a victory to applaud. In fact, in the fourth book she wins so much sympathy that the reader wonders whether Rome should be bought at this price.

The *Aeneid* occupied Virgil for 11 years and, at his death, had not yet received its final revision. In 19 BCE, planning to spend a further three years on his poem, he set out for Greece—doubtless to obtain local colour for the revision of those parts of the *Aeneid* set in Greek waters.

Writing his famous work, the Aeneid, *allowed Virgil to honour his beloved city of Rome, express his views of events unfolding around him, and achieve his goal of writing an epic poem.* Time & Life Pictures/Getty Images

On the voyage he caught a fever and returned to Italy but died soon after arrival at Brundisium. Whether the *Aeneid* would have undergone major changes cannot be guessed. The story goes that Virgil's dying wish was for his poem to be burned, but that this request was countermanded by the order of Augustus.

IMRU' AL-QAYS

(d. *c.* 500 CE)

The Arab poet Imru' al-Qays was acknowledged as the most distinguished poet of pre-Islamic times by the Prophet Muhammad, by 'Alī, the fourth caliph, and by Arab critics of the ancient Basra school. He is the author of one of the seven odes in the famed collection of pre-Islamic poetry *Al-Mu'allaqāt*.

There is no agreement as to his genealogy, but the predominant legend cites Imru' al-Qays as the youngest son of Ḥujr, the last king of Kindah. He was twice expelled from his father's court for the erotic poetry he was fond of writing, and he assumed the life of a vagabond. After his father was murdered by a rebel Bedouin tribe, the Banū Asad, Imru' al-Qays was single-minded in his pursuit of revenge. He successfully attacked and routed the Banū Asad, but, unsatisfied, he went from tribe to tribe fruitlessly seeking further help. Through King al-Ḥārith of Ghassān (northern Arabia), Imru' al-Qays was introduced to the Byzantine emperor Justinian I, who agreed to supply him with the troops that he needed to regain his kingdom. Legend has it that on his return to Arabia the emperor sent him a poisoned cloak, which caused his death at Ancyra (modern Ankara).

The philologists of the Basra school regarded Imru' al-Qays not only as the greatest of the poets of the *Mu'allaqāt* but also as the inventor of the form of the classical ode, or *qaṣīdah*, and of many of its conventions, such as the poet's weeping over the traces of deserted campsites. The opening of the long *qaṣīdah* by Imru' al-Qays that appears in the *Muʿallaqāt* is perhaps the best-known line of poetry in Arabic: "Halt, you two companions, and let us weep for the memory of a beloved and an abode mid the sand-dunes between Al-Dakhūl and Ḥawmal."

The hunting scenes and bluntly erotic narratives by Imru' al-Qays in the *Muʿallaqāt* represent important early precedents of the genres of hunt poetry and love poetry in Arabic literature. There were at least three collections (divans) of his poetry made by medieval Arab scholars, numbering as many as 68 poems. The authenticity of the greater part of them, however, is doubtful.

DU FU

(b. 712, Gongxian, Henan province, China—d. 770, on a riverboat between Danzhou [now Changsha] and Yueyang, Hunan province)

Du Fu is considered by many literary critics to be the greatest Chinese poet of all time, rivaled in that designation only by his contemporary Li Bai.

Born into a scholarly family, Du Fu received a traditional Confucian education but failed in the imperial examinations of 735. As a result, he spent much of his youth traveling. During his travels he won renown as a poet and met other poets of the period, including the great Li Bai, the unofficial poet laureate to the military expedition of Prince Lin, who was arrested when the prince was accused of intending to establish an independent kingdom and was executed. After a brief flirtation with Daoism while traveling with Li Bai, Du Fu returned to the capital and to the conventional Confucianism of his youth. He never again met Li Bai, despite his strong admiration for his freewheeling contemporary.

During the 740s Du Fu was a well-regarded member of a group of high officials, even though he was without money and official position himself and failed a second time in an imperial examination. He married, probably in 741. Between 751 and 755 he tried to attract imperial attention by submitting a succession of literary products that were couched in a language of ornamental flattery, a device that eventually resulted in a nominal position at court.

In 755, during An Lushan's rebellion, Du Fu experienced extreme personal hardships. He escaped them, however, and in 757 joined the exiled court, being given the position of censor. His memoranda to the emperor do not appear to have been particularly welcome; he was eventually relieved of his post and endured another period of poverty and hunger. Wandering about until the mid-760s, he briefly served a local warlord, a position that enabled him to acquire some land and to become a gentleman farmer, but in 768 he again started traveling aimlessly toward the south. Popular legend attributes his death (on a riverboat on the Xiang River) to overindulgence in food and wine after a 10-day fast.

Du Fu's early poetry celebrated the beauty of the natural world and bemoaned the passage of time. He soon began to write bitingly of war—seen in *Bingqu xing* (*The Ballad of the Army Carts*), a poem about conscription—and with hidden satire, as in *Liren xing* (*The Beautiful Woman*), which speaks of the conspicuous luxury of the court. As he matured, and especially during the tumultuous period of 755 to 759, his verse began to sound a note of profound compassion for humanity caught in the grip of senseless war.

Du Fu's paramount position in the history of Chinese literature rests on his superb classicism. He was highly erudite, and his intimate acquaintance with the literary tradition of the past was equaled only by his complete ease in handling the rules of prosody. His dense, compressed language makes use of all the connotative overtones of a phrase and of all the intonational potentials of the individual word, qualities that no translation can ever reveal. He was an expert in all poetic genres current in his day, but his mastery was at its height in the *lüshi*, or "regulated verse," which he refined to a point of glowing intensity.

AL-MUTANABBĪ

(b. 915, Kūfah, Iraq—d. Sept. 23, 965, near Dayr al- 'Āqūl)

Al-Mutanabbī, regarded by many as the greatest poet of the Arabic language, primarily wrote panegyrics in a flowery, bombastic, and highly influential style marked by improbable metaphors.

Al-Mutanabbī was the son of a water carrier who claimed noble and ancient southern Arabian descent. Because of his poetic talent, al-Mutanabbī received an education. When Shī'ite Qarmatians sacked Kūfah in 924, he joined them and lived among the Bedouin, learning their doctrines and Arabic. Claiming to be a prophet—hence the name al-Mutanabbī ("The Would-Be Prophet")—he led a Qarmatian revolt in Syria in 932. After its suppression and two years' imprisonment, he recanted in 935 and became a wandering poet.

He began to write panegyrics in the tradition established by the poets Abū Tammām and al-Buḥturī. A panegyric on the military victories of Sayf al-Dawlah, the Ḥamdānid poet-prince of northern Syria, resulted in al-Mutanabbī's attaching himself to the ruler's court in 948. During his time there, al-Mutanabbī lauded his patron in panegyrics that rank as masterpieces of Arabic poetry.

Among his lines of praise for Sayf al-Dawlah are ones written after the prince's recovery from illness: "Light is now returned to the sun; previously it was extinguished / As though the lack of it in a body were a kind of disease."

The latter part of this period was clouded with intrigues and jealousies that culminated in al-Mutanabbī's leaving Syria in 957 for Egypt, then ruled in name by the Ikhshīdids. Al-Mutanabbī attached himself to the regent, the Ethiopian eunuch Abū al-Misk Kāfūr, who had been born a slave. But he offended Kāfūr by lampooning him in scurrilous satirical poems and fled Egypt about 960. After further travels—including to Baghdad, where he was unable to secure patronage, and to Kūfah, where he again defended the city from attack by the Qarmatians—al-Mutanabbī lived in Shīrāz, Iran, under the protection of the emir 'Aḍūd al-Dawlah of the Būyid dynasty until 965, when he returned to Iraq and was killed by bandits near Baghdad.

Al-Mutanabbī's pride and arrogance set the tone for much of his verse, which is ornately rhetorical yet crafted with consummate skill and artistry. He gave to the traditional *qaṣīdah*, or ode, a freer and more personal development, writing in what can be called a neoclassical style that combined some elements of Iraqi and Syrian stylistics with classical features.

FERDOWSĪ

(b. *c.* 935, near Ṭūs, Iran—d. *c.* 1020–26, Ṭūs)

Ferdowsī was a Persian poet who gave to the *Shāh-nāmeh* ("Book of Kings"), the Persian national epic, its final and enduring form.

He was born in a village on the outskirts of the ancient city of Ṭūs. In the course of the centuries many legends have been woven around the poet's name—which is itself the pseudonym of Abū al-Qasem Manṣūr—but very little else, other than his birthplace, is known about the real facts of his life. The only reliable source is given by Neẓāmī-ye 'Arūẓī, a 12th-century poet who visited Ferdowsī's tomb in 1116 or 1117 and collected the traditions that were current in his birthplace less than a century after his death.

According to Neẓāmī, Ferdowsī was a *dehqān* ("landowner"), deriving a comfortable income from his estates. He had only one child, a daughter, and it was to provide her with a dowry that he set his hand to the task that was to occupy him for 35 years. The *Shāh-nāmeh* of Ferdowsī, a poem of nearly 60,000 couplets, is based mainly on a prose work of the same name compiled in the poet's early manhood in his native Ṭūs. This prose *Shāh-nāmeh* was in turn and for the most part the translation of a Pahlavi (Middle Persian) work, the *Khvatāy-nāmak*, a history of the kings of Persia from mythical times down to the reign of Khosrow II (590–628). It also contained additional material continuing the story to the overthrow of the Sāsānians by the Arabs in the middle of the 7th century. The first to undertake the versification of this chronicle of pre-Islāmic and legendary Persia was Daqīqī, a poet at the court of the Sāmānids, who came to a violent end after completing only 1,000 verses. These verses, which deal with the rise of the prophet Zoroaster, were afterward incorporated by Ferdowsī, with due acknowledgements, in his own poem.

The *Shāh-nāmeh*, finally completed in 1010, was presented to the celebrated sultan Maḥmūd of Ghazna, who by that time had made himself master of Ferdowsī's homeland, Khūrāsān. Information on the relations between poet and patron is largely legendary. According to Neẓāmī-ye 'Arūẓī, Ferdowsī came to Ghazna in person and through the good offices of the minister Aḥmad ebn Ḥasan Meymandī was able to secure the Sultan's acceptance of the poem. Unfortunately, Maḥmūd then consulted certain enemies of the minister as to the poet's reward. They suggested that Ferdowsī should be given 50,000 dirhams, and even this, they said, was too much, in view of his heretical Shī'īte tenets. Maḥmūd, a bigoted Sunnite, was influenced by their words, and in the end Ferdowsī received only 20,000 dirhams. Bitterly disappointed, he went to the bath and, on coming out, bought a draft of *foqā'* (a kind of beer) and divided the whole of the money between the bath attendant and the seller of *foqā'*.

Fearing the Sultan's wrath, he fled first to Herāt, where he was in hiding for six months, and then, by way of his native Ṭūs, to Mazanderan, where he found refuge at the court of the Sepahbād Shahreyār, whose family claimed descent from the last of the Sāsānians. There Ferdowsī composed a satire of 100 verses on Sultan Maḥmūd that he inserted in the preface of the *Shāh-nāmeh* and read it to Shahreyār, at the same time offering to dedicate the poem to him, as a descendant of the ancient kings of Persia, instead of to Maḥmūd. Shahreyār, however, persuaded him to leave the dedication to Maḥmūd, bought the satire from him for 1,000 dirhams a verse, and had it expunged from the poem. The whole text of this satire, bearing every mark of authenticity, has survived to the present.

It was long supposed that in his old age the poet had spent some time in western Persia or even in Baghdad under the protection of the Būyids, but this assumption was based upon his presumed authorship of *Yūsof o-Zalīkhā*, an epic poem on the subject of Joseph and Potiphar's wife, which, it later became known, was composed more than 100 years after Ferdowsī's death. According to the narrative of Neẓāmī-ye 'Arūẓī, Ferdowsī died inopportunely just as Sultan Maḥmūd had determined to make amends for his shabby treatment of the poet by sending him 60,000 dinars' worth of indigo. Neẓāmī does not mention the date of Ferdowsī's death. The earliest date given by later authorities is 1020 and the latest 1026; it is certain that he lived to be more than 80.

The Persians regard Ferdowsī as the greatest of their poets. For nearly a thousand years they have continued to read and to listen to recitations from his masterwork, the *Shāh-nāmeh*, in which the Persian national epic found its final and enduring form. Though written about 1,000 years ago, this work is as intelligible to the average, modern Iranian as the King James version of the Bible is to a modern English-speaker. The language, based as the poem is on a Pahlavi original, is pure Persian with only the slightest admixture of Arabic. European scholars have criticized this enormous poem for what they have regarded as its monotonous metre, its constant repetitions, and its stereotyped similes; but to the Iranian it is the history of his country's glorious past, preserved for all time in sonorous and majestic verse.

MURASAKI SHIKIBU

(b. *c.* 978, Kyōto, Japan—d. *c.* 1014, Kyōto)

Murasaki Shikibu is the name that has been given to the court lady who was the author of the *Genji monogatari* (*The Tale of Genji*), generally considered the greatest work of Japanese literature and thought to be the world's oldest full novel. Her real name, however, is unknown; it is conjectured that she acquired the sobriquet of Murasaki from the name of the heroine of her novel. The main source of knowledge about her life is the diary she kept between 1007 and 1010. This work possesses considerable interest for the delightful glimpses it affords of life at the court of the empress Jōtō mon'in, whom Murasaki Shikibu served.

Some critics believe that she wrote the entire *Tale of Genji* between 1001 (the year her husband, Fujiwara Nobutaka, died) and 1005, when she began serving at court. More probably, however, the composition of this extremely long and complex novel extended over a much greater period and was not finished until about 1010.

The Tale of Genji captures the image of a unique society of ultrarefined and elegant aristocrats, whose indispensable accomplishments were skill in poetry, music, calligraphy, and courtship. Much of it is concerned with the loves of Prince Genji and the different women in his life, all of whom are exquisitely delineated. Although the novel does not contain scenes of powerful action, it is permeated with a sensitivity to human emotions and to the beauties of nature hardly paralleled elsewhere. The tone of the novel darkens as it progresses, indicating perhaps a deepening of Murasaki Shikibu's Buddhist conviction of the vanity of the world. Some, however, believe that its last 14 chapters were written by another author. The translation (1935) of *The Tale of Genji* by Arthur Waley is a classic of English literature. Murasaki Shikibu's diary is included in *Diaries of Court Ladies of Old Japan* (1935), translated by Annie Shepley Ōmori and Kōchi Doi.

RŪMĪ

(b. *c.* Sept. 30, 1207, Balkh [now in Afghanistan]—d. Dec. 17, 1273)

Jalāl al-Dīn Rūmī, the greatest Sufi mystic and poet in the Persian language, is famous for his lyrics and for his didactic epic *Mas̄navī-yi Ma'navī* ("Spiritual Couplets"), which widely influenced mystical thought and literature throughout the Muslim world. After his death, his disciples were organized as the Mawlawīyah order.

Jalāl al-Dīn's father, Bahā' al-Dīn Walad, was a noted mystical theologian, author, and teacher. Because of either a dispute with the ruler or the threat of the approaching Mongols, Bahā' al-Dīn and his family left their native town in about 1218. According to legend, in Nīshāpūr, Iran, the family met Farīd al-Dīn 'Aṭṭār, a Persian mystical poet, who blessed young Jalāl al-Dīn. After a pilgrimage to Mecca and journeys through the Middle East, Bahā' al-Dīn and his family reached Anatolia (Rūm, hence the surname Rūmī), a region that enjoyed peace and prosperity under the rule of the Turkish Seljuq dynasty. After a short stay at Laranda (Karaman), where Jalāl al-Dīn's mother died and his first son was born, they were called to the capital, Konya, in 1228. Here, Bahā' al-Dīn Walad taught at one of the numerous madrasahs (religious schools); after his death in 1231 he was succeeded in this capacity by his son.

A year later, Burhān al-Dīn Muḥaqqiq, one of Bahā' al-Dīn's former disciples, arrived in Konya and acquainted Jalāl al-Dīn more deeply with some mystical theories that had developed in Iran. Burhān al-Dīn, who contributed considerably to Jalāl al-Dīn's spiritual formation, left Konya about 1240. Jalāl al-Dīn is said to have undertaken one or two journeys to Syria (unless his contacts with Syrian Sufi circles were already established before his family reached Anatolia); there he may have met Ibn al-'Arabī, the leading Islamic theosophist whose interpreter and stepson, Ṣadr al-Dīn al-Qunawī, was Jalāl al-Dīn's colleague and friend in Konya.

The decisive moment in Rūmī's life occurred on Nov. 30, 1244, when in the streets of Konya he met the wandering dervish—holy man—Shams al-Dīn (Sun of Religion) of Tabrīz, whom he may have first encountered in Syria. Shams al-Dīn cannot be connected with any of the traditional mystical fraternities. His overwhelming personality, however, revealed to Jalāl al-Dīn the mysteries of divine majesty and beauty. For months the two mystics lived closely together, and Rūmī neglected his disciples and family so that his scandalized entourage forced Shams to leave the town in February 1246. Jalāl al-Dīn was heartbroken; his eldest son, Sulṭān Walad, eventually brought Shams back from Syria. The family, however, could not tolerate the close relation of Jalāl al-Dīn with his beloved, and one night in 1247 Shams disappeared forever. In the 20th century it was established that Shams was indeed murdered, not without the knowledge of Rūmī's sons, who hurriedly buried him close to a well that is still extant in Konya.

This experience of love, longing, and loss turned Rūmī into a poet. His poems—*ghazals* (about 30,000 verses) and a large number of *robāʿīyāt* ("quatrains")—reflect the different stages of his love, until, as his son writes, "he found Shams in himself, radiant like the moon." The complete identification of lover and beloved is expressed by his inserting the name of Shams instead of his own pen name at the end of most of his lyrical poems. The *Dīvān-e Shams* ("The Collected Poetry of Shams") is a true translation of his experiences into poetry; its language, however, never becomes lost in lofty spiritual heights or nebulous speculation. The fresh language, propelled by its strong rhythms, sometimes assumes forms close to popular verses. There would seem to be cause for the belief, expressed by chroniclers, that much of this poetry was composed in a state of ecstasy, induced by the music of the flute or the drum, the hammering of the goldsmiths, or the sound of the water mill in Meram, where Rūmī used to go with his disciples to enjoy nature. He found in nature the reflection of the

Manuscript illumination from the Mas̆navī-yi Maʿnavī *of Rūmī, 1295–96; in the British Museum (MS. OR. 7693, fol. 225 b).* Courtesy of the trustees of the British Museum; photograph, J.R. Freeman & Co. Ltd.

radiant beauty of the Sun of Religion and felt flowers and birds partaking in his love. He often accompanied his verses by a whirling dance, and many of his poems were composed to be sung in Sufi musical gatherings.

A few years after Shams al-Dīn's death, Rūmī experienced a similar rapture in his acquaintance with an illiterate goldsmith, Ṣālāḥ al-Dīn Zarkūb. It is said that one day, hearing the sound of a hammer in front of Ṣalāḥ al-Dīn's shop in the bazaar of Konya, Rūmī began his dance. The shop owner had long been one of Rūmī's closest and most loyal disciples, and his daughter became the wife of Rūmī's eldest son. This love again inspired Rūmī to write poetry. After Ṣālāḥ al-Dīn's death, Ḥusām al-Dīn Chelebi became his spiritual love and deputy. Rūmī's main work, the *Mas̄navī-yi Ma'navī*, was composed under his influence. Ḥusām al-Dīn had asked him to follow the model of the poets 'Aṭṭār and Sanā'i, who had laid down mystical teachings in long poems, interspersed with anecdotes, fables, stories, proverbs, and allegories. Their works were widely read by the mystics and by Rūmī's disciples. Rūmī followed Ḥusām al-Dīn's advice and composed nearly 26,000 couplets of the *Mas̄navī* during the following years. It is said that he would recite his verses even in the bath or on the roads, accompanied by Ḥusām al-Dīn, who wrote them down. The *Mas̄navī* shows all the different aspects of Sufism in the 13th century, and it reflects the experience of divine love; both Ṣalāḥ al-Dīn and Ḥusām al-Dīn were, for Rūmī, renewed manifestations of Shams al-Dīn, the all-embracing light.

Rūmī lived for a short while after completing the *Mas̄navī*. He always remained a respected member of Konya society, and his company was sought by the leading officials as well as by Christian monks. Ḥusām al-Dīn was his successor and was in turn succeeded by Sulṭān

Walad, who organized the loose fraternity of Rūmī's disciples into the Mawlawīyah, known in the West as the Whirling Dervishes because of the mystical dance that constitutes their principal ritual. Sulṭān Walad's poetical accounts of his father's life are the most important source of knowledge of Rūmī's spiritual development. His mausoleum, the Green Dome, today a museum in Konya, is still a place of pilgrimage for thousands of all faiths from around the world.

DANTE

(b. *c.* May 21–June 20, 1265, Florence, Italy—d. Sept. 13/14, 1321, Ravenna)

Dante Alighieri was an Italian poet, prose writer, literary theorist, moral philosopher, and political thinker who is best known for the monumental epic poem *La commedia*, later named *La divina commedia* (*The Divine Comedy*).

Public Career and Exile

Dante was of noble ancestry, and his life was shaped by the conflict between the papal and imperial partisans called, respectively, Guelfs and Ghibellines. When an opposing political faction within the Guelfs (Dante's party) gained ascendancy in Florence, he was called in January 1302 to appear before the new government and, failing to do so, was condemned for crimes he had not committed. Again failing to appear some weeks later, Dante and others within his party were condemned to be burned to death. He soon after went into exile and never again returned to Florence.

His great friendship with the poet Guido Cavalcanti shaped Dante's later career. More important, however,

Italian Renaissance poet Dante Alighieri's Divine Comedy, *an imagined journey through heaven, hell, and purgatory, is a finely crafted rumination on humankind's existence on Earth and what lies beyond death.* David Lees/ Time & Life Pictures/Getty Images

was Beatrice, a figure in whom Dante created one of the most celebrated fictionalized women in all of literature. *La vita nuova* (*c.* 1293; *The New Life*) tells a simple story: Dante's first sight of Beatrice when both are nine years of age, her salutation when they are 18, Dante's expedients to conceal his love for her, the crisis experienced when Beatrice withholds her greeting, Dante's anguish that she is making light of him, his determination to rise above anguish and sing only of his lady's virtues, anticipations of her death, and finally the death of Beatrice, Dante's mourning, the temptation of the sympathetic *donna gentile* (a young woman who temporarily replaces Beatrice),

Beatrice's final triumph and apotheosis, and, in the last chapter, Dante's determination to write at some later time about her "that which has never been written of any woman." Yet with all of this apparently autobiographical purpose, the *Vita nuova* is strangely impersonal. The circumstances it sets down are markedly devoid of any historical facts or descriptive detail (thus making it pointless to engage in too much debate as to the exact historical identity of Beatrice).

Vita nuova is the first of two collections of verse that Dante made in his lifetime, the other being the *Il convivio* (*c.* 1304–07; *The Banquet*). Each is a *prosimetrum*, that is, a work composed of verse and prose. In each case the prose is a device for binding together poems composed over about a 10-year period. The *Vita nuova* brought together Dante's poetic efforts from before 1283 to roughly 1292–93; the *Convivio*, a bulkier and more ambitious work, contains Dante's most important poetic compositions from just prior to 1294 to the time of *The Divine Comedy*.

The *Convivio* was among the works he wrote during his difficult years of exile. In it Dante's mature political and philosophical system is nearly complete. He makes his first stirring defense of the imperial tradition and, more specifically, of the Roman Empire. He introduces the crucial concept of *horme*, that is, of an innate desire that prompts the soul to return to God. The soul, however, requires proper education through examples and doctrine; otherwise it can become misdirected toward worldly aims and society torn apart by its destructive power. Through the *Convivio* Dante felt able to explain the chaos into which Italy had been plunged, and it moved him, in hopes of remedying these conditions, to take up the epic task of *The Divine Comedy*. During this time Dante also began work on the unfinished *De vulgari eloquentia* (*c.* 1304–07; *Concerning Vernacular Eloquence*), a companion piece to the

Convivio; written in Latin, it is primarily a practical treatise in the art of poetry based upon an elevated poetic language and is one of the first great Renaissance defenses of vernacular Italian. *De monarchia* (*c.* 1313; *On Monarchy*), one of Dante's greatest polemical treatises, expands the political arguments of the *Convivio*.

The Divine Comedy

Dante's years of exile were years of difficult peregrinations from one place to another. Throughout his exile he nevertheless was sustained by work on his great poem. *The Divine Comedy* was possibly begun prior to 1308 and completed just before his death in 1321, but the exact dates are uncertain.

The Divine Comedy consists of 100 cantos, which are grouped together into three sections, or canticles, *Inferno*, *Purgatorio*, and *Paradiso*. There are 33 cantos in each canticle and one additional canto, contained in the *Inferno*, which serves as an introduction to the entire poem. For the most part the cantos range from about 136 to about 151 lines. The poem's rhyme scheme is the terza rima (*aba*, *bcb*, *cdc*, etc.).

The poem's plot can be summarized as follows: a man, generally assumed to be Dante himself, is miraculously enabled to undertake a journey that leads him to visit the souls in Hell, Purgatory, and Paradise. He has two guides: Virgil, who leads him through the *Inferno* and *Purgatorio*, and Beatrice, who introduces him to *Paradiso*. Through these fictional encounters taking place from Good Friday evening in 1300 through Easter Sunday and slightly beyond, Dante learns of the exile that is awaiting him (which had, of course, already occurred at the time of the writing). The exile of an individual becomes a microcosm of the problems of a country, and it also becomes representative of the Fall of Man.

The Divine Comedy is a profoundly Christian vision of human temporal and eternal destiny. By writing it in Italian rather than Latin, Dante almost singlehandedly made Italian a literary language. By the year 1400 no fewer than 12 commentaries devoted to detailed expositions of its meaning had appeared. Giovanni Boccaccio wrote a life of the poet and then in 1373–74 delivered the first public lectures on *The Divine Comedy*, making Dante the first of the moderns whose work found its place with the ancient classics in a university course. Dante became known as the *divino poeta*, and in an edition of his great poem published in Venice in 1555 the adjective was applied to the poem's title; thus, the simple *Commedia* became *La divina commedia*, or *The Divine Comedy*.

In his final years Dante was received honourably in many noble houses in the north of Italy, most notably by Guido Novello da Polenta, the nephew of the remarkable Francesca, in Ravenna. There, at his death, Dante was given an honourable burial attended by the leading men of letters of the time, and the funeral oration was delivered by Guido himself.

PETRARCH

(b. July 20, 1304, Arezzo, Tuscany [Italy]—d. July 18/19, 1374, Arquà, near Padua, Carrara)

Petrarch, an Italian poet and humanist, was regarded as the greatest scholar of his age. His poems addressed to Laura, an idealized beloved, contributed to the Renaissance flowering of lyric poetry, and his consciousness of the Classical past as a source of literary and philosophical meaning for the present was of great importance in paving the way for the Renaissance.

Petrarch, whose Italian name was Francesco Petrarca, undertook his first studies at Carpentras, France, and at his father's insistence he was sent to study law at Montpellier, France (1316). From there he returned to Italy with his younger brother Gherardo to continue these studies at Bologna (1320). After his father's death, in 1326, Petrarch took minor ecclesiastical orders at Avignon and entered the household of the influential cardinal Giovanni Colonna.

Petrarch had during his early youth a deep religious faith and a love of virtue. There now followed the reaction—a period of dissipation—which also coincided with the beginning of his famous chaste love for a woman known now only as Laura. Petrarch himself kept silent about everything concerning her civil status. He first saw her in the Church of St. Clare at Avignon on April 6, 1327, and loved her, although she was outside his reach, almost until his death. From this love there springs the work for which he is most celebrated, the Italian poems (*Rime*), which he affected to despise as mere trifles in the vulgar tongue but which he collected and revised throughout his life.

During the 1330s, which were years of ambition, unremitting study, and travel, Petrarch's reputation as a scholar spread. He was crowned as poet on the Capitoline Hill on April 8, 1341, afterward placing his laurel wreath on the tomb of the Apostle in St. Peter's Basilica, a symbolic gesture linking the Classical tradition with the Christian message.

He subsequently became enthusiastic for the efforts of Cola di Rienzo to revive the Roman republic and restore popular government in Rome—a sympathy that divided him still more sharply from the Avignon court and in 1346 even led to the loss of Cardinal Colonna's friendship. The Plague of 1348, known as the Black Death, saw many friends fall victim, including Laura, who died on April 6, the anniversary of Petrarch's first seeing her. Finally, in the jubilee year of 1350 he made a pilgrimage to Rome and later assigned to this year his renunciation of sensual pleasures. The time in between these landmark events was filled with diplomatic missions, study, and immense literary activity.

In 1351 he began work on a new plan for the *Rime*, which he had begun writing two decades earlier. The project was divided into two parts: the *Rime in vita di Laura* ("Poems During Laura's Life") and the *Rime in morte di Laura* ("Poems After Laura's Death"), which he now selected and arranged to illustrate the story of his own spiritual growth. The theme of his *Canzoniere* (as the poems are usually known) therefore goes beyond the apparent subject matter, his love for Laura. He also continued work on the *Epistolae metricae* (66 "letters" in Latin hexameter verses), begun in 1350; he embarked on a polemic against the conservative enemies of his new conception of education, which rejected the prevailing Aristotelianism of the schools and restored the spiritual worth of Classical writers. He also began work on his poem *Trionfi*, a generalized version of the story of the human soul in its progress from earthly passion toward fulfillment in God.

After a number of moves and intense work on the definitive versions of his various writings, Petrarch found himself in Padua in 1367. He remained there until his death, dividing his time from 1370 between Padua and Arquà, in the neighbouring Euganean hills, where he had a little house. There he wrote the defense of his humanism, *De sui ipsius et multorum ignorantia*. He was still in great demand as a diplomat. Despite suffering a stroke in 1370, he did not stop working; in addition to revisions, he composed more minor works and added new sections to his *Posteritati*, an autobiographical letter to posterity that was to have formed the conclusion to his *Seniles*; he also composed the final sections of the *Trionfi*. Petrarch died while working in his study at Arquà and was found the next morning, his head resting on a manuscript of Virgil.

GEOFFREY CHAUCER

(b. *c.* 1342/43, London?, Eng.—d. Oct. 25, 1400, London)

The Canterbury Tales by Geoffrey Chaucer, the outstanding English poet before Shakespeare, ranks as one of the greatest poetic works in English. Chaucer also contributed importantly in the second half of the 14th century to the management of public affairs as courtier, diplomat, and civil servant. But it is his avocation—the writing of poetry—for which he is remembered.

Early Years

Chaucer first appears in the records in 1357, as a member of the household of Elizabeth, countess of Ulster, wife of Lionel, third son of Edward III. By 1359 Chaucer was a member of Edward III's army in France and was captured during the unsuccessful siege of Reims, and by 1366 Chaucer had married. Chaucer's career was prospering at this time. His first important poem, *Book of the Duchess*, is among the records that provide evidence of his connection with people in high places. That poem of more than 1,300 lines, probably written in late 1369 or early 1370, is an elegy for Blanche, duchess of Lancaster, John of Gaunt's first wife, who died of plague in September 1369. Chaucer's close relationship with John, which continued through most of his life, may have commenced as early as Christmas 1357 when they, both about the same age, were present at the countess of Ulster's residence in Yorkshire.

For this first of his important poems, Chaucer used the dream-vision form, a genre made popular by the highly influential 13th-century French poem of courtly love, the *Roman de la rose*. Chaucer translated that poem, at least in part, probably as one of his first literary efforts, and he borrowed from it throughout his poetic career. The

Duchess is also indebted to contemporary French poetry and to Ovid, Chaucer's favourite Roman poet. Nothing in these borrowings, however, will account for his originality in combining dream-vision with elegy and eulogy of Blanche with consolation for John.

During the 1370s, Chaucer was at various times on diplomatic missions in Flanders, France, and Italy. His career as a diplomat and civil servant was flourishing. So much responsibility and activity in public matters appears to have left Chaucer little time for writing during this decade. The great literary event for him was that, during his missions to Italy, he encountered the work of Dante, Petrarch, and Boccaccio, which was later to have profound influence upon his own writing. Chaucer's most important work of the 1370s was *Hous of Fame*, a poem of more than 2,000 lines, also in dream-vision form. In some ways it is a failure—it is unfinished, its theme is unclear, and the diversity of its parts seems to overshadow any unity of purpose—but it gives considerable evidence of Chaucer's advancing skill as a poet. In addition to its comic aspects, the poem seems to convey a serious note: like all earthly things, fame is transitory and capricious.

THE MIDDLE YEARS

Political events of the 1380s, from the Peasants' Revolt of 1381 through the Merciless Parliament of 1388, combined with his wife's apparent death in 1387, must have kept Chaucer steadily anxious. Yet he produced a sizable body of writings during this decade, some of very high order. *The Parlement of Foules*, a playfully humorous poem of 699 lines, is a dream-vision for St. Valentine's Day, making use of the myth that each year on that day the birds gathered before the goddess Nature to choose their mates. Chaucer also translated the *Consolation of Philosophy*, written by the Roman philosopher Boethius (early 6th century), one of the most influential of medieval books. Its discussion of free will, God's foreknowledge, destiny, fortune, and true and false happiness had a deep and lasting effect upon Chaucer's thought and art. In his next poem, *Troilus and Criseyde*, the influence of Boethius's book is pervasive. Chaucer took the basic plot for this 8,239-line poem from Boccaccio's *Filostrato*. Some critics consider *Troilus and Criseyde* Chaucer's finest work, greater even than the far more widely read *Canterbury Tales*. But the two works are so different that comparative evaluation seems fruitless. Against the background of the legendary Trojan War, the love story of Troilus, son of the Trojan king Priam, and Criseyde, widowed daughter of the deserter priest Calkas, is recounted. The poem moves in leisurely fashion, with introspection and psychological insight dominating many sections.

Also in the 1380s, Chaucer produced his fourth and final dream-vision poem, *The Legend of Good Women*. Perhaps the most important fact about the *Legend* is that it shows Chaucer structuring a long poem as a collection of stories within a framework. Seemingly the static nature of the framing device for the *Legend* and the repetitive aspect of the series of stories with a single theme led him to give up this attempt as a poor job.

Last Years and *The Canterbury Tales*

Chaucer's great literary accomplishment of the 1390s was *The Canterbury Tales*. In it a group of about 30 pilgrims gather at the Tabard Inn in Southwark, across the Thames from London, and agree to engage in a storytelling contest as they travel on horseback to the shrine of Thomas à Becket in Canterbury, Kent, and back. Harry Bailly, host of the Tabard, serves as master of ceremonies for the contest. The pilgrims are introduced by vivid brief sketches in the General Prologue. Interspersed between the 24 tales told by the pilgrims are short dramatic scenes presenting lively exchanges, called links and usually involving the host and one or more of the pilgrims. Chaucer's death, in 1400, prevented him from completing the full plan for his book; the return journey from Canterbury is not included, and some of the pilgrims do not tell stories. Further, the surviving manuscripts leave room for doubt at some points as to Chaucer's intent for arranging the material. The work is nevertheless sufficiently complete to be considered a unified book rather than a collection of unfinished fragments.

Use of a pilgrimage as a framing device for the collection of stories enabled Chaucer to bring together people from many walks of life, and the storytelling contest allowed presentation of a highly varied collection of literary genres. Because of this structure, the sketches, the links, and the tales all fuse as complex presentations of the pilgrims, while at the same time the tales present remarkable examples of short stories in verse, plus two expositions in prose. Over the expanse of this intricate dramatic narrative, he presides as Chaucer the poet, Chaucer the civil servant, and Chaucer the pilgrim; somewhat slow-witted in his pose and always intrigued by human frailty but always questioning the complexity of the human condition and always seeing both the humour and the tragedy in that condition. At the end, in the Retractation with which *The Canterbury Tales* closes, Chaucer as poet and pilgrim states his conclusion that the concern for this world fades into insignificance before the prospect for the next. In view of the admonitions in The Parson's Tale, he asks forgiveness for his writings that concern "worldly vanities" and remembrance for his translation of the *Consolation* and his other works of morality and religious devotion. On that note he ends his finest work and his career as poet.

LUÍS DE CAMÕES

(b. *c.* 1524/25, Lisbon, Port.—d. June 10, 1580, Lisbon)

Luís de Camões is Portugal's great national poet. He is the author of the epic poem *Os Lusíadas* (1572; *The Lusiads*), which describes Vasco da Gama's discovery of the sea route to India.

Camões was born in Lisbon when Portuguese expansion in the East was at its peak. He was a member of the impoverished old aristocracy but well-related to the grandees of Portugal and Spain. A tradition that Camões studied at the University of Coimbra or that he followed any regular studies, for that matter, remains unproved. He may have spent 17 years in India, but his time there has not been documented. He returned to Portugal in 1570, and his *Os Lusíadas* was published in Lisbon in early 1572. In July of that year he was granted a royal pension, probably in recompense for both his service in India and his having written *Os Lusíadas*.

The title of Camões's epic poem is taken from the word *Lusiads*, which means "Portuguese" and is in turn derived from the ancient Roman name for Portugal, Lusitania. The work extols the glorious deeds of the Portuguese and their victories over the enemies of Christianity, victories not only over their fellowman but also over the forces of nature as motivated by the inimical gods of classical mythology. The courage and enterprise of Portuguese explorers had inspired the idea of a national epic during the 15th century, but it was left to Camões in the 16th century to put it into execution.

It is impossible to say for certain when he decided to do so or when he actually began to write his epic. The 10 cantos of the poem are in ottava rima and amount to 1,102 stanzas in all. After an introduction, an invocation, and a dedication to King Sebastian, the action, on both the historical and the mythological levels, begins. Da Gama's ships are already under way in the Indian Ocean, sailing up the coast of East Africa, and the Olympian gods gather to discuss the fate of the expedition (which is favoured by Venus and attacked by Bacchus). The voyagers spend several days in Melinde on the east coast of Africa, and at the king's request Vasco da Gama relates the entire history of Portugal from its origins to the inception of their great voyage (Cantos III, IV, and V). These cantos contain some of the most beautiful passages in the poem: the murder of Inês de Castro, who becomes a symbol of death for the sake of love; the battle of Aljubarrota; the vision of King Manuel I; the description of St. Elmo's fire and the waterspout; and the story of Adamastor, the giant of classical parentage who, at the Cape of Good Hope, tells da Gama he will lie in wait to destroy the fleets coming back from India.

When the passengers re-embark, the poet takes advantage of leisure hours on board to narrate the story of the Doze de Inglaterra (Canto VI, 43–69). In the meantime, Bacchus, ever ready to impede the progress of the Portuguese in the East, convokes a council of the sea gods and incites them to arrange the shipwreck of the Portuguese fleet. This is prevented by Venus (Canto VI, 85–91), and Vasco da Gama is able to reach Calicut (Kozhikode, now in Kerala state, southwestern India), the end of his voyage. There his brother, Paulo da Gama, receives the king's representative on board and explains the significance of the characters depicted on the banners that adorn the captain's ship (Cantos VII and VIII). On their homeward voyage the mariners chance upon the island that Venus has created for them, and the nymphs reward them for their labours. One of the nymphs sings of the future deeds of the Portuguese (Cantos IX and X), and the entertainment ends with a description of the universe given by

Thetis and Vasco da Gama, after which the sailors embark once more and the nymphs accompany them on their homeward journey.

In *Os Lusíadas* Camões achieved an exquisite harmony between classical learning and practical experience, delicate perception and superb artistic skill, expressing through them the gravity of thought and the finest human emotions. The epic was his eulogy of the "dangerous life" (*vida perigosa*) and was a stern warning to the Christian monarchs, who, idling their time away in petty struggles, were failing to unite against the encroaching conquests of Islam in southeastern Europe. Realistic descriptions in the poem of sensual encounters, battles, and storms and other natural phenomena transcend the thrust of classical allusions that permeate the work and make for the high-flown yet fluent style of the poem. *Os Lusíadas* reveals an astonishing command of language and variety of styles and provides a fascinating portrait of an extraordinary man and poet.

Camões also wrote dramatic and lyric poetry. In his dramatic works he tried to combine national and classical tendencies, while his sonnets, elegies, and many other poems, all published posthumously, show the poet's full powers. As a result, particularly of his epic and lyric poetry, Camões had a permanent and unparalleled impact on Portuguese and Brazilian literature alike.

MICHEL DE MONTAIGNE

(b. Feb. 28, 1533, Château de Montaigne, near Bordeaux, France—d. Sept. 23, 1592, Château de Montaigne)

In his *Essais* (*Essays*) the French writer Michel de Montaigne established a new literary form—the essay—that he used to create one of the most captivating and intimate self-portraits ever given.

As a young child Montaigne was tutored at home according to his father's ideas of pedagogy, which included the exclusive use of Latin, still the international language of educated people. As a result the boy did not learn French until he was six years old. He continued his education at the College of Guyenne and eventually at the University of Toulouse, where he studied law. He entered into the magistrature, eventually becoming a member of the Parliament of Bordeaux, one of the eight regional parliaments that constituted the French Parliament, the highest national court of justice. There, at the age of 24, he made the acquaintance of Étienne de la Boétie, a meeting that was one of the most significant events in Montaigne's life. An extraordinary friendship, based on a profound intellectual and emotional closeness and reciprocity, sprang up between Montaigne and the slightly older La Boétie, an already distinguished civil servant, humanist scholar, and writer. When La Boétie died, he left a void in Montaigne's life that no other being was ever able to fill. It is likely that Montaigne started on his writing career, six years after La Boétie's death, in order to fill the emptiness left by the loss of the irretrievable friend.

In 1570 Montaigne sold his seat in the Bordeaux Parliament and retired in 1571 to the castle of Montaigne in order to devote his time to reading, meditating, and writing. His library, installed in the castle's tower, became his refuge. It was in this round room, lined with a thousand books and decorated with Greek and Latin inscriptions, that Montaigne set out to put on paper his *essais*, that is, the probings and testings of his mind. He spent the years from 1571 to 1580 composing the first two books of the *Essays*, which comprise respectively 57 and 37 chapters of greatly varying lengths; they were published in Bordeaux in 1580.

Montaigne then set out to travel, and in the course of 15 months he visited areas of France, Germany, Switzerland, Austria, and Italy. Upon his return he assumed the position of mayor of Bordeaux at the request of King Henry III and held it for two terms, until July 1585. During his second term Montaigne played a crucial role in preserving the equilibrium between the Catholic majority and the important Protestant League representation in Bordeaux. Toward the end of this term the plague broke out in Bordeaux, soon raging out of control and killing one-third of the population.

Montaigne resumed his literary work by embarking on the third book of the *Essays*. After having been interrupted again—by a renewed outbreak of the plague that forced Montaigne and his family to seek refuge elsewhere, by military activity close to his estate, and by diplomatic duties, when Catherine de Médicis appealed to his abilities as a negotiator to mediate between herself and Henry of Navarre (a mission that turned out to be unsuccessful)—Montaigne was able to finish the work in 1587. The year 1588 was marked by both political and literary events. During a trip to Paris Montaigne was twice arrested and briefly imprisoned by members of the Protestant League because of his loyalty to Henry III. During the same trip he supervised the publication of the fifth edition of the *Essays*. He spent the last years of his life at his château, continuing to read and to reflect and to work on the *Essays*, adding new passages, which signify not so much profound changes in his ideas as further explorations of his thought and experience.

Montaigne saw his age as one of dissimulation, corruption, violence, and hypocrisy, and he considered the human being to be a creature of weakness and failure. The skepticism he expresses throughout the *Essays* is reflected in the French title of his work, *Essais*, or "Attempts," which implies not a transmission of proven knowledge or of confident opinion but a project of trial and error, of tentative exploration. Neither a reference to an established genre (for Montaigne's book inaugurated the term *essay* for the short prose composition treating a given subject in a rather informal and personal manner) nor an indication of a necessary internal unity and structure within the work, the title indicates an intellectual attitude of questioning and of continuous assessment.

The *Essays* are the record of Montaigne's thoughts, presented not in artificially organized stages but as they occurred and reoccurred to him in different shapes throughout his thinking and writing activity. They are not the record of an intellectual evolution but of a continuous accretion, and he insists on the immediacy and the authenticity of their testimony. "As my mind roams, so does my style," he wrote. The multiple digressions, the wandering developments, and the savory, concrete vocabulary all denote that fidelity to the freshness and the immediacy of the living thought.

MIGUEL DE CERVANTES

(b. Sept. 29?, 1547, Alcalá de Henares, Spain—d. April 22, 1616, Madrid)

Miguel de Cervantes was a Spanish novelist, playwright, and poet. Best known as the creator of *Don Quixote* (1605, 1615), he is the most important and celebrated figure in Spanish literature. Cervantes tried his hand in all the major literary genres save the epic. He was a notable short-story writer, and a few of those in his collection of *Novelas exemplares* (1613; *Exemplary Stories*) attain a level close to that of *Don Quixote*, on a miniature scale.

A Life Filled with Adventure

Little is known of Cervantes's early education. The supposition, based on a passage in one of the *Exemplary Stories*, that he studied for a time under the Jesuits, though not unlikely, remains conjectural. Unlike most Spanish writers of his time, including some of humble origin, he apparently did not go to a university. What is certain is that at some stage he became an avid reader of books. His first published poem, on the death of Philip II's young queen, Elizabeth of Valois, appeared in 1569. That same year he left Spain for Italy. By 1570 he had enlisted as a soldier in a Spanish infantry regiment stationed in Naples, then a possession of the Spanish crown. He was there for about a year before he saw active service.

A confrontation between the Turkish fleet and the naval forces of Venice, the papacy, and Spain was inevitable at this time. In mid-September 1571 Cervantes sailed on board the *Marquesa*, part of the large fleet under the command of Don Juan de Austria that engaged the enemy on October 7 in the Gulf of Lepanto near Corinth. The fierce battle ended in a crushing defeat for the Turks that was ultimately to break their control of the Mediterranean. There are independent accounts of Cervantes's conduct in the action, and they concur in testifying to his personal courage. Though stricken with a fever, he refused to stay below and joined the thick of the fighting. He received two gunshot wounds in the chest, and a third rendered his left hand useless for the rest of his life. He always looked back on his conduct in the battle with pride. He set sail for Spain in September 1575 with letters of commendation to the king from the duque de Sessa and Don Juan himself.

On this voyage his ship was attacked and captured by Barbary corsairs. Cervantes, together with his brother Rodrigo, was sold into slavery in Algiers, the centre of the

The facts of his life rival any of the tales of adventure Spanish author Cervantes committed to paper. A soldier and explorer who had once been sold into slavery, Cervantes was a real-life counterpart to his most famous literary character, Don Quixote, pictured here. Private Collection/The Bridgeman Art Library/Getty Images

Christian slave traffic in the Muslim world. The letters he carried magnified his importance in the eyes of his captors. This had the effect of raising his ransom price, and thus prolonging his captivity, while also, it appears, protecting him from punishment by death, mutilation, or torture when his four daring bids to escape were frustrated. His masters, the renegade Dali Mami and later Hasan Paşa, treated him with considerable leniency in the circumstances, whatever the reason. In September 1580, three years after Rodrigo had earned his freedom, Miguel's family, with the aid and intervention of the Trinitarian friars, raised the 500 gold escudos demanded for his release.

Back in Spain, Cervantes spent most of the rest of his life in a manner that contrasted entirely with his decade of action and danger. He would be constantly short of money and in tedious and exacting employment; it would be 25 years before he scored a major literary success with *Don Quixote*. His first published fiction, *La Galatea* (*Galatea: A Pastoral Romance*), in the newly fashionable genre of the pastoral romance, appeared in 1585. The publisher, Blas de Robles, paid him 1,336 reales for it, a good price for a first book. Cervantes also turned his hand to the writing of drama at this time, the early dawn of the Golden Age of the Spanish theatre. He contracted to write two plays for the theatrical manager Gaspar de Porras in 1585, one of which, *La confusa* ("Confusion"), he later described as the best he ever wrote. Many years afterward he claimed to have written 20 or 30 plays in this period, which, he noted, were received by the public without being booed off the stage or having the actors pelted with vegetables. The number is vague. Only two plays certainly survive from this time, the historical tragedy of *La Numancia* (1580s; *Numantia: A Tragedy*) and *El trato de Argel* (1580s; "The Traffic of Algiers").

Though destined to be a disappointed dramatist, Cervantes went on trying to get managers to accept his stage works. By 1587 it was clear that he was not going to make a living from literature, and he was obliged to turn in a very different direction. A series of positions as a civil servant followed. He spent time in jail several times because accounts he oversaw showed discrepancies. After 1598, information about Cervantes's life over the next four or five years is sparse.

DON QUIXOTE

In July or August 1604, Cervantes sold the rights of *El ingenioso hidalgo don Quijote de la Mancha* ("The Ingenious

Hidalgo Don Quixote of La Mancha," known as *Don Quixote*, Part I) to the publisher-bookseller Francisco de Robles for an unknown sum. License to publish was granted in September, and the book came out in January 1605. There is some evidence of its content's being known or known about before publication—to, among others, Lope de Vega, the vicissitudes of whose relations with Cervantes were then at a low point. The compositors at Juan de la Cuesta's press in Madrid are now known to have been responsible for a great many errors in the text, many of which were long attributed to the author.

Cervantes's masterpiece *Don Quixote* has been variously interpreted as a parody of chivalric romances, an epic of heroic idealism, a commentary on the author's alienation, and a critique of Spanish imperialism. While the Romantic tradition downplayed the novel's hilarity by transforming Don Quixote into a tragic hero, readers who view it as a parody accept at face value Cervantes's intention to denounce the popular yet outdated romances of his time. *Don Quixote* certainly pokes fun at the adventures of literary knights-errant, but its plot also addresses the historical realities of 17th-century Spain.

The novel was an immediate success, with multiple editions published across Europe. Thomas Shelton's English translation of the first part appeared in 1612. The name of Cervantes was soon to be as well known in England, France, and Italy as in Spain. The sale of the publishing rights, however, meant that Cervantes made no more financial profit on Part I of his novel. Nevertheless, relative success, still-unsatisfied ambition, and a tireless urge to experiment with the forms of fiction ensured that, at age 57, with less than a dozen years left to him, Cervantes was just entering the most productive period of his career.

In 1613 the 12 *Exemplary Stories* were published. Cervantes's claim in the prologue to be the first to write original novellas (short stories in the Italian manner) in Castilian is substantially justified. Their precise dates of composition are in most cases uncertain. There is some variety in the collection, within the two general categories of romance-based stories and realistic ones. *El coloquio de los perros* ("Colloquy of the Dogs," Eng. trans. in *Three Exemplary Novels*, 1952), a quasi-picaresque novella, with its frame tale *El casamiento engañoso* ("The Deceitful Marriage"), is probably Cervantes's most profound and original creation next to *Don Quixote*.

In 1614 Cervantes published *Viage del Parnaso*, a long allegorical poem in a mock-mythological and satirical vein, with a postscript in prose. Having lost all hope of seeing any more of his plays staged, he had eight of them published in 1615, together with eight short comic interludes, in *Ocho comedias, y ocho entremeses nuevos*.

It is not certain when Cervantes began writing Part II, *Segunda parte del ingenioso caballero don Quijote de la Mancha* ("Second Part of the Ingenious Knight Don Quixote of La Mancha"), but he had probably not gotten much more than halfway through by late July 1614. *Don Quixote*, Part II, emerged from the same press as its predecessor late in 1615. It was quickly reprinted outside of Spain. The second part capitalizes on the potential of the first, developing and diversifying without sacrificing familiarity.

Later Years

In his last years Cervantes mentioned several works that apparently did not get as far as the printing press, if indeed he ever actually started writing them. There was *Bernardo* (the name of a legendary Spanish epic hero), the *Semanas del jardín* ("Weeks in the Garden"; a collection of tales, perhaps like Boccaccio's *Decameron*), and the continuation to his *Galatea*. The one that was published, posthumously in 1617, was his last romance, *Los trabaios de Persiles y Sigismunda, historia setentrional* ("The Labours of Persiles and Sigismunda: A Northern Story"). In it Cervantes sought to renovate the heroic romance of adventure and love in the manner of the *Aethiopica* of Heliodorus. It was an intellectually prestigious genre destined to be very successful in 17th-century France. Intended both to edify and to entertain, the *Persiles* is an ambitious work that exploits the mythic and symbolic potential of romance. It was very successful when it appeared.

In the dedication, written three days before he died, Cervantes, "with a foot already in the stirrup," movingly bade farewell to the world. He died in 1616 and was buried in the convent of the Discalced Trinitarians in the Calle de Cantarranas (now the Calle de Lope de Vega). The exact spot is not marked.

EDMUND SPENSER

(b. 1552/53, London, Eng.—d. Jan. 13, 1599, London)

Edmund Spenser was an English poet whose long allegorical poem *The Faerie Queene* is one of the greatest in the English language.

Little is known for certain about Spenser before he entered the University of Cambridge in 1569. His first important published work, *The Shepheardes Calender* (1579 or 1580), can be called the first work of the English literary Renaissance. Following the example of Virgil and of many later poets, Spenser began his career with a series of eclogues (literally "selections," usually short poems in the form of pastoral dialogues), in which various characters, in the guise of innocent and simple shepherds, converse about life and love in a variety of elegantly managed verse forms, formulating weighty—often satirical—opinions on questions of the day. Spenser's *Calender* consists of 12 eclogues, one named after each month of the year, and was well received in its day.

Spenser appears by 1580 to have been serving Robert Dudley, earl of Leicester and to have become a member of the literary circle led by Sir Philip Sidney, Leicester's nephew, to whom the *Calender* was dedicated and who praised it in his important critical work *The Defence of Poesie* (1595). In 1580 Spenser was also made secretary to the new lord deputy of Ireland, Arthur Lord Grey, who was a friend of the Sidney family. As Grey's secretary, Spenser accompanied him on risky military campaigns as well as on more routine journeys in Ireland. Spenser may have witnessed the Smerwick massacre (1580), and his poetry is haunted by nightmare characters who embody a wild lawlessness.

For four or five years, from roughly 1584, Spenser carried out the duties of a second important official position in Ireland, deputizing for a friend as clerk of the lords president (governors) of Munster, the southernmost Irish province. In 1588 or 1589 Spenser took over the 3,000-acre (1,200-hectare) plantation of Kilcolman, near Cork. By acquiring this estate, Spenser made his choice for the future—to rise into the privileged class of what was, to all intents, a colonial land of opportunity rather than to seek power and position on the more crowded ground of the homeland, where he had made his poetic reputation. It was under these conditions that Spenser completed his greatest poem, on which he had begun work by 1580.

In its present form, *The Faerie Queene* consists of six books and a fragment (known as the "Mutabilitie Cantos"). As a setting Spenser invented the land of Faerie and its queen, Gloriana. To express himself he invented what is now known as the Spenserian stanza: a nine-line stanza, the first eight of five stresses and the last of six, whose rhyme pattern is *ababbcbcc*.

What is most characteristic of Spenser in *The Faerie Queene* is his serious view of the capacity of the romance form to act as a paradigm of human experience: the moral life as quest, pilgrimage, aspiration; as eternal war with an enemy, still to be known; and as encounter, crisis, the moment of illumination—in short, as ethics, with the added dimensions of mystery, terror, love, and victory and with all the generous virtues exalted. In *The Faerie Queene* Spenser proves himself a master: picture, music, metre, story—all elements are at one with the deeper significance of his poem, providing a moral heraldry of colours, emblems, legends, folklore, and mythical allusion, all prompting deep, instinctive responses.

The first three books of *The Faerie Queene* were published in London in 1590, together with a dedication to Queen Elizabeth and commendatory sonnets to notables of the court. Spenser saw the book through the press, made a hurried visit to Ireland, and returned speedily to London—presumably in the hope of preferment, which he received in 1591, when Elizabeth gave Spenser a small pension for life.

Back in Ireland, Spenser pressed on with his writing, and in early 1595 he published *Amoretti* and *Epithalamion*, a sonnet sequence and a marriage ode celebrating his marriage. This group of poems is unique among Renaissance sonnet sequences in that it celebrates a successful love affair culminating in marriage. Books IV, V, and VI of *The Faerie Queene* appeared in 1596 and are strikingly more ambiguous and ironic than the first three books. This burst of publication was, however, the last of his lifetime. He was buried with ceremony in Westminster Abbey.

LOPE DE VEGA

(b. Nov. 25, 1562, Madrid, Spain—d. Aug. 27, 1635, Madrid)

Lope de Vega was the outstanding dramatist of the Spanish Golden Age, author of as many as 1,800 plays and several hundred shorter dramatic pieces, of which 431 plays and 50 shorter pieces are extant. He acquired a humanistic education from his abundant though haphazard readings in erudite anthologies. In 1583 he took part in the Spanish expedition against the Azores. By this time he had established himself as a playwright in Madrid and was living from his comedias (tragicomic social dramas). He also exercised an undefined role as gentleman attendant or secretary to various nobles, adapting his role as servant or panderer according to the situation. By 1608, however, when Vega was named to a sinecure position as a familiar of the Inquisition and then prosecutor (*promotor fiscal*) of the Apostolic Chamber, he had become a famous poet and was already regarded as the "phoenix of Spanish wits."

After experiencing a deep religious crisis, he entered the first of several religious orders in 1609. From this time on he wrote almost exclusively religious works, though he also continued his theatrical work, which was financially indispensable. In 1614 he entered the priesthood, but his continued service as secretary and panderer hindered him from obtaining the ecclesiastical benefits he sought. New and scandalous romantic relationships eventually followed, in continuation of a pattern Vega pursued throughout his life. In 1627 his verse epic on the life and execution of Mary, Queen of Scots, which was dedicated to Pope Urban VIII, brought in reward a doctorate in theology of the Collegium Sapientiae and the cross of the Order of Malta, out of which came his proud use of the title *Frey* ("Brother"). His closing years were full of gloom, however, and his death in Madrid evoked national mourning.

Vega became identified as a playwright with the comedia, a comprehensive term for the new drama of Spain's Golden Age. Vega's productivity for the stage, however exaggerated by report, remains phenomenal. He claimed to have written an average of 20 sheets a day throughout his life and left untouched scarcely a vein of writing then current. Cervantes called him "the prodigy of nature."

The earliest firm date for a play written by Vega is 1593. By the beginning of the 16th century, through sheer force of creative genius and fertility of invention, Vega had given the comedia its basic formula and raised it to a peak of splendour. It was essentially a social drama, ringing a thousand changes on the accepted foundations of society: respect for crown, for church, and for the human personality, the latter being symbolized in the "point of honour" (*pundonor*) that Vega commended as the best theme of all "since there are none but are strongly moved thereby." This "point of honour" was a matter largely of convention, "honour" being equivalent, in a very limited and brittle sense, to social reputation. It followed that this was a drama less of character than of action and intrigue that rarely, if ever, grasped the true essence of tragedy.

Few of the plays that Vega wrote were perfect, and in theme they range over a vast horizon. But he had an unerring sense for the theme and detail that could move an audience conscious of being on the crest of its country's greatness to respond to a mirroring on the stage of some of the basic ingredients of that greatness. Because of him the comedia became a vast sounding board for every chord in the Spanish consciousness, a "national" drama in the truest sense.

All Vega's plays suffer from haste of composition, partly a consequence of the public's insatiable desire for novelty. His first acts are commonly his best, with the third a hasty cutting of knots or tying up of loose ends that takes scant account both of probability and of psychology. There was, too, a limit to his inventiveness in the recurrence of basic themes and situations, particularly in his cloak and sword plays. But Vega's defects, like his strength, derive from the accuracy with which he projected onto the stage the essence of his country and age. Vega's plays remain true to the great age of Spain into which he had been born and which he had come to know, intuitively rather than by study, as no one had ever known it before.

Vega's nondramatic works in verse and prose filled 21 volumes in 1776–79. Much of this vast output has withered, but its variety remains impressive. Vega wrote pastoral romances, verse histories of recent events, verse biographies of Spanish saints, long epic poems and burlesques upon such works, and prose tales, imitating or adapting works by Ariosto and Cervantes in the process. His lyric compositions—ballads, elegies, epistles, sonnets (there are 1,587 of these)—are myriad. Formally they rely much on the conceit, and in content they provide a running commentary on the poet's whole emotional life.

CHRISTOPHER MARLOWE

(baptized Feb. 26, 1564, Canterbury, Kent, Eng.—d. May 30, 1593, Deptford, near London)

The Elizabethan poet Christopher Marlowe was Shakespeare's most important predecessor in English drama. He is noted especially for his establishment of dramatic blank verse.

Marlowe obtained his Bachelor of Arts degree from the University of Cambridge in 1584. After 1587 he was in

London, writing for the theatres, occasionally getting into trouble with the authorities because of his violent and disreputable behaviour, and probably also engaging himself from time to time in the government's secret service. Marlowe won a dangerous reputation for "atheism," but this could, in Queen Elizabeth I's time, indicate merely unorthodox religious opinions. There is evidence of his unorthodoxy, notably in the denunciation of him written by the spy Richard Baines and in the letter of the playwright Thomas Kyd to the lord keeper in 1593 after Marlowe's death. Kyd alleged that certain papers "denying the deity of Jesus Christ" that were found in his room belonged to Marlowe, who had shared the room two years before. Whatever the case may be, on May 18, 1593, the Privy Council issued an order for Marlowe's arrest. On May 30, however, he was killed by Ingram Frizer at a lodging house where they and two other men had spent most of the day and where, it was alleged, a fight broke out between them over the bill.

In a playwriting career that spanned little more than six years, Marlowe's achievements were diverse and splendid. Perhaps before leaving Cambridge he had already written *Tamburlaine the Great* (in two parts, both performed by the end of 1587; published 1590), in which he established blank verse as the staple medium for later Elizabethan and Jacobean dramatic writing. Almost certainly during his later Cambridge years, Marlowe had translated Ovid's *Amores* (*The Loves*) and the first book of Lucan's *Pharsalia* from the Latin. About this time he also wrote the play *Dido, Queen of Carthage* (published in 1594 as the joint work of Marlowe and Thomas Nashe). With the production of *Tamburlaine* he received recognition and acclaim, and playwriting became his major concern in the few years that lay ahead. Both parts of *Tamburlaine* were published anonymously in 1590, and the publisher omitted certain passages that he found incongruous with the play's serious concern with history; even so, the extant *Tamburlaine* text can be regarded as substantially Marlowe's. No other of his plays or poems or translations was published during his life. His unfinished but splendid poem *Hero and Leander*, which is almost certainly the finest nondramatic Elizabethan poem apart from those produced by Edmund Spenser, appeared in 1598.

There is argument among scholars concerning the order in which the plays subsequent to *Tamburlaine* were written. It is not uncommonly held that *Faustus* —Marlowe's most famous play, in which he tells the story of the doctor-turned-necromancer Faustus, who sells his soul to the devil in exchange for knowledge and power—quickly followed *Tamburlaine* and that then Marlowe turned to a more neutral, more "social" kind of writing in *Edward II* and *The Massacre at Paris*. His last play may have been *The Jew of Malta*, in which he signally broke new ground: the main character, Barabas, is more closely incorporated within his society than either Tamburlaine, the supreme conqueror, or Faustus, the lonely adventurer against God. It is known that *Tamburlaine, Faustus*, and *The Jew of Malta* were performed by the Admiral's Men, a company whose outstanding actor was Edward Alleyn, who most certainly played Tamburlaine, Faustus, and Barabas the Jew.

WILLIAM SHAKESPEARE

(baptized April 26, 1564, Stratford-upon-Avon, Warwickshire, Eng.—d. April 23, 1616, Stratford-upon-Avon)

William Shakespeare is often called the English national poet and is considered by many to be the greatest dramatist of all time. He occupies a position unique in world literature. Other poets, such as Homer and Dante, and novelists, such as Leo Tolstoy and Charles Dickens, have transcended national barriers as well. But no writer's living reputation can compare to that of Shakespeare, whose plays, written in the late 16th and early 17th centuries for a small repertory theatre, are now performed and read more often and in more countries than ever before. The prophecy of his great contemporary, the poet and dramatist Ben Jonson, that Shakespeare "was not of an age, but for all time," has been fulfilled.

Early Life in Stratford

The parish register of Holy Trinity Church in Stratford-upon-Avon, Warwickshire, shows that he was baptized there on April 26, 1564; his birthday is traditionally celebrated on April 23. His father, John Shakespeare, was a burgess of the borough, who in 1565 was chosen an alderman and in 1568 bailiff (the position corresponding to mayor, before the grant of a further charter to Stratford in 1664). He was engaged in various kinds of trade and appears to have suffered some fluctuations in prosperity. His wife, Mary Arden, of Wilmcote, Warwickshire, came from an ancient family and was the heiress to some land. (Given the somewhat rigid social distinctions of the 16th century, this marriage must have been a step up the social scale for John Shakespeare.)

Stratford enjoyed a grammar school of good quality, and the education there was free, the schoolmaster's salary being paid by the borough. No lists of the pupils who were at the school in the 16th century have survived, but it would be absurd to suppose the bailiff of the town did not send his son there. The boy's education would consist mostly of Latin studies—learning to read, write, and speak the language fairly well and studying some of the Classical historians, moralists, and poets. Shakespeare did not go on to the university, and indeed, it is unlikely that the scholarly round of logic, rhetoric, and other studies then followed there would have interested him.

Instead, at age 18, he married. Where and exactly when are not known, but the episcopal registry at Worcester preserves a bond dated Nov. 28, 1582, and executed by two yeomen of Stratford, named Sandells and Richardson, as a security to the bishop for the issue of a license for the marriage of William Shakespeare and "Anne Hathaway of Stratford," upon the consent of her friends and upon once asking of the banns. (Anne died in 1623, seven years after Shakespeare. There is good evidence to associate her with a family of Hathaways who inhabited a beautiful farmhouse, now much visited, 2 miles [3.2 km] from Stratford.) The next date of interest is found in the records of the Stratford church, where a daughter, named Susanna, born to William Shakespeare, was baptized on May 26, 1583. On Feb. 2, 1585, twins were baptized, Hamnet and Judith. (Hamnet, Shakespeare's only son, died 11 years later.)

How Shakespeare spent the next eight years or so, until his name begins to appear in London theatre records, is not known. There are stories—given currency long after his death—of stealing deer and getting into trouble with a local magnate, Sir Thomas Lucy of Charlecote, near Stratford; of earning his living as a schoolmaster in the country; of going to London and gaining entry to the world of theatre by minding the horses of theatregoers. It has also been conjectured that Shakespeare spent some time as a member of a great household and that he was a soldier, perhaps in the Low Countries. In lieu of external evidence, such extrapolations about Shakespeare's life have often been made from the internal "evidence" of his writings. But this method is unsatisfactory. One cannot conclude, for example, from his allusions to the law that Shakespeare was a lawyer, for he was clearly a writer who without

This painting, first identified in 2009 as depicting William Shakespeare, is believed to be the only true portrait of him made during his lifetime. Authenticity has been an issue with the famous playwright for years. Many have questioned whether Shakespeare actually wrote all the works credited to him. Oli Scarff/Getty Images

difficulty could get whatever knowledge he needed for the composition of his plays.

Career in the Theatre

The first reference to Shakespeare in the literary world of London comes in 1592, when a fellow dramatist, Robert Greene, declared in a pamphlet written on his deathbed:

> *There is an upstart crow, beautified with our feathers, that with his* Tygers heart wrapt in a Players hide *supposes he is as well able to bombast out a blank verse as the best of you; and, being an absolute* Johannes Factotum, *is in his own conceit the only Shake-scene in a country.*

What these words mean is difficult to determine, but clearly they are insulting, and clearly Shakespeare is the object of the sarcasms. When the book in which they appear (*Greenes, groats-worth of witte, bought with a million of Repentance*, 1592) was published after Greene's death, a mutual acquaintance wrote a preface offering an apology to Shakespeare and testifying to his worth. This preface also indicates that Shakespeare was by then making important friends. For, although the puritanical city of London was generally hostile to the theatre, many of the nobility were good patrons of the drama and friends of the actors. Shakespeare seems to have attracted the attention of the young Henry Wriothesley, the 3rd earl of Southampton, and to this nobleman were dedicated his first published poems, *Venus and Adonis* and *The Rape of Lucrece*.

One striking piece of evidence that Shakespeare began to prosper early and tried to retrieve the family's fortunes and establish its gentility is the fact that a coat of arms was granted to John Shakespeare in 1596. Rough drafts of this grant have been preserved in the College of Arms, London, though the final document, which must have been handed to the Shakespeares, has not survived. Almost certainly William himself took the initiative and paid the fees. The coat of arms appears on Shakespeare's monument (constructed before 1623) in the Stratford church. Equally interesting as evidence of Shakespeare's worldly success was his purchase in 1597 of New Place, a large house in Stratford, which he as a boy must have passed every day in walking to school.

How his career in the theatre began is unclear, but from roughly 1594 onward he was an important member of the Lord Chamberlain's company of players (called the King's Men after the accession of James I in 1603). They had the best actor, Richard Burbage. They had the best theatre, the Globe (finished by the autumn of 1599). They had the best dramatist, Shakespeare. It is no wonder that the company prospered. Shakespeare became a full-time professional man of his own theatre, sharing in a cooperative enterprise and intimately concerned with the financial success of the plays he wrote.

Unfortunately, written records give little indication of the way in which Shakespeare's professional life molded his marvelous artistry. All that can be deduced is that for 20 years Shakespeare devoted himself assiduously to his art, writing more than a million words of poetic drama of the highest quality.

Private Life

Shakespeare had little contact with officialdom, apart from walking—dressed in the royal livery as a member of the King's Men—at the coronation of King James I in 1604. He continued to look after his financial interests.

He bought properties in London and in Stratford. In 1605 he purchased a share (about one-fifth) of the Stratford tithes—a fact that explains why he was eventually buried in the chancel of its parish church. For some time he lodged with a French Huguenot family called Mountjoy, who lived near St. Olave's Church in Cripplegate, London. The records of a lawsuit in May 1612, resulting from a Mountjoy family quarrel, show Shakespeare as giving evidence in a genial way (though unable to remember certain important facts that would have decided the case) and as interesting himself generally in the family's affairs.

No letters written by Shakespeare have survived, but a private letter to him happened to get caught up with some official transactions of the town of Stratford and so has been preserved in the borough archives. It was written by one Richard Quiney and addressed by him from the Bell Inn in Carter Lane, London, whither he had gone from Stratford on business. On one side of the paper is inscribed: "To my loving good friend and countryman, Mr. Wm. Shakespeare, deliver these." Apparently Quiney thought his fellow Stratfordian a person to whom he could apply for the loan of £30—a large sum in Elizabethan times. Nothing further is known about the transaction, but, because so few opportunities of seeing into Shakespeare's private life present themselves, this begging letter becomes a touching document. It is of some interest, moreover, that 18 years later Quiney's son Thomas became the husband of Judith, Shakespeare's second daughter.

Shakespeare's will (made on March 25, 1616) is a long and detailed document. It entailed his quite ample property on the male heirs of his elder daughter, Susanna. (Both his daughters were then married, one to the aforementioned Thomas Quiney and the other to John Hall, a respected physician of Stratford.) As an afterthought, he bequeathed his "second-best bed" to his wife; no one can be certain what this notorious legacy means. The testator's signatures to the will are apparently in a shaky hand. Perhaps Shakespeare was already ill. He died on April 23, 1616. No name was inscribed on his gravestone in the chancel of the parish church of Stratford-upon-Avon. Instead these lines, possibly his own, appeared:

Good friend, for Jesus' sake forbear
To dig the dust enclosed here.
Blest be the man that spares these stones,
And curst be he that moves my bones.

Plays and Poems

Other than *Titus Andronicus* (*c.* 1589–92), Shakespeare did not experiment with formal tragedy in his early years. The young playwright was drawn more quickly into comedy, and with more immediate success. These comedies—such as *The Two Gentlemen of Verona* (*c.* 1590–94) and *The Taming of the Shrew* (*c.* 1590–94)—revel in stories of amorous courtship in which a plucky and admirable young woman (played by a boy actor) is paired off against her male wooer. His early history plays represent a genre with very few precedents; such plays as *Richard III* (*c.* 1592–94) were immediately successful.

In the second half of the 1590s, Shakespeare brought to perfection the genre of romantic comedy that he had helped to invent with such plays as *A Midsummer Night's Dream* (*c.* 1595–96), *Much Ado About Nothing* (*c.* 1598–99), and *As You Like It* (*c.* 1598–1600). More history plays completed his dramatization of 15th-century English history. The two genres are nicely complementary: the one deals with courtship and marriage, while the other examines the career of a young man growing up to be a worthy king. The tragedy *Romeo and Juliet* (*c.* 1594–96) is unique among plays of this middle period: it combines elements of romantic comedy and tragedy, yet the tragic vision is not that of the great tragedies that were to follow.

About 1599–1600 Shakespeare turned with unsparing intensity to the exploration of darker issues such as revenge, sexual jealousy, aging, midlife crisis, and death. He began writing not only his great tragedies but a group of plays that are hard to classify in terms of genre: *All's Well That Ends Well*, *Measure for Measure*, and *Troilus and Cressida*, all of which date from 1599 to 1605. One remarkable aspect about Shakespeare's great tragedies is that they proceed through such a staggering range of human emotions, and especially the emotions that are appropriate to the mature years of the human cycle. *Hamlet* (*c.* 1599–1601) cycles through revenge, despondency, and world-weariness. *Othello* (*c.* 1603–04) centres on sexual jealousy in marriage. *King Lear* (*c.* 1605–06) is about aging, generational conflict, and feelings of ingratitude. *Macbeth* (*c.* 1606–07) explores ambition mad enough to kill a father figure who stands in the way. *Antony and Cleopatra* (*c.* 1606–07) studies the exhilarating but ultimately dismaying phenomenon of midlife crisis. Shakespeare then turned to comedies that are usually called romances or tragicomedies; *The Winter's Tale* (*c.* 1609–11) and *The Tempest* (*c.* 1611) are typical in telling stories of wandering and separation that lead eventually to tearful and joyous reunion. *The Tempest* seems to have been intended as Shakespeare's farewell to the theatre, although other plays, likely collaborations, followed.

Shakespeare's poetry dates from his early professional years, about 1592–94, during a pause in his theatrical career when the plague closed down much theatrical activity.

Venus and Adonis (1593) and *The Rape of Lucrece* (1594) are the only works that Shakespeare seems to have shepherded through the printing process. Both owe a good deal to Ovid. His sonnets are more difficult to date, since they cannot have been written all at one time; most scholars set them within the period 1593–1600. As a narrative, the sonnet sequence tells of strong attachment, of jealousy, of grief at separation, of joy at being together and sharing beautiful experiences. But their order of composition is unknown, and Shakespeare did not oversee their publication; it is also unclear whether the sonnets reflect any circumstances in Shakespeare's personal life.

JOHN DONNE

(b. sometime between Jan. 24 and June 19, 1572, London, Eng.—d. March 31, 1631, London)

John Donne, the leading English poet of the Metaphysical school and dean of St. Paul's Cathedral, London (1621–31), is often considered the greatest love poet in the English language. He is also noted for his religious verse and treatises and for his sermons, which rank among the best of the 17th century.

Life and Career

At age 12 Donne matriculated at the University of Oxford, where he studied for three years, and he then most likely continued his education at the University of Cambridge, though he took no degree from either university because as a Roman Catholic he could not swear the required oath of allegiance to the Protestant queen, Elizabeth. Following his studies Donne probably traveled in Spain and Italy and then returned to London to read law, first at Thavies

Inn (1591) and then at Lincoln's Inn (1592–94). In 1596 he took part in expeditions led by the Earl of Essex and Sir Walter Raleigh.

After his return to London in 1597, Donne became secretary to Sir Thomas Egerton, lord keeper of the great seal, in whose employ Donne remained for almost five years. The appointment itself makes it probable that Donne had become an Anglican by this time. Donne met and fell in love with Anne More, niece of Egerton's second wife and the daughter of Sir George More, who was chancellor of the garter. The two married secretly, probably in December 1601. Because of the marriage, all possibilities of a career in public service were dashed, and Donne found himself at age 30 with neither prospects for employment nor adequate funds with which to support his household. During the next 10 years Donne lived in poverty and humiliating dependence, yet he wrote and studied assiduously, producing prose works on theology and canon law and composing love lyrics, religious poetry, and complimentary and funerary verse for his patrons. In 1612 a newfound patron, Sir Robert Drury, provided the Donnes with a house in London.

In 1614 Donne had come to believe he had a religious vocation, and he finally agreed to take holy orders. He was made a royal chaplain and received, at the king's command, the degree of doctor of divinity from Cambridge. Two years after his ordination, in 1617, Anne Donne died after giving birth to a stillborn child. Grief-stricken, Donne vowed never to marry again. His bereavement turned him fully to his vocation as an Anglican divine. In 1621 he was installed as dean of St. Paul's Cathedral. The power and eloquence of Donne's sermons soon secured for him a reputation as the foremost preacher in the England of his day, and he became a favourite of both King James I and King Charles I.

POETRY

Because almost none of Donne's poetry was published during his lifetime, it is difficult to date it accurately. Most of his poems were preserved in manuscript copies made by and passed among a relatively small but admiring coterie of poetry lovers. Donne's *Anniversaries* were published in 1611–12 and were the only important poetic works by him published in his lifetime.

Donne's poetry is marked by strikingly original departures from the conventions of 16th-century English verse, particularly that of Sir Philip Sidney and Edmund Spenser. Even his early satires and elegies, which derive from classical Latin models, contain versions of his experiments with genre, form, and imagery. His poems contain few descriptive passages like those in Spenser, nor do his lines follow the smooth metrics and euphonious sounds of his predecessors. Donne replaced their mellifluous lines with a speaking voice whose vocabulary and syntax reflect the emotional intensity of a confrontation. One consequence of this is a directness of language that electrifies his mature poetry. "For Godsake hold your tongue, and let me love," begins his love poem "The Canonization," plunging the reader into the midst of an encounter between the speaker and an unidentified listener.

From these explosive beginnings, the poems develop as closely reasoned arguments or propositions that rely heavily on the use of the conceit—i.e., an extended metaphor that draws an ingenious parallel between apparently dissimilar situations or objects. Donne, however, transformed the conceit into a vehicle for transmitting multiple, sometimes even contradictory, feelings and ideas. And, changing again the practice of earlier poets, he drew his imagery from such diverse fields as alchemy, astronomy, medicine, politics, global exploration, and philosophical disputation. These conceits offer brilliant and multiple insights into the subject of the metaphor and help give rise to the much-praised ambiguity of Donne's lyrics.

Prose

Donne's earliest prose works, including *Paradoxes and Problems*, probably were begun during his days as a student at Lincoln's Inn. In 1611 Donne completed his *Essays in Divinity*, the first of his theological works. Upon recovering from a life-threatening illness, Donne in 1623 wrote *Devotions upon Emergent Occasions*, the most enduring of his prose works. Each of its 23 devotions consists of a meditation, an expostulation, and a prayer, all occasioned by some event in Donne's illness, such as the arrival of the king's personal physician or the application of pigeons to draw vapours from Donne's head. The *Devotions* correlate Donne's physical decline with spiritual sickness, until both reach a climax when Donne hears the tolling of a passing bell and questions whether the bell is ringing for him. Like Donne's poetry, the *Devotions* are notable for their dramatic immediacy and their numerous Metaphysical conceits, such as the well-known "No man is an *Iland*," by which Donne illustrates the unity of all Christians in the mystical body of Christ.

It is Donne's sermons, however, that most powerfully illustrate his mastery of prose. One-hundred and fifty-six of them were published by his son in three great folio editions (1640, 1649, and 1661). Though composed during a time of religious controversy, Donne's sermons—intellectual, witty, and deeply moving—explore the basic tenets of Christianity rather than engage in theological disputes. The power of his sermons derives from their dramatic intensity, candid personal revelations, poetic rhythms, and striking conceits.

JOHN MILTON

(b. Dec. 9, 1608, London, Eng.—d. Nov. 8?, 1674, London?)

John Milton, an English poet and pamphleteer, is considered the most significant English author after William Shakespeare. Milton is best known for *Paradise Lost*, widely regarded as the greatest epic poem in English. Together with *Paradise Regained* and *Samson Agonistes*, it confirms Milton's reputation as one of the greatest English poets.

Milton enrolled at Christ's College, Cambridge, in 1625. A year later he was "rusticated," or temporarily expelled, for a period of time because of a conflict with one of his tutors. He was later reinstated. In 1629 Milton was awarded a Bachelor of Arts degree, and in 1632 he received a Master of Arts degree. Despite his initial intent to enter the ministry, Milton did not do so, a situation that has not been fully explained. While at Cambridge he wrote poems in Latin, Italian, and English. Among the most important of these are the companion poems *L'Allegro* and *Il Penseroso*, both published later in *Poems* (1645); Milton's first published poem in English, *On Shakespeare*, composed in 1630 and published anonymously in the Second Folio (1632) of Shakespeare's plays; and *On the Morning of Christ's Nativity*. In 1632–39 he engaged in private study—writing the masque *Comus* (first performed 1634) and the elegy *Lycidas* (1638)—and toured Europe, spending most of his time in Italy. The Florentine academies especially appealed to Milton, and he befriended young members of the Italian literati, whose similar humanistic interests he found gratifying. Invigorated by their admiration for him, he corresponded with his Italian friends after his return to England. While in Florence, Milton also met with Galileo, who was under virtual house arrest.

Having returned from abroad in 1639, Milton turned his attention from poetry to prose. In doing so, he entered

Images from John Milton's Paradise Lost *underscore the epic poem's sense of despair and regret. Patterned after the biblical story of Adam and Eve, the work also details Satan's battle with Jesus for immortal souls.* Hulton Archive/Getty Images

the controversies surrounding the abolition of the Church of England and of the Royalist government, at times replying to, and often attacking vehemently, English and Continental polemicists who targeted him as the apologist of radical religious and political dissent. His best-known prose is in the pamphlets *Areopagitica* (1644), on freedom of the press, and *Of Education* (1644). He mounted a cogent, radical argument, informed by the concepts of personal liberty and individual volition, for divorce in four tracts published 1643–45. He also wrote tracts against the Church of England and against the monarchy. Among the antimonarchical polemics of 1649–55 is *The Tenure of Kings and Magistrates* (1649), composed after Milton had become allied to those who sought to form an English republic but probably written before and during the trial of King Charles I though not published until after his death on Jan. 30, 1649; it urges the abolition of tyrannical kingship and the execution of tyrants. Thereafter, Milton was appointed secretary for foreign tongues (also called Latin secretary) for the Council of State, the executive body of the Commonwealth under Oliver Cromwell. Milton was entrusted with the duties of translating foreign correspondence, drafting replies, composing papers in which national and international affairs of state were addressed, and serving as an apologist for the Commonwealth against attacks from abroad.

He lost his sight about 1651 and thereafter dictated his works. After the Restoration he was arrested as a prominent defender of the Commonwealth but was soon released. His focus returned to poetry. Abandoning an earlier plan to compose an epic on the legendary British king Arthur, Milton instead turned to biblical subject matter and to a Christian idea of heroism. *Paradise Lost*, considered the greatest epic poem in English, was the result. It was first published in 10 books in 1667 and then in 12 books in 1674, at a length of almost 11,000 lines. It uses blank verse and reworks Classical epic conventions to recount the Fall of Man. *Paradise Lost* is ultimately not only about the downfall of Adam and Eve but also about the clash between Satan and the Son. Many readers have admired Satan's splendid recklessness, if not heroism, in confronting the Godhead. Satan's defiance, anger, willfulness, and resourcefulness define a character who strives never to yield. *Paradise Regained* (1671) is a shorter epic in which Christ overcomes Satan the tempter. It unfolds as a series of debates—an ongoing dialectic—in which Jesus analyzes and refutes Satan's arguments. Though *Paradise Regained* lacks the vast scope of *Paradise Lost*, it fulfills its purpose admirably by pursuing the idea of Christian heroism as a state of mind. More so than *Paradise Lost*, it dramatizes the inner workings of the mind of Jesus, his perception, and the interplay of faith and reason in his debates with Satan. Milton's third great long poem, *Samson Agonistes* (1671), is a dramatic poem in which the Old Testament figure conquers self-pity and despair to become God's champion.

Among prose works published late in Milton's life or after his death are *History of Britain*, which was incomplete when published in 1670, and an unfinished work on theology, which was discovered in 1832. The exact date and location of Milton's death remain unknown; he likely died from complications of the gout (possibly renal failure). He was buried inside St. Giles Cripplegate Church in London.

JEAN RACINE

(baptized Dec. 22, 1639, La Ferté-Milon, France—d. April 21, 1699, Paris)

Jean Racine was a dramatic poet and historiographer renowned for his mastery of French classical tragedy. He was not only a contemporary of Molière, the father of modern French comedy, but his career intersected with that of the man who rivalled him for the title of the greatest of all French playwrights.

Orphaned at an early age, Racine was educated in a Jansenist convent, and he chose drama in defiance of his upbringing. His first play, *Amasie*, was never produced and has not survived. His career as a dramatist began with the production by Molière's troupe of his play *La Thébaïde ou les frères ennemis* ("The Thebaide or the Enemy Brothers") at the Palais-Royal Theatre in 1664. Molière's troupe also produced Racine's next play, *Alexandre le grand* (*Alexander the Great*), which premiered at the Palais Royal in 1665. This play was so well received that Racine secretly negotiated with the Hôtel de Bourgogne, a rival troupe, to present a "second premiere" of *Alexandre*. The break with Molière was irrevocable; Racine even seduced Molière's leading actress, Thérèse du Parc, into joining him personally and professionally.

Molière hardly slackened his theatrical activity, however. Born Jean-Baptiste Poquelin in 1622 to a prosperous upholsterer, Molière had left home to become an actor in 1643, joining forces with the Béjart family. He cofounded the troupe known as the Illustre Théâtre and toured the French provinces (1645–58), writing plays and acting in them. After his troupe was established in a permanent theatre in Paris under the patronage of Louis XIV, he won acclaim in the court and among bourgeois audiences for his comedy *Les Précieuses ridicules* (1659; *The Affected Young Ladies*). His other major plays include *L'École des femmes* (1662; *The School for Wives*), *Tartuffe* (1664; initially banned by religious authorities), *Le Misanthrope* (1666), and *Le Malade imaginaire* (1673; *The Imaginary Invalid*), among others. His plays represent a portrait of all levels of 17th-century French society and are marked by their good-humoured and intelligent mockery of human vices, vanities, and follies. Taken ill during a performance in February 1673, he died of a hemorrhage within a day. As he had not been given the sacraments or the opportunity of formally renouncing the actor's profession, he was buried without ceremony.

Racine, after having made off with Thérèse du Parc in 1665, saw her star in his successful *Andromaque* (1667), which explored his theme of the tragic folly of passionate love. The three-act comedy *Les Plaideurs* (1668; *The Litigants*) offered Racine the opportunity to demonstrate his skill in Molière's privileged domain, as well as the occasion to display his expertise in Greek, of which he had better command than almost any nonprofessional classicist in France. The result, a brilliant satire of the French legal system, was an adaptation of Aristophanes' *The Wasps* that found much more favour at court than on the Parisian stage. The great tragedies *Britannicus* (1669), *Bérénice* (1670), and *Bajazet* (1672) followed. *Bérénice* marked the decisive point in Racine's theatrical career, for with this play he found a felicitous combination of elements that he would use, without radical alteration, for the rest of his secular tragedies: a love interest, a relatively uncomplicated plot, striking rhetorical passages, and a highly poetic use of time.

Phèdre (1677) is Racine's supreme accomplishment because of the rigour and simplicity of its organization, the emotional power of its language, and the profusion of its images and meanings. Racine presents Phaedra as consumed by an incestuous passion for her stepson, Hippolytus. Receiving false information that her husband, King Theseus, is dead, Phaedra declares her love to Hippolytus, who is horrified. Theseus returns and is falsely informed that Hippolytus has been the aggressor toward Phaedra. Theseus invokes the aid of the god Neptune to destroy his son, after which Phaedra kills herself out of guilt and sorrow. A structural pattern of cycles and circles in *Phèdre* reflects a conception of human existence as essentially changeless, recurrent, and therefore asphyxiatingly tragic. The play constitutes a daring representation of the contagion of sin and its catastrophic results. After writing his masterpiece, Racine retired to become official historian to Louis XIV. His final plays, *Esther* (1689) and *Athalie* (1691), were commissioned by the king's wife, Mme de Maintenon. Racine died in 1699 from cancer of the liver.

APHRA BEHN

(b. 1640?, Harbledown?, Kent, Eng.—d. April 16, 1689, London)

Aphra Behn, an English dramatist, fiction writer, and poet, was the first Englishwoman known to earn her living by writing. Her origin remains a mystery, in part because Behn may have deliberately obscured her early life. One tradition identifies Behn as the child known only as Ayfara or Aphra, who traveled in the 1650s with a couple named Amis to Suriname, which was then an English possession. She was more likely the daughter of a barber, Bartholomew Johnson, who may or may not have sailed with her and the rest of her family to Suriname in 1663. She returned to England in 1664 and married a merchant named Behn; he died (or the couple separated) soon after. Her wit and talent having brought her into high esteem, she was employed by King Charles II in secret service in the Netherlands in 1666. Unrewarded and briefly imprisoned for debt, she began to write to support herself.

Behn's early works were tragicomedies in verse. In 1670 her first play, *The Forc'd Marriage*, was produced, and *The Amorous Prince* followed a year later. Her sole tragedy, *Abdelazer*, was staged in 1676. However, she turned increasingly to light comedy and farce over the course of the

1670s. Many of these witty and vivacious comedies, notably *The Rover* (two parts, produced 1677 and 1681), were commercially successful. *The Rover* depicts the adventures of a small group of English Cavaliers in Madrid and Naples during the exile of the future Charles II. *The Emperor of the Moon*, first performed in 1687, presaged the harlequinade, a form of comic theatre that evolved into the English pantomime.

Though Behn wrote many plays, her fiction today draws more interest. Her short novel *Oroonoko* (1688) tells the story of an enslaved African prince whom Behn claimed to have known in South America. Its engagement with the themes of slavery, race, and gender, as well as its influence on the development of the English novel, helped to make it, by the turn of the 21st century, her best-known work. Behn's other fiction includes the multipart epistolary novel *Love-Letters Between a Nobleman and His Sister* (1684–87) and *The Fair Jilt* (1688).

Behn's versatility, like her output, was immense; she wrote other popular works of fiction, and she often adapted works by older dramatists. She also wrote poetry, the bulk of which was collected in *Poems upon Several Occasions, with A Voyage to the Island of Love* (1684) and *Lycidus; or, The Lover in Fashion* (1688). Behn's charm and generosity won her a wide circle of friends, and her relative freedom as a professional writer, as well as the subject matter of her works, made her the object of some scandal.

BASHŌ

(b. 1644, Ueno, Iga province, Japan—d. Nov. 28, 1694, Ōsaka)

Bashō is the supreme Japanese haiku poet. He greatly enriched the 17-syllable haiku form and made it an accepted medium of artistic expression.

Interested in haiku from an early age, Bashō—in full Matsuo Bashō, a pseudonym of Matsuo Munefusa—at first put his literary interests aside and entered the service of a local feudal lord. After his lord's death in 1666, however, Bashō abandoned his samurai (warrior) status to devote himself to poetry. Moving to the capital city of Edo (now Tokyo), he gradually acquired a reputation as a poet and critic. In 1679 he wrote his first verse in the "new style" for which he came to be known:

On a withered branch
A crow has alighted:
Nightfall in autumn.

The simple descriptive mood evoked by this statement and the comparison and contrast of two independent phenomena became the hallmark of Bashō's style. He attempted to go beyond the stale dependence on form and ephemeral allusions to current gossip that had been characteristic of haiku, which in his day had amounted to little but a popular literary pastime. Instead he insisted that the haiku must be at once unhackneyed and eternal. Following the Zen philosophy he studied, Bashō attempted to compress the meaning of the world into the simple pattern of his poetry, disclosing hidden hopes in small things and showing the interdependence of all objects.

In 1684 Bashō made the first of many journeys that figure so importantly in his work. His accounts of his travels are prized not only for the haiku that record various sights along the way but also for the equally beautiful prose passages that furnish the backgrounds. *Oku no hosomichi* (1694; *The Narrow Road to the Deep North*), describing his visit to northern Japan, is one of the loveliest works of Japanese literature.

On his travels Bashō also met local poets and competed with them in composing the linked verse (*renga*), an art in which he so excelled that some critics believe his *renga* were his finest work. When Bashō began writing *renga* the link between successive verses had generally depended on a pun or play on words, but he insisted that poets must go beyond mere verbal dexterity and link their verses by "perfume," "echo," "harmony," and other delicately conceived criteria.

One term frequently used to describe Bashō's poetry is *sabi*, which means the love of the old, the faded, and the unobtrusive, a quality found in the verse

Scent of chrysanthemums . . .
And in Nara
All the ancient Buddhas.

Here the musty smell of the chrysanthemums blends with the visual image of the dusty, flaking statues in the old capital. Living a life that was in true accord with the gentle spirit of his poetry, Bashō maintained an austere, simple hermitage that contrasted with the general flamboyance of his times. On occasion he withdrew from society altogether, retiring to Fukagawa, site of his Bashō-an ("Cottage of the Plantain Tree"), a simple hut from which the poet derived his pen name. Later men, honouring both the man and his poetry, revered him as the saint of the haiku.

The Narrow Road to Oku (1996), Donald Keene's translation of *Oku no hosomichi*, provides the original text and a modern-language version by Kawabata Yasunari. *The Monkey's Straw Raincoat and Other Poetry of the Basho School* (1981), a translation by Earl Miner and Hiroko Odagiri, presents a celebrated linked-verse sequence in which Bashō took part, along with a commentary.

SOR JUANA INÉS DE LA CRUZ

(b. Nov. 12, 1651?, San Miguel Nepantla, Viceroyalty of New Spain [now in Mexico]—d. April 17, 1695, Mexico City)

The poet, dramatist, scholar, and nun who came to be known as Sor Juana Inés de la Cruz was an outstanding writer of the Latin American colonial period and of the Hispanic Baroque.

Juana Ramírez de Asbaje was born out of wedlock to a family of modest means in either 1651 or, according to a baptismal certificate, 1648. Her mother was a Creole and her father Spanish. Juana's mother sent the gifted child to live with relatives in Mexico City. There her prodigious intelligence attracted the attention of the viceroy, Antonio Sebastián de Toledo, marquis de Mancera. He invited her to court as a lady-in-waiting in 1664 and later had her knowledge tested by some 40 noted scholars. In 1667, given what she called her "total disinclination to marriage" and her wish "to have no fixed occupation which might curtail my freedom to study," Sor (Spanish: "Sister") Juana began her life as a nun with a brief stay in the order of the Discalced Carmelites. She moved in 1669 to the more lenient Convent of Santa Paula of the Hieronymite order in Mexico City, and there she took her vows.

Convent life afforded Sor Juana time to study and write and the opportunity to teach music and drama to the girls in Santa Paula's school. She also functioned as the convent's archivist and accountant. In her convent cell, Sor Juana amassed one of the largest private libraries in the New World, together with a collection of musical and scientific instruments. The patronage of the viceroy and vicereine of New Spain, notably that of the marquis and marquise de la Laguna from 1680 to 1688, helped her maintain her exceptional freedom. They visited her, favoured her, and had her works published in Spain. For her part,

Sor Juana, though cloistered, became the unofficial court poet in the 1680s.

Sor Juana was the last great writer of the Hispanic Baroque and the first great exemplar of colonial Mexican culture. She employed all of the poetic models then in fashion, including sonnets, romances (ballad form), and so on. She drew on a vast stock of Classical, biblical, philosophical, and mythological sources. She wrote moral, satiric, and religious lyrics, along with many poems of praise to court figures. Though it is impossible to date much of her poetry, it is clear that, even after she became a nun, Sor Juana wrote secular love lyrics. She also authored both allegorical religious dramas and entertaining cloak-and-dagger plays. Notable in the popular vein are the *villancicos* (carols) that she composed to be sung in the cathedrals of Mexico City, Puebla, and Oaxaca.

Sor Juana celebrated woman as the seat of reason and knowledge rather than passion. Her poem *Hombres necios* ("Foolish Men") accuses men of the illogical behaviour that they criticize in women. Her many love poems in the first person show a woman's *desengaño* ("disillusionment") with love, given the strife, pain, jealousy, and loneliness that it occasions. Sor Juana's most significant full-length plays involve the actions of daring, ingenious women. Sor Juana also occasionally wrote of her native Mexico. The short play that introduces her religious drama *El divino Narciso* (1689; *The Divine Narcissus*, in a bilingual edition) blends the Aztec and Christian religions. Her various carols contain an amusing mix of Nahuatl (a Mexican Indian language) and Hispano-African and Spanish dialects. Sor Juana's most important and most difficult poem, known as the *Primero sueño* (1692; *First Dream*), is both personal and universal. The date of its writing is unknown. It employs the convoluted poetic forms of the Baroque to recount the torturous quest of the soul for knowledge.

Sor Juana achieved considerable renown in Mexico and in Spain. With renown came disapproval from church officials. Sor Juana broke with her Jesuit confessor, Antonio Núñez de Miranda, in the early 1680s because he had publicly maligned her. The nun's privileged situation began definitively to collapse after the departure for Spain of her protectors, the marquis and marquise de la Laguna. In November 1690, Manuel Fernández de Santa Cruz, bishop of Puebla, published without Sor Juana's permission her critique of a 40-year-old sermon by the Portuguese Jesuit preacher António Vieira. Fernández de Santa Cruz titled the critique *Carta atenagórica* ("Letter Worthy of Athena"). Using the female pseudonym of Sister Filotea, he also admonished Sor Juana to concentrate on religious rather than secular studies. Sor Juana responded to the bishop of Puebla in March 1691 with her magnificent self-defense and defense of all women's right to knowledge, the *Respuesta a sor Filotea de la Cruz* ("Reply to Sister Filotea of the Cross"). In the autobiographical section of the document, Sor Juana traces the many obstacles that her powerful "inclination to letters" had forced her to surmount throughout her life.

Yet by 1694 Sor Juana had succumbed in some measure to external or internal pressures. She curtailed her literary pursuits. Her library and collections were sold for alms. She returned to her previous confessor, renewed her religious vows, and signed various penitential documents. Sor Juana died while nursing her sister nuns during an epidemic.

DANIEL DEFOE

(b. 1660, London, Eng.—d. April 24, 1731, London)

Daniel Defoe was an English novelist, pamphleteer, and journalist. He remains best known as the author of *Robinson Crusoe* (1719–22) and *Moll Flanders* (1722).

Although intended for the Presbyterian ministry, Defoe decided against this, and by 1683 had set up as a merchant. He dealt in many commodities, traveled widely at home and abroad, and became an acute and intelligent economic theorist.

In 1692, however, after prospering for a while, Defoe went bankrupt. The main reason for his bankruptcy was the loss that he sustained in insuring ships during the war with France—he was one of 19 "merchants insurers" ruined in 1692. He suffered further severe losses in 1703, when his prosperous brick-and-tile works near Tilbury failed during his imprisonment for political offenses, and he did not actively engage in trade after this time.

With Defoe's interest in trade went an interest in politics, both foreign and domestic. The first of many political pamphlets by him appeared in 1683. He was a supporter of William of Orange—"*William*, the Glorious, Great, and Good, and Kind," as Defoe was to call him—and Defoe supported him loyally, becoming his leading pamphleteer. In 1701, in reply to attacks on the "foreign" king, Defoe published his vigorous and witty poem *The True-Born Englishman*, an enormously popular work. The most famous and skillful of all his pamphlets, "The Shortest-Way With The Dissenters" (1702), was published anonymously but resulted in his being fined and sentenced to stand three times in the pillory, a prosecution that was likely primarily political, driven by an attempt to force him into betraying certain political allies. Although apprehensive of his punishment, Defoe had spirit enough, while awaiting his ordeal, to write the audacious "Hymn To The Pillory" (1703). This helped to turn the occasion into something of a triumph, with the pillory garlanded, the mob drinking his health, and the poem on sale in the streets.

Perhaps Defoe's most remarkable achievement at this time was his periodical, the *Review*. He wrote this serious, forceful, and long-lived paper practically single-handedly from 1704 to 1713. At first a weekly, it became a thrice-weekly publication in 1705, and Defoe continued to produce it even when, for short periods in 1713, his political enemies managed to have him imprisoned again on various pretexts. It was, effectively, the main government organ. But, in addition to politics as such, Defoe discussed current affairs in general, religion, trade, manners, morals, and so on. His work undoubtedly had a considerable influence on the development of later essay periodicals (such as Richard Steele and Joseph Addison's *The Tatler* and *The Spectator*) and of the newspaper press.

With George I's accession (1714), Defoe continued to write for the government of the day and to carry out intelligence work. At about this time (perhaps prompted by a severe illness), he wrote the most popular of his many didactic works, *The Family Instructor* (1715). His writings to this point in his career would not necessarily have procured literary immortality for Defoe; this he achieved when in 1719 he turned to an extended work of prose fiction and (drawing partly on the memoirs of voyagers and castaways such as Alexander Selkirk) produced *Robinson Crusoe*. A German critic has called it a "world-book," a label justified not only by the enormous number of translations, imitations, and adaptations that have appeared but by the almost mythic power with which Defoe creates a hero and a situation with which every reader can in some sense identify.

Here (as in his works of the remarkable year 1722, which saw the publication of *Moll Flanders*, *A Journal of the Plague Year*, and *Colonel Jack*) Defoe displays his finest gift as a novelist—his insight into human nature. The men and women he writes about are all, it is true, placed in unusual circumstances; they are all, in one sense or another, solitaries; they all struggle, in their different ways, through a life that is a constant scene of jungle warfare; they all become, to some extent, obsessive. They are also ordinary human beings, however, and Defoe, writing always in the first person, enters into their minds and analyzes their motives. His novels are given verisimilitude by their matter-of-fact style and their vivid concreteness of detail; the latter may seem unselective, but it effectively helps to evoke a particular, circumscribed world. Defoe's range is narrow, but within that range he is a novelist of considerable power, and his plain, direct style, as in almost all of his writing, holds the reader's interest.

In 1724 he published his last major work of fiction, *Roxana*, though in the closing years of his life, despite failing health, he remained active and enterprising as a writer. In 1724–26 were published the three volumes of Defoe's animated and informative *Tour Through the Whole Island of Great Britain*, based in large part on his visits to Scotland, especially at the time of the Act of Union in 1707.

JONATHAN SWIFT

(b. Nov. 30, 1667, Dublin, Ire.—d. Oct. 19, 1745, Dublin)

The Anglo-Irish author Jonathan Swift is among the foremost prose satirists in the English language. Besides the celebrated novel *Gulliver's Travels* (1726), he wrote such shorter works as *A Tale of a Tub* (1704) and *A Modest Proposal* (1729).

In 1682 Swift entered Trinity College, Dublin, where he was granted his Bachelor of Arts degree in 1686 and continued in residence as a candidate for his Master of Arts degree until 1689. But the Roman Catholic disorders that had begun to spread through Dublin after the Glorious Revolution (1688–89) in Protestant England caused Swift, a Protestant, to seek security in England. In 1692 he received the degree of M.A. at the University of Oxford.

During a return visit to Ireland, he took orders in the Anglican church, being ordained priest in January 1695.

Between 1691 and 1694 Swift wrote a number of poems, notably six odes. But his true genius did not find expression until he turned from verse to prose satire and composed, between 1696 and 1699, *A Tale of a Tub*. Published anonymously in 1704, this work is outstanding for its exuberance of satiric wit and energy and is marked by an incomparable command of stylistic effects, largely in the nature of parody.

After 1699, Swift returned to Dublin as chaplain and secretary to the earl of Berkeley, who was then going to Ireland as a lord justice. During the ensuing years he was in England on some four occasions—in 1701, 1702, 1703, and 1707 to 1709—and won wide recognition in London for his intelligence and his wit as a writer. Early in 1700 he was preferred to several posts in the Irish church. His public writings of this period show that he kept in close touch with affairs in both Ireland and England. Swift's works brought him to the attention of a circle of Whig writers led by Joseph Addison, but Swift was uneasy about many policies of the Whig administration. He was a Whig by birth, education, and political principle, but he was also passionately loyal to the Anglican church, and he came to view with apprehension the Whigs' growing determination to yield ground to the Nonconformists.

A momentous period began for Swift when, in 1710, he once again found himself in London. A Tory ministry headed by Robert Harley (later earl of Oxford) and Henry St. John (later Viscount Bolingbroke) was replacing that of the Whigs. Swift's reactions to such a rapidly changing world are vividly recorded in his *Journal to Stella*, a series of letters written between his arrival in England in 1710 and 1713. The astute Harley made overtures to Swift and won him over to the Tories. Swift quickly became the Tories' chief pamphleteer and political writer. He was rewarded for his services in April 1713 with his appointment as dean of St. Patrick's Cathedral in Dublin. With the accession of George I, the Tories were a ruined party, and Swift's career in England was at an end. He withdrew to Ireland, where he was to pass most of the remainder of his life.

After a period of seclusion, Swift gradually regained his energy. He turned again to verse, which he continued to write throughout the 1720s and early '30s, producing the impressive poem *Verses on the Death of Doctor Swift*, among others. By 1720 he was also showing a renewed interest in public affairs. In his Irish pamphlets of this period he came to grips with many of the problems, social and economic, then confronting Ireland. Of his Irish writings, *A Modest Proposal* remains perhaps the best known. It is a grimly ironic letter of advice in which a public-spirited citizen suggests that Ireland's overpopulation and dire economic conditions could be alleviated if the babies of poor Irish parents were sold as edible delicacies to be eaten by the rich.

Swift's greatest satire, *Gulliver's Travels*, was published in 1726. It is uncertain when he began this work, but it appears from his correspondence that he was writing in earnest by 1721 and had finished the whole by August 1725. Its success was immediate. This work, which is told in Gulliver's "own words," is the most brilliant as well as the most bitter and controversial of his satires. In each of its four books the hero, Lemuel Gulliver, embarks on a voyage, but shipwreck or some other hazard usually casts him up on a strange land. *Gulliver's Travels*'s matter-of-fact style and its air of sober reality confer on it an ironic depth that defeats oversimple explanations. Is it essentially comic, or is it a misanthropic depreciation of humankind? Pulling in different directions, this irony creates the tensions that are characteristic of Swift's best work, and reflects his vision of humanity's ambiguous position between bestiality and reasonableness.

Swift remained active throughout most of the 1730s—Dublin's foremost citizen and Ireland's great patriot dean. In the autumn of 1739 a great celebration was held in his honour. He had, however, begun to fail physically and later suffered a paralytic stroke, with subsequent aphasia. After his death in 1745, he was buried in St. Patrick's Cathedral.

VOLTAIRE

(b. Nov. 21, 1694, Paris, France—d. May 30, 1778, Paris)

Voltaire (the pseudonym of François-Marie Arouet) is one of the greatest of all French writers, known especially as a courageous crusader against tyranny, bigotry, and cruelty. He studied law but abandoned it to become a writer.

After the death of Louis XIV, in 1715, under the morally relaxed Regency, Voltaire became the wit of Parisian society, and his epigrams were widely quoted. In 1718, after the success of *Oedipe*, the first of his tragedies, he was acclaimed as the successor of the great classical dramatist Jean Racine and thenceforward adopted the name of Voltaire. (The origin of this pen name remains doubtful.) He continued to write for the theatre all his life.

Voltaire was twice imprisoned in the Bastille for his remarks and in 1726 was exiled to England, where his philosophical interests deepened; he also learned English, and to the end of his life he was able to speak and write it fluently. He returned to France in 1728 or 1729. His epic poem *La Henriade* (1728) was well received, but his lampoons of the Regency and his liberal religious opinions caused offense. His *Lettres philosophiques* (1734) spoke out against established religious and political systems: they contrast

Although he began a law career and was also a noted philosopher, Voltaire achieved his greatest success as a writer. Through his poems and plays, he became an advocate for the downtrodden and oppressed in his native France. Hulton Archive/Getty Images

the Empiricist psychology of the English philosopher John Locke with the conjectural lucubrations of the French philosopher René Descartes. A philosopher worthy of the name disdains empty, a priori speculations, Voltaire argues; he instead observes the facts and reasons from them.

The frankness of Voltaire's attack created an uproar. When a warrant of arrest was issued in 1734, he fled Paris and settled at Cirey in Champagne with Mme du Châtelet, who became his patroness and mistress. There he continued his theatrical writing, and he also turned to scientific research and the systematic study of religions and culture. Because of a lawsuit, he followed Mme du Châtelet to Brussels in May 1739, and thereafter they were constantly on the move between Belgium, Cirey, and Paris. After her death, in 1749, he spent periods in Berlin and Geneva; in 1754 he settled in Switzerland, and in 1758 he bought Ferney, a property on the Swiss border which, together with Tourney in France, enabled him, by crossing the frontier, to safeguard himself against police incursion from either country.

A period of intense and wide-ranging work followed, and there was scarcely a subject of importance on which he did not speak. In addition to his many works on philosophical and moral problems, he wrote *contes* ("tales"), including *Zadig* (1747), which is a kind of allegorical autobiography in which the Babylonian sage Zadig, like Voltaire, suffers persecution, is pursued by ill fortune, and ends by doubting the tender care of Providence for human beings, and *Micromégas* (1752), which measures the littleness of man in the cosmic scale. His best-known work, *Candide* (1759), is a satire on philosophical optimism. In it, the youth Candide, disciple of Doctor Pangloss (himself a disciple of the philosophical optimism of Leibniz), saw and suffered such misfortune that he was unable to believe that this was "the best of all possible worlds." Having retired with his companions to the shores of the Propontis, he discovered that the secret of happiness was "to cultivate one's garden," a practical philosophy excluding excessive idealism and nebulous metaphysics.

Voltaire's fame was now worldwide. As the "Innkeeper of Europe," as he was called, he welcomed such literary figures as James Boswell, Giovanni Casanova, Edward Gibbon, the Prince de Ligne, and the fashionable philosophers of Paris. He kept up an enormous correspondence—with the Philosophes, with his actresses and actors, and with those high in court circles, such as the duc de Richelieu (grandnephew of the Cardinal de Richelieu), the duc de Choiseul, and Mme du Barry, Louis XV's favourite. He renewed his correspondence with Frederick II and exchanged letters with Catherine II of Russia. His main interest at this time, however, was his opposition to *l'infâme*, a word he used to designate the church, especially when it was identified with intolerance.

Voltaire's epic poetry, lyrical verse, and plays are virtually unknown today, but his *contes* are continually republished, and his letters are regarded as one of the great monuments of French literature. Yet it was the theatre that brought Voltaire back to Paris in 1778. Wishing to direct the rehearsals of *Irène*, he made his triumphal return to the city he had not seen for 28 years. His health was profoundly impaired by the ensuing excitement, and he died several months later.

HENRY FIELDING

(b. April 22, 1707, Sharpham Park, Somerset, Eng.—d. Oct. 8, 1754, Lisbon, Port.)

Henry Fielding was a novelist and playwright who is considered one of the founders of the English novel.

He began his literary career as a playwright who wrote satirical plays often targeting political corruption of the times. The passage in 1737 of the Licensing Act, by which all new plays had to be approved and licensed by the Lord Chamberlain before production, ended this work. Fielding then became a barrister but had little success. He probably wrote *Shamela* (1741), a burlesque of Samuel Richardson's novel *Pamela* that he never claimed.

Fielding's *Joseph Andrews* also satirizes *Pamela*, with Joseph, Pamela's virtuous footman brother, resisting the attempts of a highborn lady to seduce him. The parodic intention soon becomes secondary, and the novel develops into a masterpiece of sustained irony and social criticism. At its centre is Parson Adams, one of the great comic figures of literature. Fielding explains in his preface that he is writing "a comic Epic-Poem in Prose." He was certainly inaugurating a new genre in fiction.

Journalistic work after the Jacobite Rebellion of 1745 made Fielding a trusted supporter of the government. His reward came in 1748, when he was appointed justice of the peace (or magistrate) for Westminster and Middlesex, with his own courthouse, which was also his residence, in Bow Street in central London. Together with his blind half brother, John Fielding, also a magistrate, he turned an office without honour—it carried no salary—into one of great dignity and importance and established a new tradition of justice and the suppression of crime in London. Among other things, Fielding strengthened the police force at his disposal by recruiting a small body of able and energetic "thieftakers"—the Bow Street Runners.

The History of Tom Jones, a Foundling (1749), with its great comic gusto, vast gallery of characters, and contrasted scenes of high and low life in London and the provinces, has always constituted the most popular of his works. Like its predecessor, *Joseph Andrews*, it is constructed around a romance plot. The hero, whose true identity remains unknown until the denouement, loves the beautiful Sophia Western, and at the end of the book he wins her hand. Numerous obstacles have to be overcome before he achieves this, however, and in the course of the action the various sets of characters pursue each other from one part of the country to another, giving Fielding an opportunity to paint an incomparably vivid picture of England in the mid-18th century. The introductory chapters at the beginning of each book make it clear how carefully Fielding had considered the problem of planning the novel. No novelist up until then had so clear an idea of what a novel should be, so that it is not surprising that *Tom Jones* is a masterpiece of literary engineering.

Amelia (1751), a much more sombre work, anticipates the Victorian domestic novel, being a study of the relationship between a man and his wife. It is also Fielding's most intransigent representation of the evils of the society in which he lived, and he clearly finds the spectacle no longer comic.

SAMUEL JOHNSON

(b. Sept. 18, 1709, Lichfield, Staffordshire, Eng.—d. Dec. 13, 1784, London)

Samuel Johnson, an English critic, biographer, essayist, poet, and lexicographer, is regarded as one of the greatest figures of 18th-century life and letters.

Johnson was the son of a poor bookseller. In 1728 he entered Pembroke College, Oxford. He stayed only 13 months, until December 1729, because he lacked the funds to continue. Johnson then became undermaster at Market Bosworth grammar school in 1732 but was unhappy there;

with only £20 inheritance from his father, he left his position with the feeling that he was escaping prison. In 1735 Johnson married Elizabeth Porter, a widow 20 years his senior. His wife's marriage settlement enabled him to open a school in Edial, near Lichfield, the following year. One of his students, David Garrick, would become the greatest English actor of the age and a lifelong friend, though their friendship was not without its strains. The school soon proved a failure, however, and he and Garrick left for London in 1737.

A year later Johnson began his long association with *The Gentleman's Magazine*, often considered the first modern magazine, with a wide range of poetry and prose. In the mid-1740s he began to work toward two of his major literary accomplishments. His *Miscellaneous Observations on the Tragedy of Macbeth* (1745), intended as a preliminary sample of his work, was his first significant Shakespeare criticism, which remains his greatest work of literary criticism. The work culminated in his editing an edition of Shakespeare, which appeared in eight volumes in 1765. Johnson edited and annotated the text and wrote a preface.

In 1746 he wrote *The Plan of a Dictionary of the English Language* and signed a contract for *A Dictionary of the English Language*, which was eventually published in two volumes in 1755—six years later than planned, but remarkably quickly for so extensive an undertaking. There had been earlier English dictionaries, but none on the scale of Johnson's. In addition to giving etymologies, not the strong point of Johnson and his contemporaries, and definitions, in which he excelled, Johnson illustrated usage with quotations drawn almost entirely from writing from the Elizabethan period to his own time.

Johnson's other works include *The Vanity of Human Wishes* (1749), his most impressive poem as well as the first work published with his name, and the long fiction *Rasselas* (originally published as *The Prince of Abissinia: A Tale*), which he wrote in 1759, during the evenings of a single week, in order to be able to pay for the funeral of his mother. His many essays appeared in the periodicals *The Rambler* (1750–52), *The Literary Magazine* (from 1756), and *The Universal Chronicle* (in a series known as *The Idler*, 1758–60), among others.

In 1765 Johnson received an honorary Doctor of Laws degree from Trinity College, Dublin, and 10 years later he was awarded the Doctor of Civil Laws from the University of Oxford. He never referred to himself as Dr. Johnson, though a number of his contemporaries did; James Boswell's consistent use of the title in his famous biography of Johnson, *The Life of Samuel Johnson, LL.D.* (1791), made it popular.

In the early 1770s Johnson wrote a series of political pamphlets supporting positions favourable to the government but in keeping with his own views. His subsequent works include *A Journey to the Western Islands of Scotland* (1775), based on travels with Boswell, and *Prefaces, Biographical and Critical, to the Works of the English Poets* (conventionally known as *The Lives of the Poets*), which was conceived modestly as short prefatory notices to an edition of English poetry but which expanded in scope so that Johnson's prefaces alone filled the first 10 volumes (1779–81) and the poetry grew to 56 volumes.

While Johnson is well remembered for his aphorisms—which contributed to his becoming, after Shakespeare, the most frequently quoted of English writers—his criticism is, perhaps, the most significant part of his writings. Through his *Dictionary*, his edition of Shakespeare, and his *Lives of the Poets* in particular, he helped invent what we now call "English Literature."

JOHANN WOLFGANG VON GOETHE

(b. Aug. 28, 1749, Frankfurt am Main [Germany]—d. March 22, 1832, Weimar, Saxe-Weimar)

Johann Wolfgang von Goethe was a poet, playwright, novelist, scientist, statesman, theatre director, critic, and amateur artist. He is considered the greatest German literary figure of the modern era.

Goethe is the only German literary figure whose range and international standing equal those of Germany's supreme philosophers (who have often drawn on his works and ideas) and composers (who have often set his works to music). In the literary culture of the German-speaking countries, he has had so dominant a position that, since the end of the 18th century, his writings have been described as "classical." In a European perspective he appears as the central and unsurpassed representative of the Romantic movement, broadly understood. He could be said to stand in the same relation to the culture of the era that began with the Enlightenment and continues to the present day as William Shakespeare does to the culture of the Renaissance and Dante to the culture of the High Middle Ages. His *Faust*, though eminently stageworthy when suitably edited, is also Europe's greatest long poem since John Milton's *Paradise Lost*, if not since Dante's *The Divine Comedy*.

Early Works

From April 1770 until August 1771 Goethe studied in Strasbourg for the doctorate. However, he had now emerged from his Christian period, and for his dissertation he chose a potentially shocking subject from ecclesiastical law concerning the nature of ancient Jewish religion. The dissertation, which questioned the status of the Ten Commandments, proved too scandalous to be accepted, as perhaps he intended, and he took instead the Latin oral examination for the licentiate in law (which by convention also conferred the title of doctor).

He later returned to Frankfurt. There he created a first draft over six weeks in the autumn of 1771 of *Geschichte Gottfriedens von Berlichingen mit der eisernen Hand, dramatisirt* ("The History of Gottfried von Berlichingen with the Iron Hand, Dramatized"), later titled simply *Götz von Berlichingen*. It was eventually translated by Sir Walter Scott, who was inspired by Goethe's example to think of using his own local history as the material for his novels. It also contains, however, an invented love-intrigue, focusing on the weak-willed Weislingen, a man who is unable to remain faithful to a worthy woman and betrays his class origins for the sake of a brilliant career. *Götz* was not published immediately but became known to a few friends in manuscript, and Goethe, already well-connected at the cultivated local court of Darmstadt, was asked to start reviewing for a new intellectual Frankfurt journal, the *Frankfurter Gelehrte Anzeigen* ("Frankfurt Review of Books"), which was hostile to the enlightened despotism of the German princely states, notably Prussia and Austria. He thereby effectively became part of the literary movement subsequently known as the Sturm und Drang ("Storm and Stress").

The years from 1773 to 1776 proved to be the most productive period in Goethe's life; poems and other works, mainly fragments, poured out. *Die Leiden des jungen Werthers* (*The Sorrows of Young Werther*), written in two months early in 1774, appeared that autumn and captured the imagination of a generation. It was almost immediately translated into French and in 1779 into English. The uncompromising concentration on the principal character's viewpoint—no one else's letters are communicated to the reader—permits the depiction from within of emotional and intellectual disintegration and partly accounts for the strength of the public reaction. Much moral outrage was generated by a work that appeared to condone both adultery and suicide, but for 35 years Goethe was known in the first instance as the author of *Werther*.

A Change in Perspective

In 1775, after an invitation to visit the court of the young new duke of Weimar, Goethe arrived at Weimar, where he accepted an appointment to the ducal court; he would remain there, on the whole, for the rest of his life. His presence helped to establish Weimar as a literary and intellectual centre. But Goethe was never entirely at ease in his role of Weimar courtier and official, and his literary output suffered. Until 1780, he continued to produce original and substantial works—particularly, in 1779, a prose drama, *Iphigenie auf Tauris* (*Iphigenia in Tauris*). Thereafter, however, he found it increasingly difficult to complete anything, and the flow of poetry, which had been getting thinner, all but dried up. He kept himself going as a writer by forcing himself to write one book of a novel, *Wilhelm Meisters theatralische Sendung* (*The Theatrical Mission of Wilhelm Meister*), each year until 1785. In a rough-and-tumble, ironic way, reminiscent of the English novelist Henry Fielding, the novel tells the story of a gifted young man who aims for stardom in a reformed German national theatrical culture. At first the plot was transparently autobiographical, but Goethe's own development gradually diverged from that of his hero, and the novel remained in manuscript during his lifetime. For 10 years Goethe turned away completely from publishing; the last lengthy work of his to be printed before the silence was *Stella* in 1776.

Goethe spent most of the years from 1786 to 1788 in Italy, away from the court and its pressures and disappointments. As a geologist, he climbed Vesuvius; as a connoisseur of ancient art, he visited Pompeii and Herculaneum. He consulted others about his own drawing and joined the circle of the British ambassador in Naples, Sir William Hamilton, and the actress who was later to be, as Emma, Lady Hamilton, the ambassador's wife and Lord Nelson's mistress. In Sicily he had reached a landscape impregnated with a Greek past, in which Homer's *Odyssey* seemed not fanciful but realistic; later he even toyed with the idea that Homer might have been a Sicilian. What Goethe came to value most about this time was not the opportunity of seeing ancient and Renaissance works of art and architecture firsthand but rather the opportunity of living as nearly as possible what he thought of as the ancient way of life, experiencing the benign climate and fertile setting in which human beings and nature were in harmony. His return to Weimar in June 1788 was extremely reluctant.

New Ventures

By his 40th birthday, in 1789, Goethe had all but completed the collected edition of his works, but he seems not to have known where to go next as a poet. A drama failed; he tinkered with satires and translations. Perhaps by way of compensation, he turned to science. In 1790 he published his theory of the principles of botany, *Versuch, die Metamorphose der Pflanzen zu erklären* ("Essay in Elucidation of the Metamorphosis of Plants"; Eng. trans. in *Goethe's Botany*), an attempt to show that all plant forms are determined by a process of alternating expansion and contraction of a basic unit, the leaf. In 1791, however, a completely new scientific issue began to obsess him: the theory of colour. Convinced that Newton was wrong to assume that white light could be broken into light of different colours, Goethe proposed a new approach of his own.

In 1794 the poet and dramatist Friedrich Schiller suggested that he and Goethe should collaborate on a new journal, *Die Horen* (*The Horae*), intended to give literature a voice in an age increasingly dominated by politics. The friendship with Schiller began a new period in Goethe's life, in some ways one of the happiest and, from a literary point of view, one of the most productive. In *The Horae* he published a collection of short stories, *Unterhaltungen deutscher Ausgewanderten* ("Conversations of German Émigrés"; Eng. trans. *The German Refugees*), which were found tedious, and the *Roman Elegies*, which were found scandalous, and serialized a translation of the autobiography of Florentine Mannerist artist Benvenuto Cellini, which was acceptable but unexciting.

Schiller soon lost interest in the journal, which ceased publication after three years. Perhaps it had served its purpose simply by initiating the collaboration with Goethe, which was closer, longer, and on a higher level than any comparable friendship in world literature. The poets began a correspondence, which ran to over a thousand letters, and for over 10 years they discussed each other's works and projects, as well as those of their contemporaries, in conversation and writing. Both profited incalculably from the relationship. But in early 1805 Schiller and Goethe both fell seriously ill. Schiller died. Goethe recovered but felt that, with Schiller dead, he had lost "the half of my existence."

In 1806 Napoleon routed the Prussian armies at the Battle of Jena. Weimar, 12 miles from the battle, was subsequently occupied and sacked, though Goethe's house was spared, thanks to Napoleon's admiration for the author of *Werther*. In 1808 he met Napoleon during the Congress of Erfurt and was made a knight of the Legion of Honour. He became reconciled to Napoleon's rule, regarding it as a more or less legitimate successor to the Holy Roman Empire, and, in the relatively peaceful interval after the Austrian war against France in 1809, a new serenity entered his writing. But that ended during the years 1814–17, after the overthrow of Napoleon's dominion by allied troops at the Battle of Leipzig (1813). Alienation from the modern age is the undertone in all his work of this period.

Later Years

In his final years he experienced a time of extraordinary, indeed probably unparalleled literary achievement by a man of advanced age. He prepared a final collected edition of his works, initially in 40 volumes, the *Ausgabe letzter Hand* ("Edition of the Last Hand"). He wrote a fourth section of his autobiography, completing the story of his life up to his departure for Weimar in 1775; he compiled an account of his time in Rome in 1787–88, *Zweiter Römischer Aufenthalt* (1829; "Second Sojourn in Rome"); and above all he wrote part two of *Faust*, of which only a few passages had been drafted in 1800.

Work on *Faust* accompanied Goethe throughout his adult life. Of a possible plan in 1769 to dramatize the story of the man who sold his soul to the Devil in exchange for earthly fulfillment, perhaps including his ultimate redemption, no firm evidence survives. The first published version,

Faust: ein Fragment, appeared in 1790, with *Faust: Part One* following in 1808 and *Faust: Part Two* in 1832. *Part Two* is, in a sense, a poetic reckoning with Goethe's own times, with their irresistible dynamism and their alienation from his Classical ideal of fulfilled humanity. As with much of Goethe's later work, its richness, complexity, and literary daring began to be appreciated only in the 20th century.

The year 1829 brought celebrations throughout Germany of Goethe's 80th birthday. In the spring of 1832, having caught a cold, he died of a heart attack.

ROBERT BURNS

(b. Jan. 25, 1759, Alloway, Ayrshire, Scot.—d. July 21, 1796, Dumfries, Dumfriesshire)

Robert Burns, considered the national poet of Scotland, wrote lyrics and songs in the Scottish dialect of English. He was also famous for his amours and his rebellion against orthodox religion and morality.

Watching his father die a worn-out and bankrupt man in 1784 helped to make Burns both a rebel against the social order of his day and a bitter satirist of all forms of religious and political thought that condoned or perpetuated inhumanity. He received some formal schooling from a teacher as well as sporadically from other sources. He acquired a superficial reading knowledge of French and a bare smattering of Latin, and he read most of the important 18th-century English writers as well as Shakespeare, Milton, and Dryden. His knowledge of Scottish literature was confined in his childhood to orally transmitted folk songs and folk tales together with a modernization of the late 15th-century poem *Wallace*.

Proud, restless, and full of a nameless ambition, the young Burns did his share of hard work on his family's

Robert Burns, engraving from A Biographical Dictionary of Eminent Scotsmen, *1870*. © Photos.com/Jupiterimages

farm. He developed rapidly throughout 1784 and 1785 as an "occasional" poet who more and more turned to verse to express his emotions of love, friendship, or amusement or his ironical contemplation of the social scene. But these were not spontaneous effusions by an almost-illiterate peasant. Burns was a conscious craftsman; his entries in the commonplace book that he had begun in 1783 reveal that from the beginning he was interested in the technical problems of versification. Though he wrote poetry for his own amusement and that of his friends, Burns remained dissatisfied. In the midst of personal and economic troubles he published *Poems, Chiefly in the Scottish Dialect* in 1786. Its success with simple country folk and sophisticated Edinburgh critics alike was immediate and overwhelming. It included a handful of first-rate Scots poems: *The Twa Dogs*, *Scotch Drink*, *The Holy Fair*, *An Address to the Deil*, *The Death and Dying Words of Poor Maillie*, *To a Mouse*, *To a Louse*, and some others, including a number of verse letters addressed to various friends. In addition, there were six gloomy and histrionic poems in English, four songs, of which only one, "It Was Upon a Lammas Night," showed promise of his future greatness as a song writer.

Burns moved to Edinburgh in 1786 and was lionized, patronized, and showered with well-meant but dangerous advice. After a number of amorous and other adventures there and several trips to other parts of Scotland, he settled in the summer of 1788 at a farm in Ellisland, Dumfriesshire. At Edinburgh, too, he arranged for a new and enlarged edition (1787) of his *Poems*, but little of significance was added.

In Edinburgh Burns had met James Johnson, a keen collector of Scottish songs who was bringing out a series of volumes of songs with the music and who enlisted

Burns's help in finding, editing, improving, and rewriting items. Burns was enthusiastic and soon became virtual editor of Johnson's *The Scots Musical Museum*. Later, he became involved with a similar project for George Thomson, but Thomson was a more consciously genteel person than Johnson, and Burns had to fight with him to prevent him from "refining" words and music and so ruining their character. Johnson's *The Scots Musical Museum* (1787–1803) and the first five volumes of Thomson's *A Select Collection of Original Scotish Airs for the Voice* (1793–1818) contain the bulk of Burns's songs. Burns spent the latter part of his life in assiduously collecting and writing songs to provide words for traditional Scottish airs. He obtained a post in the excise service in 1789 and moved to Dumfries in 1791, where he lived until his death. He wrote numerous "occasional" poems and did an immense amount of work for the two song collections, in addition to carrying out his duties as exciseman.

It is by his songs that Burns is best known, and it is his songs that have carried his reputation around the world. Burns is without doubt the greatest songwriter Great Britain has produced. He wrote all his songs to known tunes, sometimes writing several sets of words to the same air in an endeavour to find the most apt poem for a given melody. Many songs which, it is clear from a variety of evidence, must have been substantially written by Burns he never claimed as his. He never claimed "Auld Lang Syne," for example, which he described simply as an old fragment he had discovered, but the song we have is almost certainly his, though the chorus and probably the first stanza are old. (Burns wrote it for a simple and moving old air that is *not* the tune to which it is now sung, as Thomson set it to another tune.) The full extent of Burns's work on Scottish song will probably never be known.

WILLIAM WORDSWORTH

(b. April 7, 1770, Cockermouth, Cumberland, Eng.—d. April 23, 1850, Rydal Mount, Westmorland)

William Wordsworth was an English poet whose *Lyrical Ballads* (1798), written with Samuel Taylor Coleridge, helped launch the English Romantic movement.

Wordsworth, orphaned at age 13, entered St. John's College, Cambridge in 1787. Repelled by the competitive pressures there, he elected to idle his way through the university. The most important thing he did in his college years was to devote his summer vacation in 1790 to a long walking tour through revolutionary France. There he was caught up in the passionate enthusiasm that followed the fall of the Bastille and became an ardent republican sympathizer.

After graduation and another brief trip to France, Wordsworth found himself unprepared for any profession, rootless, virtually penniless, and bitterly hostile to his own country's opposition to the French. He lived in London in the company of radicals like William Godwin and learned to feel a profound sympathy for the abandoned mothers, beggars, children, vagrants, and victims of England's wars who began to march through the sombre poems he began writing at this time. This dark period ended in 1795, when a friend's legacy made possible Wordsworth's reunion with his beloved sister Dorothy—the two were never again to live apart—and their move in 1797 to Alfoxden House, near Bristol. There Wordsworth became friends with a fellow poet, Samuel Taylor Coleridge, and they formed a partnership that would change both poets' lives and alter the course of English poetry.

Their partnership was rooted in one marvelous year (1797–98) in which they "together wantoned in wild Poesy."

Stimulated by Coleridge and under the healing influences of nature and his sister, Wordsworth began to compose the short lyrical and dramatic poems for which he is best remembered. Some of these were affectionate tributes to Dorothy, some were tributes to daffodils, birds, and other elements of "Nature's holy plan," and some were portraits of simple rural people intended to illustrate basic truths of human nature. Many of these short poems were written to a daringly original program formulated jointly by Wordsworth and Coleridge, and aimed at breaking the decorum of Neoclassical verse. These poems appeared in 1798 in a slim, anonymously authored volume entitled *Lyrical Ballads*, which opened with Coleridge's long poem *The Rime of the Ancient Mariner* and closed with Wordsworth's *Tintern Abbey*. All but three of the intervening poems were Wordsworth's. The manifesto and the accompanying poems thus set forth a new style, a new vocabulary, and new subjects for poetry, all of them foreshadowing 20th-century developments.

About 1798 Wordsworth began writing the autobiographical poem that would absorb him intermittently for the next 40 years, and which was eventually published in 1850 under the title *The Prelude, or, Growth of a Poet's Mind. The Prelude* extends the quiet autobiographical mode of reminiscence that Wordsworth had begun in *Tintern Abbey* and traces the poet's life from his school days through his university life and his visits to France, up to 1799.

In the company of Dorothy, Wordsworth spent the winter of 1798–99 in Germany. Upon his return to England—where he took possession of Dove Cottage, at Grasmere, Westmorland, where he was to reside for eight of his most productive years—Wordsworth incorporated several new poems in the second edition of *Lyrical Ballads* (1800), notably two tragic pastorals of country life, *The Brothers* and *Michael.* These poems, together with the brilliant lyrics that were assembled in Wordsworth's second verse collection, *Poems, in Two Volumes* (1807), help to make up what is now recognized as his great decade, stretching from his meeting with Coleridge in 1797 until 1808.

In his middle period Wordsworth invested a good deal of his creative energy in odes, the best known of which is *On the Power of Sound.* He also produced a large number of sonnets, most of them strung together in sequences.

In 1808 Wordsworth and his family moved from Dove Cottage to larger quarters in Grasmere, and five years later they settled at Rydal Mount, near Ambleside, where Wordsworth spent the remainder of his life. In 1813 he accepted the post of distributor of stamps for the county of Westmorland.

Through all these years Wordsworth was assailed by vicious and tireless critical attacks by contemptuous reviewers. But by the mid-1830s his reputation had been established with both critics and the reading public. Wordsworth succeeded his friend Robert Southey as Britain's poet laureate in 1843 and held that post until his own death in 1850. Wordsworth's last years were given over partly to "tinkering" his poems, as the family called his compulsive and persistent habit of revising his earlier poems through edition after edition. *The Prelude*, for instance, went through four distinct manuscript versions (1798–99, 1805–06, 1818–20, and 1832–39) and was published only after the poet's death in 1850. Most readers find the earliest versions of *The Prelude* and other heavily revised poems to be the best, but flashes of brilliance can appear in revisions added when the poet was in his seventies.

SIR WALTER SCOTT, 1ST BARONET

(b. Aug. 15, 1771, Edinburgh, Scot.—d. Sept. 21, 1832, Abbotsford, Roxburgh)

The Scottish novelist, poet, historian, and biographer Sir Walter Scott is often considered both the inventor and the greatest practitioner of the historical novel.

In 1786 Scott was apprenticed to his father as writer to the signet, a Scots equivalent of the English solicitor (attorney). His study and practice of law were somewhat desultory, for his immense youthful energy was diverted into social activities and miscellaneous readings in Italian, Spanish, French, German, and Latin. In the mid-1790s Scott became interested in German Romanticism, Gothic novels, and Scottish border ballads. His first published work, *The Chase, and William and Helen* (1796), was a translation of two ballads by the German Romantic balladeer G.A. Bürger. Scott's interest in border ballads finally bore fruit in his collection of them entitled *Minstrelsy of the Scottish Border*, 3 vol. (1802–03). His attempts to "restore" the orally corrupted versions back to their original compositions sometimes resulted in powerful poems that show a sophisticated Romantic flavour. The work made Scott's name known to a wide public, and he followed up his first success with a full-length narrative poem, *The Lay of the Last Minstrel* (1805), which ran into many editions. The poem's clear and vigorous storytelling, Scottish regionalist elements, honest pathos, and vivid evocations of landscape were repeated in further poetic romances, including *The Lady of the Lake* (1810), which was the most successful of these pieces.

Scott led a highly active literary and social life during these years, but his finances now took the first of several disastrous turns. He had become a partner in a printing (and later publishing) firm owned by James Ballantyne and

Sir Walter Scott, 1st Baronet, 1870. © Photos.com/Jupiterimages

his irresponsible brother John. By 1813 this firm was hovering on the brink of financial disaster, and although Scott saved the company from bankruptcy, from that time onward everything he wrote was done partly in order to make money and pay off the lasting debts he had incurred. Another ruinous expenditure was the country house he was having built at Abbotsford, which he stocked with enormous quantities of antiquarian objects.

By 1813 Scott had begun to tire of narrative poetry. That year he rediscovered the unfinished manuscript of a novel he had started in 1805, and in the early summer of 1814 he wrote with extraordinary speed almost the whole of his novel, which he titled *Waverley*. A story of the Jacobite rebellion of 1745, it reinterpreted and presented with living force the manners and loyalties of a vanished Scottish Highland society. The book was published anonymously, as were all of the many novels he wrote down to 1827.

In *Waverley* and succeeding novels Scott's particular literary gifts—as a born storyteller and a master of dialogue who possessed a flair for picturesque incidents and a rich, ornate, seemingly effortless literary style—could be utilized to their fullest extent. These immensely popular novels, now known as the *Waverley* novels, include *Guy Mannering* (1815) and *The Antiquary* (1816), which with *Waverley* completed a sort of trilogy covering the period from the 1740s to just after 1800. The first of four series of novels published under the title *Tales of My Landlord* was composed of *The Black Dwarf* and the masterpiece *Old Mortality* (1816). These were followed by the masterpieces *Rob Roy* (1817) and *The Heart of Midlothian* (1818), and then by *The Bride of Lammermoor* and *A Legend of Montrose* (both 1819). He then turned to themes from English history and elsewhere and wrote *Ivanhoe* (1819), a novel set in 12th-century England and one that remains his most popular book. Two more masterpieces were *Kenilworth* (1821), set in Elizabethan England, and the highly successful *Quentin Durward* (1823), set in 15th-century France. The best of his later novels are *Redgauntlet* (1824) and *The Talisman* (1825), the latter being set in Palestine during the Crusades.

Scott's immense earnings in those years contributed to his financial downfall. Eager to own an estate and to act the part of a bountiful laird, he anticipated his income and involved himself in exceedingly complicated and ultimately disastrous financial agreements with his publisher, Archibald Constable, and his agents, the Ballantynes. When Constable was unable to meet his liabilities and went bankrupt, he dragged down the Ballantynes and Scott in his wake because their financial interests were inextricably intermingled. Scott assumed personal responsibility for both his and the Ballantynes' liabilities and thus dedicated himself for the rest of his life to paying off debts amounting to about £120,000.

The result was reckless haste in the production of all his later books and compulsive work whose strain shortened his life, though his rapidity and ease of writing remained largely unimpaired, as did his popularity. Scott's creditors were not hard with him during this period, however, and he was generally revered as the grand old man of English letters. In 1827 Scott's authorship of the *Waverley* novels was finally made public. In 1831 his health deteriorated sharply, and he tried a continental tour with a long stay at Naples to aid recovery. He was taken home and died in 1832.

SAMUEL TAYLOR COLERIDGE

(b. Oct. 21, 1772, Ottery St. Mary, Devonshire, Eng.—d. July 25, 1834, Highgate, near London)

Samuel Taylor Coleridge was an English lyrical poet, critic, and philosopher. His *Lyrical Ballads*, written with William Wordsworth, heralded the English Romantic movement, and his *Biographia Literaria* (1817) is the most significant work of general literary criticism produced in the English Romantic period.

In 1791 Coleridge entered Jesus College, Cambridge. In his third year there, oppressed by financial difficulties, he went to London and enlisted as a dragoon under the assumed name of Silas Tomkyn Comberbache. Despite his unfitness for the life, he remained until discovered by his friends; he was then bought out by his brothers and restored to Cambridge. A chance meeting with the poet Robert Southey led to a close association between the two men and a plan, eventually aborted, to set up a utopian community in Pennsylvania.

Despite these difficulties, Coleridge's intellect flowered in an extraordinary manner during this period, as he embarked on an investigation of the nature of the human mind, joined by William Wordsworth, with whom he had become acquainted in 1795. Together they entered upon one of the most influential creative periods of English literature. Coleridge was developing a new, informal mode of poetry in which he could use a conversational tone and rhythm to give unity to a poem, best exemplified by *Frost at Midnight*.

That poem was an element of Coleridge's exploration of the possibility that all religions and mythical traditions, with their general agreement on the unity of God and the immortality of the soul, sprang from a universal life consciousness, which was expressed particularly through the phenomena of human genius. While these speculations were at their most intense, Coleridge, according to his own account, composed under the influence of laudanum the mysterious poetic fragment known as *Kubla Khan*. The exotic imagery and rhythmic chant of this poem have led many critics to conclude that it should be read as a "meaningless reverie," but it is, like *Frost at Midnight*, a complex poem about the nature of human genius.

Coleridge was enabled to explore similar themes in *The Rime of the Ancient Mariner*, composed during the autumn and winter of 1797–98. For this, his most famous poem, he drew upon the ballad form. The main narrative, infused with supernatural elements, tells how a sailor who has committed a crime against the life principle by slaying an albatross suffers from torments, physical and mental, in which the nature of his crime is made known to him. The placing of it at the beginning of *Lyrical Ballads* (1798) was evidently intended by Coleridge and Wordsworth to provide a context for the sense of wonder in common life that marks many of Wordsworth's contributions.

The decade following the publication of *Lyrical Ballads* were troubled years for Coleridge. He split with Wordsworth, and opium retained its powerful hold on him; the writings that survive from this period are redolent of unhappiness, with self-dramatization veering toward self-pity. In spite of this, however, there also appear signs of a slow revival. A course of lectures on Shakespeare he delivered during the winter of 1811–12 attracted a large audience. Coleridge's play *Osorio*, written many years before, was also produced at Drury Lane with the title *Remorse* in January 1813.

After Coleridge read the 17th-century archbishop Robert Leighton's commentary on the First Letter of Peter, Christianity, hitherto one point of reference for Coleridge, became his "official" creed. By aligning himself with the Anglican church of the 17th century at its best, he hoped to find a firm point of reference that would both keep him in communication with orthodox Christians of his time (thus giving him the social approval he always needed, even if only from a small group of friends) and enable him to pursue his former intellectual explorations in the hope of reaching a Christian synthesis that might help to revitalize the English church both intellectually and emotionally.

One effect was a sense of liberation and an ability to produce large works again. He drew together a collection of his poems (published in 1817 as *Sibylline Leaves*) and wrote *Biographia Literaria* (1817), a rambling and discursive but highly influential work in which he outlined the evolution of his thought and developed an extended critique of Wordsworth's poems. For the general reader *Biographia Literaria* is a misleading volume, since it moves bewilderingly between autobiography, abstruse philosophical discussion, and literary criticism. But over the whole work hovers Coleridge's veneration for the power of imagination.

His final decades were more settled years. His election as a fellow of the Royal Society of Literature in 1824 brought him an annuity and a sense of recognition. In 1830 he joined the controversy that had arisen around the issue of Catholic Emancipation by writing his last prose work, *On the Constitution of the Church and State*. The third edition of Coleridge's *Poetical Works* appeared in time for him to see it before his final illness and death in 1834.

Coleridge's achievement has been given more widely varying assessments than that of any other English literary artist, though there is broad agreement that his enormous potential was never fully realized in his works.

JANE AUSTEN

(b. Dec. 16, 1775, Steventon, Hampshire, Eng.—d. July 18, 1817, Winchester, Hampshire)

Jane Austen is the English writer who first gave the novel its distinctly modern character through her treatment of ordinary people in everyday life. Austen also created the comedy of manners of middle-class life in the England of her time in her novels.

Austen was born in the Hampshire village of Steventon, where her father, the Reverend George Austen, was rector. She was the seventh child in a family of eight. Her closest companion throughout her life was her elder sister, Cassandra, who also remained unmarried. Their father was a scholar who encouraged the love of learning in his children. His wife, Cassandra, was a woman of ready wit, famed for her impromptu verses and stories. The great family amusement was acting.

Jane Austen's lively and affectionate family circle provided a stimulating context for her writing. Moreover, her experience was carried far beyond Steventon rectory by an extensive network of relationships by blood and friendship. It was this world—of the minor landed gentry and the country clergy, in the village, the neighbourhood, and the country town, with occasional visits to Bath and to London—that she was to use in the settings, characters, and subject matter of her novels.

Her earliest-known writings date from about 1787, and between then and 1793 she wrote a large body of material that has survived in three manuscript notebooks. These contain plays, verses, short novels, and other prose and show Austen engaged in the parody of existing literary forms, notably sentimental fiction. Her passage to a more serious view of life from the exuberant high spirits and extravagances of her earliest writings is evident in *Lady Susan*, a short novel-in-letters written about 1793–94 (and not published until 1871).

In 1802 it seems likely that Austen agreed to marry Harris Bigg-Wither, the 21-year-old heir of a Hampshire family, but the next morning changed her mind. There

Jane Austen penned plays, poems, and short stories as a young lady and continued storytelling until her final illness made it impossible. Austen's productivity is rivaled only by her longevity. She remains a beloved author to this day. Hulton Archive/Getty Images

are also a number of mutually contradictory stories connecting her with someone with whom she fell in love but who died very soon after. Since Austen's novels are so deeply concerned with love and marriage, there is some point in attempting to establish the facts of these relationships. Unfortunately, the evidence is unsatisfactory and incomplete.

The earliest of her novels, *Sense and Sensibility*, was begun about 1795. Between October 1796 and August 1797 Austen completed the first version of *Pride and Prejudice*. In 1797 her father wrote to offer it to a London publisher for publication, but the offer was declined. *Northanger Abbey*, the last of the early novels, was written about 1798 or 1799, probably under the title "Susan." In 1803 the manuscript of "Susan" was sold to the publisher Richard Crosby for £10. He took it for immediate publication, but, although it was advertised, unaccountably it never appeared during her lifetime.

After years of unsettled lodgings, as a result of the family's move to Bath, Austen's brother Edward was able in 1809 to provide his mother and sisters with a large cottage in the village of Chawton, within his Hampshire estate, not far from Steventon. The prospect of settling at Chawton had already given Austen a renewed sense of purpose, and she began to prepare *Sense and Sensibility* and *Pride and Prejudice* for publication. Two years later Thomas Egerton agreed to publish *Sense and Sensibility*, which came out, anonymously, in November 1811. Both of the leading reviews, the *Critical Review* and the *Quarterly Review*, welcomed its blend of instruction and amusement. Meanwhile, in 1811 Austen had begun the most serious of her novels, *Mansfield Park*, which was finished in 1813 and published in 1814. *Pride and Prejudice* seems to have been the fashionable novel of its season. Between January 1814 and March 1815 she wrote *Emma*, which appeared in

December 1815; of her novels it is the most consistently comic in tone. *Persuasion* (written August 1815–August 1816) was published posthumously, with *Northanger Abbey*, in December 1817.

The years after 1811 seem to have been the most rewarding of her life. She had the satisfaction of seeing her work in print and well reviewed and of knowing that the novels were widely read. They were so much enjoyed by the Prince Regent (later George IV) that he had a set in each of his residences; and *Emma*, at a discreet royal command, was "respectfully dedicated" to him.

For the last 18 months of her life, she was busy writing. In January 1817 she began *Sanditon*, a robust and self-mocking satire on health resorts and invalidism. This novel remained unfinished owing to Austen's declining health. In April she made her will, and in May she was taken to Winchester to be under the care of an expert surgeon. She died on July 18, and six days later she was buried in Winchester Cathedral. Her authorship was announced to the world at large by her brother Henry, who supervised the publication of *Northanger Abbey* and *Persuasion*. There was no recognition at the time that regency England had lost its keenest observer and sharpest analyst.

GEORGE GORDON BYRON, 6TH BARON BYRON

(b. Jan. 22, 1788, London, Eng.—d. April 19, 1824, Missolonghi, Greece)

Lord Byron was a British Romantic poet and satirist whose poetry and personality captured the imagination of Europe.

In 1805 Byron entered Trinity College, Cambridge, where he piled up debts at an alarming rate and indulged in the conventional vices of undergraduates there. His

first published volume of poetry, *Hours of Idleness*, appeared in 1807. A sarcastic critique of the book in *The Edinburgh Review* provoked his retaliation in 1809 with a couplet satire, *English Bards and Scotch Reviewers*, in which he attacked the contemporary literary scene. This work gained him his first recognition.

In 1809 Byron took his seat in the House of Lords, and then embarked on a grand tour of Europe. In Greece Byron began *Childe Harolde's Pilgrimage*, which he continued in Athens. In March 1810 he sailed for Constantinople (now Istanbul, Turkey), visited the site of Troy, and swam the Hellespont (present-day Dardanelles) in imitation of Leander. In March 1812, the first two cantos of *Childe Harold's Pilgrimage* were published by John Murray, and Byron "woke to find himself famous." The poem describes the travels and reflections of a young man who, disillusioned with a life of pleasure and revelry, looks for distraction in foreign lands. Besides furnishing a travelogue of Byron's own wanderings through the Mediterranean, the first two cantos express the melancholy and disillusionment felt by a generation weary of the wars of the post-Revolutionary and Napoleonic eras.

During the summer of 1813, Byron apparently entered into intimate relations with his half sister Augusta, now married to Colonel George Leigh. He then carried on a flirtation with Lady Frances Webster as a diversion from this dangerous liaison. The agitations of these two love affairs and the sense of mingled guilt and exultation they aroused in Byron are reflected in a series of gloomy and remorseful verse tales he wrote at this time, including *The Corsair* (1814), which sold 10,000 copies on the day of publication.

Seeking to escape his love affairs in marriage, Byron proposed in September 1814 to Anne Isabella (Annabella)

Milbanke. The marriage took place in January 1815, and Lady Byron gave birth to a daughter, Augusta Ada, in December 1815. Annabella soon after left Byron to live with her parents, amid swirling rumours centring on his relations with Augusta Leigh and his bisexuality. Wounded by the general moral indignation directed at him, Byron went abroad in April 1816, never to return to England.

Byron sailed up the Rhine River into Switzerland and settled at Geneva, near Percy Bysshe Shelley and Mary Godwin, who had eloped, and Godwin's stepdaughter by a second marriage, Claire Clairmont, with whom Byron had begun an affair in England. In Geneva he wrote the third canto of *Childe Harold* (1816), which, perhaps predictably, follows Harold from Belgium up the Rhine River into Switzerland. At the end of the summer the Shelley party left for England, where Claire gave birth to Byron's illegitimate daughter Allegra in January 1817. In May he arrived in Rome, gathering impressions that he recorded in a fourth canto of *Childe Harold* (1818). He also wrote *Beppo*, a poem in ottava rima that satirically contrasts Italian with English manners.

In the light, mock-heroic style of *Beppo* Byron found the form in which he would write his greatest poem, *Don Juan*, a satire in the form of a picaresque verse tale. The first two cantos of *Don Juan* were begun in 1818 and published in July 1819. Byron transformed the legendary libertine Don Juan into an unsophisticated, innocent young man who, though he delightedly succumbs to the beautiful women who pursue him, remains a rational norm against which to view the absurdities and irrationalities of the world.

Shelley and other visitors in 1818 found Byron grown fat, with hair long and turning gray, looking older than his years, and sunk in sexual promiscuity. But a chance meeting with Countess Teresa Gamba Guiccioli, who was only 19 years old and married to a man nearly three times her age, reenergized Byron and changed the course of his life. He won the friendship of her father and brother, Counts Ruggero and Pietro Gamba, respectively, who initiated him into the secret society of the Carbonari and its revolutionary aims to free Italy from Austrian rule. Byron wrote cantos III, IV, and V of *Don Juan* at this time; it and a number of other works were published in 1821.

After collaborating with Shelley and Leigh Hunt on a periodical, Byron's attention wandered. Cantos VI to XVI of *Don Juan* were published in 1823–24 by Hunt's brother John, after Byron quarrelled with his publisher. From April 1823 Byron aided the Greeks in their struggle for independence from the Turks. He made efforts to unite the various Greek factions and took personal command of a brigade of Souliot soldiers, reputedly the bravest of the Greeks. But a serious illness in February 1824 weakened him, and in April he contracted the fever from which he died. Deeply mourned, he became a symbol of disinterested patriotism and a Greek national hero. His body was brought back to England and, refused burial in Westminster Abbey, was placed in the family vault near Newstead.

PERCY BYSSHE SHELLEY

(b. Aug. 4, 1792, Field Place, near Horsham, Sussex, Eng.—d. July 8, 1822, at sea off Livorno, Tuscany [Italy])

Percy Bysshe Shelley was an English Romantic poet whose passionate search for personal love and social justice was gradually channeled from overt actions into poems that rank with the greatest in the English language.

Shelley was the heir to rich estates acquired by his grandfather, Bysshe (pronounced "Bish") Shelley. Between the spring of 1810 and that of 1811, he published two Gothic novels and two volumes of juvenile verse. In the fall of 1810 Shelley entered University College, Oxford; he was expelled the following year. Late in August 1811, Shelley eloped with Harriet Westbrook, the younger daughter of a London tavern owner; by marrying her, he betrayed the acquisitive plans of his grandfather and father, who tried to starve him into submission but only drove the strong-willed youth to rebel against the established order. Early in 1812, Shelley, Harriet, and her older sister Eliza Westbrook went to Dublin, where Shelley circulated pamphlets advocating political rights for Roman Catholics, autonomy for Ireland, and freethinking ideals.

Lack of money finally drove Shelley to moneylenders in London, where in 1813 he issued *Queen Mab*, his first major poem—a nine-canto mixture of blank verse and lyric measures that attacks the evils of the past and present (commerce, war, the eating of meat, the church, monarchy, and marriage) but ends with resplendent hopes for humanity when freed from these vices. In June 1813 Harriet Shelley gave birth to their daughter Ianthe, but a year later Shelley fell in love with Mary Wollstonecraft Godwin, daughter of William Godwin and his first wife, *née* Mary Wollstonecraft. Against Godwin's objections, Shelley and Mary Godwin eloped to France on July 27, 1814. Following travels through France, Switzerland, and Germany, they returned to London, where they were shunned by the Godwins and most other friends.

By mid-May 1816, Shelley, Mary, and Mary's stepsister Claire Clairmont hurried to Geneva to intercept Lord Byron, with whom Claire had begun an affair. During this memorable summer, Shelley composed the poems "Hymn to Intellectual Beauty" and "Mont Blanc," and Mary began her novel *Frankenstein*, the novel for which she would become best known. Shelley's party returned to England in September, settling in Bath. Late in the year, Harriet Shelley drowned herself in London, and on Dec. 30, 1816, Shelley and Mary were married with the Godwins' blessing.

In March 1817 the Shelleys settled near Peacock at Marlow, where Shelley wrote his twelve-canto romance-epic *Laon and Cythna; or, The Revolution of the Golden City* and Mary Shelley finished *Frankenstein*. They compiled *History of a Six Weeks' Tour* jointly from the letters and journals of their trips to Switzerland. In November, *Laon and Cythna* was suppressed by its printer and publisher, who feared that Shelley's idealized tale of a peaceful national revolution, bloodily suppressed by a league of king and priests, violated the laws against blasphemous libel. After revisions, it was reissued in 1818 as *The Revolt of Islam*. Because Shelley's health suffered from the climate and his financial obligations outran his resources, the Shelleys and Claire Clairmont went to Italy, where Byron was residing.

Thus far, Shelley's literary career had been politically oriented. But in Italy, far from the daily irritations of British politics, Shelley deepened his understanding of art and literature and, unable to reshape the world to conform to his vision, he concentrated on embodying his ideals within his poems.

In early 1818–19 Shelley wrote *Prometheus Unbound* and outlined *The Cenci*, a tragedy on the Elizabethan model based on a case of incestuous rape and patricide in sixteenth-century Rome. He completed this drama during the summer of 1819. Memorable characters, classic five-act structure, powerful and evocative language, and moral ambiguities still make *The Cenci* theatrically effective. Even so, it is a less notable achievement than *Prometheus Unbound: A Lyrical Drama*, the keystone of Shelley's poetic achievement, which Shelley completed at Florence in the autumn of 1819. Both plays appeared about 1820.

After moving to Pisa in 1820, Shelley was stung by hostile reviews into expressing his hopes more guardedly. In 1821, however, he reasserted his uncompromising idealism. *Epipsychidion* (in couplets) mythologizes his infatuation with Teresa ("Emilia") Viviani, a convent-bound young admirer, into a Dantesque fable of how human desire can be fulfilled through art. His essay *A Defence of Poetry* (published 1840) eloquently declares that the poet creates humane values and imagines the forms that shape the social order: thus each mind recreates its own private universe, and "Poets are the unacknowledged legislators of the World."

After the Shelleys moved to Lerici in 1822, Percy Shelley began *The Triumph of Life*, a dark fragment on which he was at work until he sailed to Leghorn to welcome his friend Leigh Hunt, who had arrived to edit a periodical called *The Liberal*. Shelley drowned on July 8, 1822, when his boat sank during the stormy return voyage to Lerici.

After her husband's death, Mary Shelley returned to England and devoted herself to publicizing Shelley's writings and educating their only surviving child, Percy Florence Shelley. She published her late husband's *Posthumous Poems* (1824) and also edited his *Poetical Works* (1839), with long and invaluable notes, and his prose works. Her *Journal* is a rich source of Shelley biography, and her letters are an indispensable adjunct. By 1840 she had disseminated his fame and most of his writings.

JOHN KEATS

(b. Oct. 31, 1795, London, Eng.—d. Feb. 23, 1821, Rome, Papal States [Italy])

John Keats was an English Romantic lyric poet who devoted his short life to the perfection of a poetry marked by vivid imagery, great sensuous appeal, and an attempt to express a philosophy through classical legend.

The son of a livery-stable manager, Keats received relatively little formal education. He was apprenticed to a surgeon in 1811, but he broke off his apprenticeship in 1814 and went to live in London, where he worked as a dresser, or junior house surgeon, at Guy's and St. Thomas' hospitals. After 1817 he devoted himself entirely to poetry.

His first mature poem is the sonnet *On First Looking Into Chapman's Homer* (1816), which was inspired by his excited reading of George Chapman's classic 17th-century translation of the *Iliad* and the *Odyssey*. Keats's first book, *Poems*, was published in March 1817. The volume is remarkable only for some delicate natural observation and some obvious Spenserian influences.

In 1817 Keats began work on *Endymion*, his first long poem, which appeared in 1818. This work is divided into four 1,000-line sections, and its verse is composed in loose rhymed couplets. The poem narrates a version of the Greek legend of the moon goddess Diana's (or Cynthia's) love for Endymion, a mortal shepherd, but Keats put the emphasis on Endymion's love for Diana rather than on hers for him and thus transformed the tale to express the widespread Romantic theme of the attempt to find in actuality an ideal love that has been glimpsed heretofore only in imaginative longings.

In the summer of 1818 Keats went on a walking tour in the Lake District (of northern England) and Scotland, and his exposure and overexertions on that trip brought on the first symptoms of the tuberculosis of which he was to die. On his return to London a brutal criticism of his early poems appeared in *Blackwood's Magazine*, followed by a similar attack on *Endymion* in the *Quarterly Review*. Contrary to later assertions, Keats met these reviews with a calm assertion of his own talents, and he went on steadily writing poetry. But there were family troubles, and Keats also met Fanny Brawne, a near neighbour in Hampstead, with whom he soon fell hopelessly and tragically in love. The relation with Brawne had a decisive effect on Keats's development.

It was during the year 1819 that all his greatest poetry was written—*Lamia*, *The Eve of St. Agnes*, the great odes (*On Indolence*, *On a Grecian Urn*, *To Psyche*, *To a Nightingale*, *On Melancholy*, and *To Autumn*), and the two versions of *Hyperion*. This poetry was composed under the strain of illness and his growing love for Brawne; and it is an astonishing body of work, marked by careful and considered development, technical, emotional, and intellectual. *The Eve of St. Agnes* may be considered the perfect culmination of Keats's earlier poetic style. Written in the first flush of his meeting with Brawne, it conveys an atmosphere of passion and excitement in its description of the elopement of a pair of youthful lovers.

The odes are Keats's most distinctive poetic achievement. In the *Ode to a Nightingale* a visionary happiness in communing with the nightingale and its song is contrasted with the dead weight of human grief and sickness, and the transience of youth and beauty—strongly brought home to Keats in recent months by the death of one of his brothers. This theme is taken up more distinctly in the *Ode on a Grecian Urn*. The figures of the lovers depicted on the Greek urn become for him the symbol of an enduring but unconsummated passion that subtly belies the poem's celebrated conclusion, "Beauty is truth, truth beauty,—that is all ye know on earth, and all ye need to know."

Keats's fragmentary poetic epic, *Hyperion*, exists in two versions, the second being a revision of the first with the addition of a long prologue in a new style, which makes it into a different poem. *Hyperion* was begun in the autumn of 1818, and all that there is of the first version was finished by April 1819. These two versions cover the period of Keats's most intense experience, both poetical and personal. The poem is his last attempt, in the face of increasing illness and frustrated love, to come to terms with the conflict between absolute value and mortal decay that appears in other forms in his earlier poetry.

The poems *Isabella*, *Lamia*, *The Eve of St. Agnes*, and *Hyperion* and the odes were all published in the famous 1820 volume, the one that gives the true measure of his powers. He had been increasingly ill throughout 1819, and by the beginning of 1820 the evidence of tuberculosis was clear. He realized that it was his death warrant, and from that time sustained work became impossible. Keats sailed for Italy in September 1820; when he reached Rome, he had a relapse and died there.

ALEKSANDR PUSHKIN

(b. May 26 [June 6, New Style], 1799, Moscow, Russia—d. Jan. 29 [Feb. 10], 1837, St. Petersburg)

The Russian poet, novelist, dramatist, and short-story writer Aleksandr Sergeyevich Pushkin has often been considered his country's greatest poet and the founder of modern Russian literature.

In 1817 Pushkin accepted a post in the foreign office at St. Petersburg, where he was elected to Arzamás, an exclusive literary circle founded by his uncle's friends. In his political verses and epigrams, widely circulated in manuscript, he made himself the spokesman for the ideas and aspirations of those who were to take part in the Decembrist rising of 1825, the unsuccessful culmination of a Russian revolutionary movement in its earliest stage.

For these political poems, Pushkin was banished from St. Petersburg in May 1820 to a remote southern province.

Sent first to Yekaterinoslav (now Dnipropetrovsk, Ukraine), he was there taken ill. While convalescing, he traveled in the northern Caucasus and later to the Crimea. The impressions he gained provided material for his "southern cycle" of romantic narrative poems, published 1820–23. Although this cycle of poems confirmed the reputation of the author of *Ruslan i Lyudmila* (1820; *Ruslan and Ludmila*), his first major work, and Pushkin was hailed as the leading Russian poet of the day, he himself was not satisfied with it. In May 1823 he started work on his central masterpiece, the novel in verse *Yevgeny Onegin* (1833), on which he continued to work intermittently until 1831. *Yevgeny Onegin* unfolds a panoramic picture of Russian life. The characters it depicts and immortalizes—Onegin, the disenchanted skeptic; Lensky, the romantic, freedom-loving poet; and Tatyana, the heroine, a profoundly affectionate study of Russian womanhood—are typically Russian and are shown in relationship to the social and environmental forces by which they are molded.

Remarks in letters intercepted by police resulted in Pushkin being exiled to his mother's estate of Mikhaylovskoye, near Pskov, at the other end of Russia. Although the two years at Mikhaylovskoye were unhappy for Pushkin, they were to prove one of his most productive periods. Alone and isolated, he embarked on a close study of Russian history; he came to know the peasants on the estate and interested himself in noting folktales and songs. During this period the specifically Russian features of his poetry became steadily more marked. He wrote the provincial chapters of *Yevgeny Onegin* as well as one of his major works, the historical tragedy *Boris Godunov* (1831). Written just before the Decembrist uprising, *Boris Godunov* treats the burning question of the relations between the ruling classes, headed by the tsar, and the masses; it is the moral and political significance of the latter, "the judgment of the people," that Pushkin emphasizes. Pushkin's ability to create psychological and dramatic unity, despite the episodic construction, and to heighten the dramatic tension by economy of language, detail, and characterization make this outstanding play a revolutionary event in the history of Russian drama.

After the suppression of the Decembrist uprising, the new tsar Nicholas I, aware of Pushkin's immense popularity and knowing that he had taken no part in the Decembrist "conspiracy," allowed him to return to Moscow in the autumn of 1826. During a long conversation between them, the tsar met the poet's complaints about censorship with a promise that in the future he himself would be Pushkin's censor and told him of his plans to introduce several pressing reforms from above and, in particular, to prepare the way for liberation of the serfs.

Pushkin saw, however, that without the support of the people, the struggle against autocracy was doomed. He considered that the only possible way of achieving essential reforms was from above, "on the tsar's initiative." This is the reason for his persistent interest in the age of reforms at the beginning of the 18th century and in the figure of Peter the Great, the "tsar-educator," whose example he held up to the present tsar in, among other works, the poem *Medny vsadnik* (1837; *The Bronze Horseman*). The poem describes how the "little hero," Yevgeny, driven mad by the drowning of his sweetheart, wanders through the streets. Seeing the bronze statue of Peter I seated on a rearing horse and realizing that the tsar, seen triumphing over the waves, is the cause of his grief, Yevgeny threatens him. In a climax of growing horror, he is pursued through the streets by the "Bronze Horseman." The poem's descriptive and emotional powers give it an unforgettable impact and make it one of the greatest in Russian literature.

It was during this period that Pushkin's genius came to its fullest flowering, despite his being surveilled by the police and struggling against the tsar's censorship. His art acquired new dimensions, and almost every one of the many works written between 1829 and 1836 opened a new chapter in the history of Russian literature.

In 1831, Pushkin married Natalya Nikolayevna Goncharova and settled in St. Petersburg. Once more he took up government service. The social life at court, which he was now obliged to lead and which his wife enjoyed, was ill-suited to creative work, but he stubbornly continued to write. Alongside the theme of Peter the Great, the motif of a popular peasant rising acquired growing importance in his work, as is shown in particular by the most important of his prose works, the historical novel of the Pugachov Rebellion, *Kapitanskaya dochka* (1836; *The Captain's Daughter*). In court circles he was regarded with mounting suspicion and resentment, however, and his repeated petitions to be allowed to retire to the country and devote himself entirely to literature were all rejected. In 1837, Pushkin was mortally wounded defending his wife's honour in a duel forced on him by influential enemies.

VICTOR HUGO

(b. Feb. 26, 1802, Besançon, France—d. May 22, 1885, Paris)

Victor Hugo was a poet, novelist, and dramatist, and the most important of the French Romantic writers. Though regarded in France as one of that country's greatest poets, he is better known abroad for such novels as *Notre-Dame de Paris* (1831) and *Les Misérables* (1862).

Victor Hugo, photograph by Nadar (Gaspard-Félix Tournachon). Archives Photographiques, Paris

The son of a general, Hugo was an accomplished poet before age 20. With his verse drama *Cromwell* (1827), though immensely long and almost impossible to stage, he emerged as an important figure in Romanticism. The production of his verse tragedy *Hernani*, on Feb. 25, 1830, gained victory for the young Romantics over the Classicists in what came to be known as the battle of *Hernani*. In this play Hugo extolled the Romantic hero in the form of a noble outlaw at war with society, dedicated to a passionate love and driven on by inexorable fate.

Hugo gained wider fame in 1831 with his historical novel *Notre-Dame de Paris* (Eng. trans. *The Hunchback of Notre-Dame*), an evocation of life in medieval Paris during the reign of Louis XI. The novel condemns a society that, in the persons of Frollo the archdeacon and Phoebus the soldier, heaps misery on the hunchback Quasimodo and the gypsy girl Esmeralda.

So intense was Hugo's creative activity in the 1830s and 1840s that he also continued to pour out plays. There were two motives for this: first, he needed a platform for his political and social ideas, and, second, he wished to write parts for a young and beautiful actress, Juliette Drouet, with whom he had begun a liaison in 1833. The first of these plays was another verse drama, *Le Roi s'amuse* (1832; Eng. trans. *The King's Fool*).

Hugo's literary achievement was recognized in 1841 by his election, after three unsuccessful attempts, to the French Academy and by his nomination in 1845 to the Chamber of Peers. From this time he almost ceased to publish, partly because of the demands of society and political life but also as a result of personal loss: his daughter Léopoldine, recently married, was accidentally drowned with her husband in September 1843. He found relief above all in working on a new novel, which became

Les Misérables, published in 1862 after work on it had been set aside for a time and then resumed.

Hugo's republican views drove him into exile—at first enforced, then voluntary—between 1851 and 1870. During this exile he produced the most extensive part of all his writings and the most original, including *Les Châtiments* (1853; "The Punishments"), among the most powerful satirical poems in the French language, and *Les Contemplations* (1856), which contains the purest of his poetry.

Hugo then returned to prose and took up his abandoned novel, *Les Misérables*. Its extraordinary success with readers of every type when it was published in 1862 brought him instant popularity in his own country, and its speedy translation into many languages won him fame abroad. The novel's name means "the wretched," or "the outcasts," but English translations generally carry the French title. The story centres on the convict Jean Valjean, a victim of society who has been imprisoned for 19 years for stealing a loaf of bread. *Les Misérables* is a vast panorama of Parisian society and its underworld, and it contains many famous episodes and passages, among them a chapter on the Battle of Waterloo and the description of Jean Valjean's rescue of his daughter's husband by means of a flight through the sewers of Paris.

Hugo's enormous output is unique in French literature; it is said that he wrote each morning 100 lines of verse or 20 pages of prose. "The most powerful mind of the Romantic movement," as he was described in 1830, laureate and peer of France in 1845, he went on to assume the role of an outlawed sage who, with the easy consciousness of authority, put down his insights and prophetic visions in prose and verse, becoming at last the genial grandfather of popular literary portraiture and the national poet who gave his name to a street in every town in France.

NATHANIEL HAWTHORNE

(b. July 4, 1804, Salem, Mass., U.S.—d. May 19, 1864, Plymouth, N.H.)

The American novelist and short-story writer Nathaniel Hawthorne was a master of the allegorical and symbolic tale. One of the greatest fiction writers in American literature, he is best known for *The Scarlet Letter* (1850) and *The House of the Seven Gables* (1851).

Hawthorne did not distinguish himself as a young man. Instead, he spent nearly a dozen years reading and trying to master the art of writing fiction. His first novel, *Fanshawe*, which he published at his own expense in 1825, upon graduation from Bowdoin College, he considered a failure. Hawthorne, however, soon found his own voice, style, and subjects, and by 1830 he had published such impressive and distinctive stories as "The Hollow of the Three Hills" and "An Old Woman's Tale." By 1832, "My Kinsman, Major Molineux" and "Roger Malvin's Burial," two of his greatest tales—and among the finest in the language—had appeared. "Young Goodman Brown," perhaps the greatest tale of witchcraft ever written, appeared in 1835.

His first signed book, *Twice-Told Tales*, was published in 1837. By 1842, Hawthorne's writing had brought him a sufficient income to allow him to marry Sophia Peabody; the couple rented the Old Manse in Concord and began a happy period that Hawthorne would later record in his essay "The Old Manse."

The presence of some of the leading social thinkers and philosophers of his day, such as Ralph Waldo Emerson, Henry Thoreau, and Bronson Alcott, in Concord made the village the centre of the philosophy of Transcendentalism. Hawthorne welcomed the companionship of his Transcendentalist neighbours, but he had little to say to them. His new short-story collection, *Mosses from an Old Manse*, appeared in 1846, a year after he had moved to Salem, where he had been appointed to the position of surveyor of the Custom House.

In a few months of concentrated effort in 1848, he produced his masterpiece, *The Scarlet Letter*. (The bitterness he felt over his dismissal from the Salem Custom House in 1848, which had been a political appointment, is apparent in "The Custom House" essay prefixed to the novel.) *The Scarlet Letter* tells the story of two lovers kept apart by the ironies of fate, their own mingled strengths and weaknesses, and the Puritan community's interpretation of moral law, until at last death unites them under a single headstone. The book made Hawthorne famous and was eventually recognized as one of the greatest of American novels.

Determined to leave Salem forever, Hawthorne moved to Lenox, located in the mountain scenery of the Berkshires in western Massachusetts. There he began work on *The House of the Seven Gables* (1851), the story of the Pyncheon family, who for generations had lived under a curse until it was removed at last by love. At Lenox he enjoyed the stimulating friendship of Herman Melville, who lived in nearby Pittsfield. This friendship, although important for the younger writer and his work, was much less so for Hawthorne.

In 1853, when his friend Franklin Pierce assumed the presidency of the United States, Hawthorne was appointed to a consulship in Liverpool, Lancashire. The position was terminated in 1857, and then he spent a year and a half sightseeing in Italy. Determined to produce yet another romance, he finally retreated to a seaside town in England and quickly produced *The Marble Faun*. In writing it, he drew heavily upon the experiences and impressions he had recorded in a notebook kept during his Italian tour to give substance to an allegory of the Fall of Man, a theme that had usually been assumed in his earlier works but that now received direct and philosophic treatment.

Back in Concord in 1860, Hawthorne devoted himself entirely to his writing but was unable to make any progress with his plans for a new novel. The drafts of unfinished works he left are mostly incoherent. Some two years before his death he began to age very suddenly. His hair turned white, his handwriting changed, he suffered frequent nosebleeds, and he took to writing the figure "64" compulsively on scraps of paper. He died in his sleep on a trip with Pierce in search of health.

Hawthorne's high rank among American fiction writers is the result of at least three considerations. First, Hawthorne was a skillful craftsman with an impressive sense of form; second, he had profound moral insight; third, he was a master of allegory and symbolism. Hawthorne was also the master of a literary style that is remarkable for its directness, its clarity, its firmness, and its sureness of idiom. Hawthorne's work initiated the most durable tradition in American fiction, that of the symbolic romance that assumes the universality of guilt and explores the complexities and ambiguities of man's choices. His greatest short stories and *The Scarlet Letter* are marked by a depth of psychological and moral insight seldom equaled by any American writer.

EDGAR ALLAN POE

(b. Jan. 19, 1809, Boston, Mass., U.S.—d. Oct. 7, 1849, Baltimore, Md.)

Edgar Allan Poe was an American short-story writer, poet, critic, and editor who is famous for his cultivation of mystery and the macabre. His tale *The Murders in the Rue Morgue* (1841) initiated the modern detective story,

Edgar Allan Poe. U.S. Signal Corps/National Archives, Washington, D.C.

and the atmosphere in his tales of horror is unrivaled in American fiction. His *The Raven* (1845) numbers among the best-known poems in the national literature.

Poe was the son of the English-born actress Elizabeth Arnold Poe and David Poe, Jr., an actor from Baltimore. After his mother died in Richmond, Virginia, in 1811, he was taken into the home of John Allan, a Richmond merchant (presumably his godfather), and of his childless wife. He was later taken to Scotland and England (1815–20), where he was given a classical education that was continued in Richmond. For 11 months in 1826 he attended the University of Virginia, but his gambling losses at the university so incensed his guardian that he refused to let him continue, and Poe returned to Richmond to find his sweetheart, (Sarah) Elmira Royster, engaged. He went to Boston, where in 1827 he published a pamphlet of youthful Byronic poems, *Tamerlane, and Other Poems*. Poverty forced him to join the army under the name of Edgar A. Perry, but, on the death of Poe's foster mother, John Allan purchased his release from the army and helped him get an appointment to the U.S. Military Academy at West Point. Before going, Poe published a new volume at Baltimore, *Al Aaraaf, Tamerlane, and Minor Poems* (1829). He successfully sought expulsion from the academy, where he was absent from all drills and classes for a week.

He proceeded to New York City and brought out a volume of *Poems*, containing several masterpieces, some showing the influence of John Keats, Percy Bysshe Shelley, and Samuel Taylor Coleridge. He then returned to Baltimore, where he began to write stories. In 1833 his *MS. Found in a Bottle* won $50 from a Baltimore weekly, and by 1835 he was in Richmond as editor of the *Southern Literary Messenger*. There he made a name as a critical reviewer and married his young cousin Virginia Clemm, who was only

13. Poe seems to have been an affectionate husband and son-in-law.

Poe was dismissed from his job in Richmond, apparently for drinking, and went to New York City. While in New York City in 1838 he published a long prose narrative, *The Narrative of Arthur Gordon Pym*, combining (as so often in his tales) much factual material with the wildest fancies. It is considered one inspiration of Herman Melville's *Moby Dick*. In 1839 he became coeditor of *Burton's Gentleman's Magazine* in Philadelphia. There a contract for a monthly feature stimulated him to write *William Wilson* and *The Fall of the House of Usher*, stories of supernatural horror. The latter contains a study of a neurotic now known to have been an acquaintance of Poe, not Poe himself.

Later in 1839 Poe's *Tales of the Grotesque and Arabesque* appeared (dated 1840). He resigned from *Burton's* about June 1840 but returned in 1841 to edit its successor, *Graham's Lady's and Gentleman's Magazine*, in which he printed the first detective story, *The Murders in the Rue Morgue*. In 1843 his *The Gold-Bug* won a prize of $100 from the Philadelphia *Dollar Newspaper*, which gave him great publicity. In 1844 he returned to New York, wrote *The Balloon-Hoax* for the *Sun*, and became subeditor of the *New York Mirror* under N. P. Willis, thereafter a lifelong friend. In the *New York Mirror* of Jan. 29, 1845, there appeared, from advance sheets of the *American Review*, his most famous poem, *The Raven*, which gave him national fame at once.

Poe then became editor of the *Broadway Journal*, a short-lived weekly, in which he republished most of his short stories, in 1845. During this last year the now-forgotten poet Frances Sargent Locke Osgood pursued Poe. Virginia did not object, but "Fanny's" indiscreet writings about her literary love caused great scandal. His *The*

Raven and Other Poems and a selection of his *Tales* came out in 1845, and in 1846 Poe moved to a cottage at Fordham (now part of New York City), where he wrote *The Literati of New York City* for *Godey's Lady's Book* (May–October 1846). These gossipy sketches on personalities of the day led to a libel suit.

Poe's wife, Virginia, died in January 1847. The following year he went to Providence, Rhode Island, to woo Sarah Helen Whitman, a poet. There was a brief engagement. Poe had close but platonic entanglements with Annie Richmond and with Sarah Anna Lewis, who helped him financially. He composed poetic tributes to all of them. In 1848 he also published the lecture *Eureka*, a transcendental "explanation" of the universe, which has been hailed as a masterpiece by some critics and as nonsense by others. In 1849 he went south, had a wild spree in Philadelphia, but got safely to Richmond, where he finally became engaged to Elmira Royster, by then the widowed Mrs. Shelton, and spent a happy summer with only one or two relapses. He enjoyed the companionship of childhood friends and an unromantic friendship with a young poet, Susan Archer Talley.

Poe had some forebodings of death when he left Richmond for Baltimore late in September. There he died, although whether from drinking, heart failure, or other causes is still uncertain.

CHARLES DICKENS

(b. Feb. 7, 1812, Portsmouth, Hampshire, Eng.—d. June 9, 1870, Gad's Hill, near Chatham, Kent)

Charles Dickens is generally considered the greatest British novelist of the Victorian period. His origins were middle class, if of a newfound and precarious respectability; one grandfather had been a domestic servant, and the other an embezzler. His father, a clerk in the navy pay office, was well paid, but his extravagance and ineptitude often brought the family to financial embarrassment or disaster. In 1824 the family reached bottom. Charles, the eldest son, had been withdrawn from school and was now sent to do manual work in a factory, and his father went to prison for debt. These shocks deeply affected Charles. Though abhorring this brief descent into the working class, he began to gain that sympathetic knowledge of their life and privations that informed his writings. His schooling, interrupted and unimpressive, ended at 15. He became a clerk in a solicitor's office, then a shorthand reporter in the law courts (thus gaining a knowledge of the legal world often used in the novels), and finally a parliamentary and newspaper reporter.

Much drawn to the theatre, Dickens nearly became a professional actor in 1832. In 1833 he began contributing stories and descriptive essays to magazines and newspapers; these attracted attention and were reprinted as *Sketches by "Boz"* (February 1836). The same month, he was invited to provide a comic serial narrative to accompany engravings by a well-known artist; seven weeks later the first installment of *Pickwick Papers* appeared. Within a few months *Pickwick*, his first novel, was the rage and Dickens the most popular author of the day. Resigning from his newspaper job, he undertook to edit a monthly magazine, *Bentley's Miscellany*, in which he serialized his second novel, *Oliver Twist* (1837–39).

Finding serialization congenial and profitable, he repeated the *Pickwick* pattern of 20 monthly parts in *Nicholas Nickleby* (1838–39); then he experimented with shorter weekly installments for *The Old Curiosity Shop* (1840–41) and *Barnaby Rudge* (1841). Exhausted at last, he then took a five-month vacation in America, touring strenuously and receiving quasi-royal honours as a literary celebrity but offending national sensibilities by protesting against the absence of copyright protection.

Novels continued to tumble forth: *Martin Chuzzlewit* (1843–44), *Dombey and Son* (1846–48), *Bleak House* (1852–53), *Little Dorrit* (1855–57). Dickens's popularity was ever-expanding. He had about him "a sort of swell and overflow as of a prodigality of life," an American journalist said, and he cut a dandyish figure in London. His journalistic ambitions at last found a permanent form in *Household Words* (1850–59) and its successor, *All the Year Round* (1859–88), to which he contributed some serialized novels—including *Hard Times* (1854), *A Tale of Two Cities* (1859), and *Great Expectations* (1860–61)—and essays. But in the novels of the 1850s Dickens is politically more despondent, emotionally more tragic. The satire is harsher, the humour less genial and abundant, the "happy endings" more subdued than in the early fiction. This turn was the result partly of political reasons, partly of marital troubles. (The actress Ellen Ternan, 27 years his junior, seems to have become his mistress in the 1860s.)

In April 1858 Dickens began a series of paid public readings, the immediate impulse being to find some energetic distraction from his domestic unhappiness. His readings drew on more permanent elements in him and his art: his remarkable histrionic talents, his love of theatricals and of seeing and delighting an audience, and the eminently performable nature of his fiction. Moreover, he could earn more by reading than by writing, and more certainly; it was easier to force himself to repeat a performance than create a book. His initial repertoire consisted entirely of Christmas books but was soon amplified by episodes from the novels and magazine Christmas stories. A performance usually consisted of two items. Of the 16 eventually performed, the most popular were *The*

Trial from Pickwick and *A Christmas Carol* (1834). Comedy predominated, though pathos was important in the repertoire, and horrifics were startlingly introduced in the last reading he devised, *Sikes and Nancy*, with which he petrified his audiences and half killed himself. Intermittently, until shortly before his death, he gave seasons of readings in London and embarked upon hard-working tours through the provinces and (in 1867–68) the United States. Altogether he performed about 471 times.

Tired and ailing though he was in his later years, Dickens remained inventive and adventurous in his final novels. *A Tale of Two Cities* was an experiment, relying less than before on characterization, dialogue, and humour. *Great Expectations*, though not his most ambitious, is his most finely achieved novel. *Our Mutual Friend* (1864–65), a large inclusive novel, offers a critique of monetary and class values. The unfinished *Edwin Drood* (1870) would likely have been his most elaborate treatment of the themes of crime, evil, and psychological abnormality that had recurred throughout his novels. His farewell reading tour was abandoned when, in April 1869, he collapsed. He died suddenly in June 1870 and was buried in Westminster Abbey.

Dickens enjoyed a wider popularity than had any previous author during his lifetime. Much in his work could appeal to simple and sophisticated, to the poor and to the Queen, and technological developments as well as the qualities of his work enabled his fame to spread worldwide very quickly. The most abundantly comic of English authors, he was much more than a great entertainer. The range, compassion, and intelligence of his apprehension of his society and its shortcomings enriched his novels and made him both one of the great forces in 19th-century literature and an influential spokesman of the conscience of his age.

ROBERT BROWNING

(b. May 7, 1812, London, Eng.—d. Dec. 12, 1889, Venice [Italy])

Robert Browning was perhaps the greatest English poet of the Victorian age, noted for his mastery of the dramatic monologue and of psychological portraiture.

Browning received only a slight formal education, although his father gave him a grounding in Greek and Latin. His first published work, *Pauline: A Fragment of a Confession* (1833, anonymous), although formally a dramatic monologue, embodied many of his own adolescent passions and anxieties. Although it received some favourable comment, it was attacked by John Stuart Mill, who condemned the poet's exposure and exploitation of his own emotions and his "intense and morbid self-consciousness." It was perhaps Mill's critique that determined Browning never to confess his own emotions again in his poetry but to write objectively. In 1835 he published *Paracelsus* and in 1840 *Sordello*, both poems dealing with men of great ability striving to reconcile the demands of their own personalities with those of the world. *Paracelsus* was well received, but *Sordello*, which made exacting demands on its reader's knowledge, was almost universally declared incomprehensible.

Encouraged by the actor Charles Macready, Browning devoted his main energies for some years to verse drama, a form that he had already adopted for *Strafford* (1837). Between 1841 and 1846, in a series of pamphlets under the general title of *Bells and Pomegranates*, he published seven more plays in verse, including *Pippa Passes* (1841), *A Blot in the 'Scutcheon* (produced in 1843), and *Luria* (1846). These, and all his earlier works except *Strafford*, were printed at his family's expense. Although Browning enjoyed writing for the stage, he was not successful in the theatre, since his strength lay in depicting, as he had himself observed

Robert Browning. © Photos.com/Jupiterimages

of *Strafford*, "Action in Character, rather than Character in Action."

By 1845 the first phase of Browning's life was near its end. In that year he met Elizabeth Barrett. In her *Poems* (1844) Barrett had included lines praising Browning, who wrote to thank her (January 1845). In May they met and soon discovered their love for each other. Barrett had, however, been for many years an invalid, confined to her room and thought incurable. Her father, moreover, was a dominant and selfish man, jealously fond of his daughter, who in turn had come to depend on his love. When her doctors ordered her to Italy for her health and her father refused to allow her to go, the lovers, who had been corresponding and meeting regularly, were forced to act. They were married secretly in September 1846; a week later they left for Pisa.

Throughout their married life, although they spent holidays in France and England, their home was in Italy, mainly at Florence, where they had a flat in Casa Guidi. Their income was small, although after the birth of their son, Robert, in 1849 Mrs. Browning's cousin John Kenyon made them an allowance of £100 a year, and on his death in 1856 he left them £11,000.

Browning produced comparatively little poetry during his married life. *Men and Women* (1855) was a collection of 51 poems—dramatic lyrics such as *Memorabilia*, *Love Among the Ruins*, and *A Toccata of Galuppi's*; the great monologues such as *Fra Lippo Lippi*, *How It Strikes a Contemporary*, and *Bishop Blougram's Apology*; and a very few poems in which implicitly (*By the Fireside*) or explicitly (*One Word More*) he broke his rule and spoke of himself and of his love for his wife. *Men and Women*, however, had no great sale, and many of the reviews were unfavourable and unhelpful. Disappointed for the first time by the reception of his work, Browning in the following years wrote little, sketching and modeling in clay by day and enjoying the society of his friends at night. At last Mrs. Browning's health, which had been remarkably restored by her life in Italy, began to fail. On June 29, 1861, she died in her husband's arms. In the autumn he returned slowly to London with his young son.

His first task on his return was to prepare his wife's *Last Poems* for the press. At first he avoided company, but gradually he accepted invitations more freely and began to move in society. Another collected edition of his poems was called for in 1863, but *Pauline* was not included. When his next book of poems, *Dramatis Personae* (1864)—including *Abt Vogler*, *Rabbi Ben Ezra*, *Caliban upon Setebos*, and *Mr. Sludge, "The Medium"*—reached two editions, it was clear that Browning had at last won a measure of popular recognition.

In 1868–69 he published his greatest work, *The Ring and the Book*, based on the proceedings in a murder trial in Rome in 1698. Grand alike in plan and execution, it was at once received with enthusiasm, and Browning was established as one of the most important literary figures of the day. For the rest of his life he was much in demand in London society. He spent his summers with friends in France, Scotland, or Switzerland or, after 1878, in Italy.

The most important works of his last years, when he wrote with great fluency, were long narrative or dramatic poems, often dealing with contemporary themes. While staying in Venice in 1889, Browning caught a cold, became seriously ill, and died on December 12. He was buried in Westminster Abbey.

CHARLOTTE BRONTË

(b. April 21, 1816, Thornton, Yorkshire, Eng.—d. March 31, 1855, Haworth, Yorkshire)

Charlotte Brontë was an English novelist best known for *Jane Eyre* (1847), a strong narrative of a woman in conflict with her natural desires and social condition. The novel gave new truthfulness to Victorian fiction.

Her father was Patrick Brontë (1777–1861), an Anglican clergyman. Irish-born, he had changed his name from the more commonplace Brunty. After serving in several parishes, he moved with his wife, Maria Branwell Brontë, and their six small children to Haworth amid the Yorkshire moors in 1820, having been awarded a rectorship there. Soon after, Mrs. Brontë and the two eldest children (Maria and Elizabeth) died, leaving the father to care for the remaining three girls—Charlotte, Emily, and Anne—and a boy, Patrick Branwell. Their upbringing was aided by an aunt, Elizabeth Branwell, who left her native Cornwall and took up residence with the family at Haworth.

In 1824 Charlotte and Emily, together with their elder sisters before their deaths, attended Clergy Daughters' School at Cowan Bridge, near Kirkby Lonsdale, Lancashire. The fees were low, the food unattractive, and the discipline harsh. Charlotte condemned the school (perhaps exaggeratedly) long years afterward in *Jane Eyre*, under the thin disguise of Lowood. Charlotte and Emily returned home in June 1825, and for more than five years the Brontë children learned and played there, writing and telling romantic tales for one another and inventing imaginative games played out at home or on the desolate moors.

In 1831 Charlotte was sent to Miss Wooler's school at Roe Head, near Huddersfield, where she stayed a year and made some lasting friendships. Her correspondence with one of her friends, Ellen Nussey, continued until her death, and has provided much of the current knowledge of her life. In 1832 she came home to teach her sisters but in 1835 returned to Roe Head as a teacher. The work, with its inevitable restrictions, was uncongenial to Charlotte. She fell into ill health and melancholia and in the summer of 1838 terminated her engagement.

In 1839 Charlotte declined a proposal from the Rev. Henry Nussey, her friend's brother, and some months later one from another young clergyman. At the same time Charlotte's ambition to make the practical best of her talents and the need to pay Branwell's debts urged her to spend some months as governess with the Whites at Upperwood House, Rawdon. Branwell's talents for writing and painting, his good classical scholarship, and his social charm had engendered high hopes for him; but he was fundamentally unstable, weak willed, and intemperate. He went from job to job and took refuge in alcohol and opium.

Meanwhile his sisters had planned to open a school together, which their aunt had agreed to finance. The plan would eventually fail, but in February 1842 Charlotte and Emily went to Brussels as pupils to improve their qualifications in French and acquire some German. The talent displayed by both brought them to the notice of Constantin Héger, a fine teacher and a man of unusual perception. After a brief trip home, Charlotte returned to Brussels as a pupil-teacher. She stayed there during 1843 but was lonely and depressed. Her friends had left Brussels, and Madame Héger appears to have become jealous of her. The nature of Charlotte's attachment to Héger and the degree to which she understood herself have been much discussed. She offered him an innocent but ardent devotion, but he tried to repress her emotions.

By 1846 Charlotte, Emily, and Anne were trying to place the three novels they had written. Charlotte failed to place *The Professor: A Tale* but had, however, nearly finished *Jane Eyre: An Autobiography*, begun in August 1846 in Manchester, where she was staying with her father, who had gone there for an eye operation. When Smith, Elder and Company, declining *The Professor*, declared themselves willing to consider a three-volume novel with more action and excitement in it, she completed and submitted it at once. *Jane Eyre* was accepted, published less than eight weeks later (on Oct. 16, 1847), and had an immediate success, far greater than that of the books that her sisters published the same year. Central to its success is the fiery conviction with which it presented a thinking, feeling woman, craving for love but able to renounce it at the call of impassioned self-respect and moral conviction.

The months that followed were tragic ones. Branwell died in September 1848, Emily in December, and Anne in May 1849. Charlotte completed *Shirley: A Tale* in the empty parsonage, and it appeared in October. In the following years Charlotte went three times to London as the guest of her publisher; there she met the novelist William Makepeace Thackeray and sat for her portrait by George Richmond. She stayed in 1851 with the writer Harriet Martineau and also visited her future biographer, Mrs. Elizabeth Gaskell, in Manchester and entertained her at Haworth. *Villette* came out in January 1853. Meanwhile, in 1851, she had declined a third offer of marriage, this time from James Taylor, a member of Smith, Elder and Company. Her father's curate, Arthur Bell Nicholls (1817–1906), an Irishman, was her fourth suitor. It took some months to win her father's consent, but they were married on June 29, 1854. She began another book, *Emma*, of which some pages remain. Her pregnancy, however, was accompanied by exhausting sickness, and she died in 1855. Her first novel, *The Professor*, which is based on her experiences in Brussels, was published posthumously in 1857.

HENRY DAVID THOREAU

(b. July 12, 1817, Concord, Mass., U.S.—d. May 6, 1862, Concord)

The American essayist, poet, and practical philosopher Henry David Thoreau is renowned for having lived the doctrines of Transcendentalism as recorded in his masterwork, *Walden* (1854), and for having been a vigorous advocate of civil liberties, as evidenced in the essay "Civil Disobedience" (1849).

Thoreau entered Harvard University in 1833. Graduating in the middle ranks of the class of 1837, he searched for a teaching job and secured one at his old grammar school in Concord. But he was no disciplinarian, and he resigned after two shaky weeks. A canoe trip that he and his brother John took along the Concord and Merrimack rivers in 1839 confirmed in him the opinion that he ought to be not a schoolmaster but a poet of nature.

Sheer chance made his entrance to writing easier, for he came under the benign influence of the essayist and poet Ralph Waldo Emerson, who had settled in Concord during Thoreau's sophomore year at Harvard. By the autumn of 1837, they were becoming friends. Emerson sensed in Thoreau a true disciple—that is, one with so much Emersonian self-reliance that he would still be his own man. Thoreau saw in Emerson a guide, a father, and a friend. With his magnetism Emerson attracted others to Concord. Out of their heady speculations and affirmatives came New England Transcendentalism.

In Emerson's company Thoreau's hope of becoming a poet looked not only proper but feasible. He wrote some poems—a good many, in fact—for several years. Captained by Emerson, the Transcendentalists started a magazine, *The Dial*; the inaugural issue, dated July 1840, carried

Thoreau's poem *Sympathy* and his essay on the Roman poet Aulus Persius Flaccus.

The Dial published more of Thoreau's poems and then, in July 1842, the first of his outdoor essays, "Natural History of Massachusetts." Then followed more lyrics, such as *To the Maiden in the East*, and another nature essay, "A Winter Walk." *The Dial* ceased publication with the April 1844 issue, having published a richer variety of Thoreau's writing than any other magazine ever would.

By early 1845 Thoreau felt more restless than ever, until he decided to take up an idea of a Harvard classmate who had once built a waterside hut in which one could loaf or read. In the spring Thoreau picked a spot by Walden Pond, a small lake south of Concord on land Emerson owned. Once settled, after building his home, he restricted his diet for the most part to the fruit and vegetables he found growing wild and the beans he planted. When not occupied with fishing, swimming, or rowing, he spent long hours observing and recording the local flora and fauna, reading, and writing.

Out of such activity and thought came *Walden*, a series of 18 essays describing Thoreau's experiment in basic living. Several of the essays provide his original perspective on the meaning of work and leisure and describe his experiment in living as simply and self-sufficiently as possible, while in others Thoreau describes the various realities of life at Walden Pond: his intimacy with the small animals he came in contact with; the sounds, smells, and look of woods and water at various seasons; the music of wind in telegraph wires. The physical act of living day by day at Walden Pond is what gives the book authority, while Thoreau's command of a clear, straightforward but elegant style helped raise it to the level of a literary classic.

Midway in his Walden sojourn Thoreau had spent a night in jail. On an evening in July 1846 he encountered

Sam Staples, the constable and tax gatherer. Staples asked him amiably to pay his poll tax, which Thoreau had omitted paying for several years. He declined, and Staples locked him up. The next morning a still-unidentified lady, perhaps his aunt, Maria, paid the tax. Thoreau reluctantly emerged, did an errand, and then went huckleberrying. A single night, he decided, was enough to make his point that he could not support a government that endorsed slavery and waged an imperialist war against Mexico. His defense of the private, individual conscience against the expediency of the majority found expression in his most famous essay, "Civil Disobedience," which was first published in May 1849 under the title "Resistance to Civil Government."

When Thoreau left Walden in 1847, he passed the peak of his career. Slowly his Transcendentalism drained away as he became a surveyor in order to support himself. But as Thoreau became less of a Transcendentalist he became more of an activist—above all, a dedicated abolitionist. As much as anyone in Concord, he helped to speed fleeing slaves north on the Underground Railroad. He lectured and wrote against slavery. In the abolitionist John Brown he found a father figure beside whom Emerson paled. By now Thoreau was in poor health, and when Brown's raid on Harpers Ferry failed and he was hanged in 1859, Thoreau suffered a psychic shock that probably hastened his own death, apparently of tuberculosis.

EMILY BRONTË

(b. July 30, 1818, Thornton, Yorkshire, Eng.—d. Dec. 19, 1848, Haworth, Yorkshire

Emily Brontë was an English novelist and poet who produced but one novel, *Wuthering Heights* (1847), a highly imaginative novel of passion and hate set on the Yorkshire moors.

Her father held a number of curacies: Hartshead-cum-Clifton, Yorkshire, was the birthplace of his elder daughters, Maria and Elizabeth (who died young), and nearby Thornton that of Emily and her siblings Charlotte, Patrick Branwell, and Anne. In 1820 the father became rector of Haworth, remaining there for the rest of his life.

After the death of their mother in 1821, the children were left very much to themselves in the bleak moorland rectory. The children were educated, during their early life, at home, except for a single year that Charlotte and Emily spent at the Clergy Daughters' School at Cowan Bridge in Lancashire. In 1835, when Charlotte secured a teaching position at Miss Wooler's school at Roe Head, Emily accompanied her as a pupil but suffered from homesickness and remained only three months. In 1838 Emily spent six exhausting months as a teacher in Miss Patchett's school at Law Hill, near Halifax, and then resigned.

To keep the family together at home, Charlotte planned to keep a school for girls at Haworth. In February 1842 she and Emily went to Brussels to learn foreign languages and school management. Although Emily pined for home and for the wild moorlands, it seems that in Brussels she was better appreciated than Charlotte. Her passionate nature was more easily understood than Charlotte's decorous temperament. In October, however, when her aunt died, Emily returned permanently to Haworth.

In 1845 Charlotte came across some poems by Emily, and this led to the discovery that all three sisters—Charlotte, Emily, and Anne—had written verse. A year later they published jointly a volume of verse, *Poems by Currer, Ellis and Acton Bell*, the initials of these pseudonyms being those of the sisters. The book of verse contained 21 of Emily's poems, and a consensus of later criticism has accepted the fact that Emily's verse alone reveals true poetic genius. The venture cost the sisters about £50 in all, and only two copies were sold.

By midsummer of 1847, Emily's *Wuthering Heights* and Anne's *Agnes Grey* had been accepted for joint publication by J. Cautley Newby of London, but publication of the three volumes was delayed until the appearance of their sister Charlotte's *Jane Eyre*, which was immediately and hugely successful. *Wuthering Heights*, when published in December 1847, did not fare well; critics were hostile, calling it too savage, too animal-like, and clumsy in construction. Only later did it come to be considered one of the finest novels in the English language. It is distinguished from other novels of the period by its dramatic and poetic presentation, its abstention from all comment by the author, and its unusual structure.

Soon after its publication, Emily's health began to fail rapidly. She had been ill for some time, but now her breathing became difficult, and she suffered great pain. She died of tuberculosis in December 1848. Emily was perhaps the greatest of the three Brontë sisters, but the record of her life is extremely meagre, for she was silent and reserved and left no correspondence of interest. Her single novel darkens rather than solves the mystery of her spiritual existence.

WALT WHITMAN

(b. May 31, 1819, West Hills, Long Island, N.Y., U.S.—d. March 26, 1892, Camden, N.J.)

Walt Whitman was an American poet, journalist, and essayist whose verse collection *Leaves of Grass* is a landmark in the history of American literature.

Whitman attended public school in Brooklyn, began working at the age of 12, and learned the printing trade.

Walt Whitman started out editing newspaper articles in New York City, but he took greater satisfaction in his later years writing poetry. His Leaves of Grass *is considered one of the greatest works of American literature.* Library of Congress Prints and Photographs Division

He was employed as a printer in Brooklyn and New York City, taught in country schools on Long Island, and became a journalist. At the age of 23 he edited a daily newspaper in New York, and in 1846 he became editor of the *Brooklyn Daily Eagle*, a fairly important newspaper of the time. Discharged from the *Eagle* early in 1848 because of his support for the Free Soil faction of the Democratic Party, he went to New Orleans, La., where he worked for three months on the *Crescent* before returning to New York via the Mississippi River and the Great Lakes. After another abortive attempt at Free Soil journalism, he built houses and dabbled in real estate in New York from about 1850 until 1855.

Whitman had spent a great deal of his 36 years walking and observing in New York City and Long Island. He had visited the theatre frequently, and he had developed a strong love of music, especially opera. During these years he had also read extensively at home and in the New York libraries, and he began experimenting with a new style of poetry. While a schoolteacher, printer, and journalist he had published sentimental stories and poems in newspapers and popular magazines, but they showed almost no literary promise.

By the spring of 1855 Whitman had enough poems in his new style for a thin volume. Unable to find a publisher, he sold a house and printed the first edition of *Leaves of Grass* at his own expense. No publisher's or author's name appeared on the first edition in 1855, but the cover had a portrait of Whitman. Though little appreciated upon its appearance, *Leaves of Grass* was warmly praised by the poet and essayist Ralph Waldo Emerson, who wrote to Whitman on receiving the poems that it was "the most extraordinary piece of wit and wisdom" America had yet contributed.

Whitman continued practicing his new style of writing in his private notebooks, and in 1856 the second edition of *Leaves of Grass* appeared. This collection contained revisions of the poems of the first edition and a new one, the *Sun-down Poem* (later to become *Crossing Brooklyn Ferry*). The second edition was also a financial failure, and once again Whitman edited a daily newspaper, the *Brooklyn Times*, but was unemployed by the summer of 1859. In 1860 a Boston publisher brought out the third edition of *Leaves of Grass*, greatly enlarged and rearranged, but the outbreak of the American Civil War bankrupted the firm.

During the Civil War, Whitman took a temporary post in the paymaster's office in Washington. He spent his spare time visiting wounded and dying soldiers in the Washington hospitals. In January 1865 he became a clerk in the Department of the Interior; in May he was promoted but in June was dismissed because the secretary of the Interior thought that *Leaves of Grass* was indecent. Whitman then obtained a post in the attorney general's office, largely through the efforts of his friend, the journalist William O'Connor, who wrote a vindication of Whitman.

In May 1865 a collection of war poems entitled *Drum Taps* showed Whitman's readers a new kind of poetry, moving from the oratorical excitement with which he had greeted the falling-in and arming of the young men at the beginning of the Civil War to a disturbing awareness of what war really meant. The *Sequel to Drum Taps*, published in the autumn of 1865, contained his great elegy on President Abraham Lincoln, *When Lilacs Last in the Dooryard Bloom'd*.

The fourth edition of *Leaves of Grass*, published in 1867, contained much revision and rearrangement, and in the late 1860s Whitman's work began to receive greater recognition. In January 1873 his first stroke left him partly paralyzed. Additional editions of *Leaves of Grass* followed, and the book finally reached the form in which it was henceforth to be published. *The Complete Poems and Prose* was published in 1888, along with the eighth edition of *Leaves of Grass*. The ninth, or "authorized," edition appeared in 1892, the year of Whitman's death.

Under the influence of the Romantic movement in literature and art, Whitman held the theory that the chief function of the poet was to express his own personality in his verse. The first edition of *Leaves of Grass* also appeared during the most nationalistic period in American literature, when critics were calling for a literature commensurate with the size, natural resources, and potentialities of the North American continent. From this time on throughout his life Whitman attempted to dress the part and act the role of the shaggy, untamed poetic spokesman of the proud young nation. For the expression of this persona he also created a form of free verse without rhyme or metre, but abounding in oratorical rhythms and chanted lists of American place-names and objects.

HERMAN MELVILLE

(b. Aug. 1, 1819, New York City—d. Sept. 28, 1891, New York City)

The American novelist, short-story writer, and poet Herman Melville is best known for his novels of the sea, including his masterpiece, *Moby Dick* (1851).

Born to a wealthy New York family that suffered great financial losses, Melville had little formal schooling and began a period of wanderings at sea in 1839, when he served as cabin boy on a merchant ship. The summer voyage did not dedicate Melville to the sea. After a grinding search for work, he eventually sailed on the whaler *Acushnet*, from New Bedford, Mass., on a voyage to the South Seas.

In June 1842 the *Acushnet* anchored in present-day French Polynesia. Melville's adventures here, somewhat romanticized, became the subject of his first novel, *Typee* (1846). In July Melville and a companion jumped ship and, according to *Typee*, spent about four months as guest-captives of the reputedly cannibalistic Typee people. Actually, in August he was registered in the crew of the Australian whaler *Lucy Ann*. Whatever its precise correspondence with fact, however, *Typee* was faithful to the imaginative impact of the experience on Melville.

Although Melville was down for a 120th share of the whaler's proceeds, the voyage had been unproductive. He joined a mutiny that landed the mutineers in a Tahitian jail, from which he escaped without difficulty. On these events and their sequel, Melville based his second book, *Omoo* (1847). Lighthearted in tone, with the mutiny shown as something of a farce, it describes Melville's travels through the islands. In November he signed as a harpooner on his last whaler, the *Charles & Henry*, out of Nantucket, Mass. Six months later he disembarked at Lahaina, in the Hawaiian Islands. In August 1843 he signed as an ordinary seaman on the frigate *United States*, which in October 1844 discharged him in Boston.

Typee provoked immediate enthusiasm and outrage, and then a year later *Omoo* had an identical response. In 1847 Melville began a third book, *Mardi* (1849), and became a regular contributor of reviews and other pieces to a literary journal. When *Mardi* appeared, public and critics alike found its wild, allegorical fantasy and medley of styles incomprehensible. It began as another Polynesian adventure but quickly set its hero in pursuit of the mysterious Yillah, "all beauty and innocence," a symbolic quest that ends in anguish and disaster. Concealing his disappointment at the book's reception, Melville quickly wrote *Redburn* (1849) and *White-Jacket* (1850). The critics

Herman Melville, etching after a portrait by Joseph O. Eaton. Library of Congress, Washington, D.C. (Digital File Number: cph 3c35949)

acclaimed *White-Jacket*, and its powerful criticism of abuses in the U.S. Navy won it strong political support. But both novels, however much they seemed to revive the Melville of *Typee*, had passages of profoundly questioning melancholy.

Melville had promised his publishers for the autumn of 1850 the novel first entitled *The Whale*, finally *Moby Dick*. His delay in submitting it was caused by his explorations into the unsuspected vistas opened for him by Nathaniel Hawthorne, whose *Scarlet Letter* he had read in the spring of 1850 and who became Melville's neighbour when Melville bought a farm near Hawthorne's home. Their relationship reanimated Melville's creative energies. On his side, it was dependent, almost mystically intense. To the cooler, withdrawn Hawthorne, such depth of feeling so persistently and openly declared was uncongenial. The two men gradually drew apart.

Book jacket for Moby Dick *by Herman Melville; Saddleback Educational Publishing, 2005.* Saddleback Educational Publishing.

Moby Dick was published in London in October 1851 and a month later in America. It brought its author neither acclaim nor reward. Basically its story is simple. Captain Ahab pursues the white whale, Moby Dick, which finally kills him.

At that level, it is an intense, superbly authentic narrative of whaling. In the perverted grandeur of Captain Ahab and in the beauties and terrors of the voyage of the *Pequod*, however, Melville dramatized his deeper concerns: the equivocal defeats and triumphs of the human spirit and its fusion of creative and murderous urges.

Increasingly a recluse, Melville embarked almost at once on *Pierre* (1852). It was an intensely personal work, revealing the sombre mythology of his private life framed in terms of a story of an artist alienated from his society. When published, it was another critical and financial disaster. Near breakdown, and having to face in 1853 the disaster of a fire at his New York publishers that destroyed most of his books, Melville persevered with writing. His contributions to *Putnam's Monthly Magazine*—"Bartleby the Scrivener" (1853), "The Encantadas" (1854), and "Benito Cereno" (1855)—reflected the despair and the contempt for human hypocrisy and materialism that possessed him increasingly. *The Confidence-Man* (1857), a despairing satire on an America corrupted by the shabby dreams of commerce, was the last of his novels to be published in his lifetime. Three American lecture tours were followed by his final sea journey, in 1860, when he joined his brother Thomas for a voyage around Cape Horn. He abandoned the trip in San Francisco. He then abandoned the novel for poetry for a time.

His return to prose culminated in his last work, the novel *Billy Budd*, which remained unpublished until 1924. Provoked by a false charge, the sailor Billy Budd accidentally kills the satanic master-at-arms. In a time of threatened mutiny he is hanged, going willingly to his fate. The manuscript ends with the date April 19, 1891. Five months later Melville died. By the end of the 1840s he was among the most celebrated of American writers, yet his death evoked but a single obituary notice.

GEORGE ELIOT

(b. Nov. 22, 1819, Chilvers Coton, Warwickshire, Eng.—d. Dec. 22, 1880, London)

George Eliot, the pseudonym of Mary Ann (or Marian) Evans, was an English Victorian novelist who developed the method of psychological analysis characteristic of modern fiction.

Evans had a strong evangelical piety instilled in her as a girl. In 1841 she moved with her father to Coventry, where she soon broke with her upbringing after she became acquainted with a prosperous ribbon manufacturer, Charles Bray, a self-taught freethinker who campaigned for radical causes.

In 1851 Evans moved to London to become a freelance writer, and, after a brief return to Coventry, she served for three years as subeditor of *The Westminster Review*, which under her influence enjoyed its most brilliant run since the days of John Stuart Mill. At evening parties in London she met many notable literary figures in an atmosphere of political and religious radicalism, including the subeditor of *The Economist*, Herbert Spencer, whose *Social Statics* (1851) had just been published. Evans shared many of Spencer's interests and saw so much of him that it was soon rumoured that they were engaged. Though he did not become her husband, he introduced her to the two men who did.

One of those men was George Henry Lewes, a versatile Victorian journalist. In 1841 he had married Agnes Jervis, by whom he had four sons. But after two subsequent pregnancies by another man, Lewes ceased in 1851 to regard her as his wife. He had, however, condoned the adultery and was therefore precluded from suing for divorce. At this moment of dejection, his home hopelessly broken, he met Evans. They consulted about articles and

She may have been forced to achieve literary success under a male pseudonym, but today George Eliot (Mary Ann Evans) is noted more for her style and contributions to modern literature than her gender. Hulton Archive/Getty Images

went to plays and operas that Lewes reviewed for *The Leader*. Convinced that his break with Agnes was irrevocable, Evans determined to live openly with Lewes as his wife. In July 1854, after the publication of her translation of Feuerbach's *Essence of Christianity*, they went to Germany together. In all but the legal form it was a marriage, and it continued happily until Lewes's death in 1878.

At Weimar and Berlin Evans wrote some of her best essays for *The Westminster* and translated Spinoza's *Ethics* (still unpublished), while Lewes worked on his groundbreaking life of Goethe. By his pen alone he had to support his three surviving sons at school in Switzerland as well as Agnes, whom he gave £100 a year, which was continued until her death in 1902. She turned to early memories and, encouraged by Lewes, wrote a story about a childhood episode in Chilvers Coton parish. Published in *Blackwood's Magazine* (1857) as *The Sad Fortunes of the Reverend Amos Barton*, it was an instant success. Two more tales, *Mr. Gilfil's Love-Story* and *Janet's Repentance*, also based on local events, appeared serially in the same year, and Blackwood republished all three as *Scenes of Clerical Life*, 2 vol. (1858) under the pseudonym George Eliot. It would become her pen name for the rest of her professional career.

Adam Bede, 3 vol. (1859), her first long novel, she described as "a country story—full of the breath of cows and the scent of hay." Its masterly realism brought to English fiction the same truthful observation of minute detail that Ruskin was commending in the Pre-Raphaelites. But what was new in this very popular novel was the combination of deep human sympathy and rigorous moral judgment. In *The Mill on the Floss*, 3 vol. (1860), Evans returned again to the scenes of her early life. The first half of the book, with its remarkable portrayal of childhood, is irresistibly appealing, and throughout there are scenes that reach a new level of psychological subtlety.

During their visit to Florence in 1860, Lewes suggested Savonarola as a good subject. Evans grasped it enthusiastically and began to plan *Romola* (1862–63). First, however, she wrote *Silas Marner* (1861). Its brevity and perfection of form made this story of the weaver whose lost gold is replaced by a strayed child the best known of her books. *Romola* was planned as a serial for *Blackwood's*, until an offer of £10,000 from *The Cornhill Magazine* induced Evans to desert her old publisher. Rather than divide the book into the 16 installments the editor wanted, she accepted £3,000 less, an evidence of artistic integrity few writers would have shown. It was published in 14 parts between July 1862 and August 1863.

Her next two novels are laid in England at the time of agitation for passage of the Reform Bill. In *Felix Holt, the Radical*, 3 vol. (1866), she drew the election riot from recollection of one she saw at Nuneaton in December 1832. *Middlemarch* (8 parts, 1871–72) is by general consent George Eliot's masterpiece. Every class of Middlemarch society is depicted from the landed gentry and clergy to the manufacturers and professional men, the shopkeepers, publicans, farmers, and labourers. Several strands of plot are interwoven to reinforce each other by contrast and parallel. Yet the story depends not on close-knit intrigue but on showing the incalculably diffusive effect of the unhistoric acts of anonymous individuals.

Daniel Deronda (8 parts, 1876) is built on the contrast between Mirah Cohen, a poor Jewish girl, and the upper class Gwendolen Harleth, who marries for money and regrets it. The hero, Daniel, after discovering that he is Jewish, marries Mirah and departs for Palestine to establish a home for his nation. The best part of *Daniel Deronda* is the keen analysis of Gwendolen's character, which seems to many critics the peak of George Eliot's achievement.

In 1863 the Leweses bought the Priory, 21, North Bank, Regent's Park, where their Sunday afternoons became a brilliant feature of Victorian life. There on Nov. 30, 1878, Lewes died. For nearly 25 years he had fostered Evans's genius and managed all the practical details of life, which now fell upon her. Most of all she missed the encouragement that alone made it possible for her to write. For some years her investments had been in the hands of John Walter Cross, a banker introduced to the Leweses by Herbert Spencer. On May 6, 1880, they were married. Cross was 40; she was in her 61st year. After a wedding trip in Italy they returned to her country house at Witley before moving to 4, Cheyne Walk, Chelsea, where she died in December. She was buried at Highgate Cemetery.

CHARLES BAUDELAIRE

(b. April 9, 1821, Paris, France—d. Aug. 31, 1867, Paris)

Charles Baudelaire was a French poet, translator, and literary and art critic whose reputation rests primarily on *Les Fleurs du mal* (1857; *The Flowers of Evil*), which was perhaps the most important and influential poetry collection published in Europe in the 19th century.

Regular acts of indiscipline led to his being expelled from the prestigious Lycée Louis-le-Grand after a trivial incident in April 1839. After passing his *baccalauréat* examinations while enrolled at the Collège Saint-Louis, Baudelaire became a nominal student of law at the École de Droit while in reality leading a "free life" in the Latin Quarter. There he made his first contacts in the literary world and also contracted the venereal disease that would eventually kill him, probably from a prostitute nicknamed Sarah la Louchette ("Squint-Eyed Sarah"), whom he celebrated in some of his most affecting early poems.

Charles Baudelaire, photograph by Étienne Carjat, 1863. Courtesy of the Bibliothèque Nationale, Paris

Baudelaire embarked on a protracted voyage to India in June 1841, but he effectively jumped ship in Mauritius and, after a few weeks there and in Réunion, returned to France in February 1842. He came into his inheritance in April 1842 and rapidly proceeded to dissipate it on the lifestyle of a dandified man of letters, spending freely on clothes, books, paintings, expensive food and wines, and, not least, hashish and opium. It was shortly after returning from the South Seas that Baudelaire met Jeanne Duval, who, first as his mistress and then, after the mid-1850s, as his financial charge, was to dominate his life for the next 20 years. Jeanne would inspire Baudelaire's most anguished and sensual love poetry, her perfume and, above all, her magnificent flowing black hair provoking such masterpieces of the exotic-erotic imagination as *La Chevelure* ("The Head of Hair"). Baudelaire's continuing extravagance exhausted half his fortune in two years, and he also fell prey to cheats and moneylenders, thus laying the foundation for an accumulation of debt that would cripple him for the rest of his life.

In 1847 Baudelaire discovered the work of Edgar Allan Poe. Overwhelmed by what he saw as the almost preternatural similarities between the American writer's thought and temperament and his own, he embarked upon the task of translation that was to provide him with his most regular occupation and income for the rest of his life. His translation of Poe's *Mesmeric Revelation* appeared as early as July 1848, and thereafter translations appeared regularly in reviews before being collected in book form in *Histoires extraordinaires* (1856; "Extraordinary Tales") and *Nouvelles Histoires extraordinaires* (1857; "New Extraordinary Tales"), each preceded by an important critical introduction by Baudelaire.

Baudelaire's growing reputation as Poe's translator and as an art critic at last enabled him to publish some of his poems. In June 1855 the *Revue des deux mondes* published a sequence of 18 of his poems under the general title of *Les Fleurs du mal*. The poems, which Baudelaire had chosen for their original style and startling themes, brought him notoriety. The following year Baudelaire signed a contract with the publisher Poulet-Malassis for a full-length poetry collection to appear with that title. When the first edition of *Les Fleurs du mal* was published in June 1857, 13 of its 100 poems were immediately arraigned for offences to religion or public morality. After a one-day trial on Aug. 20, 1857, six of the poems were ordered to be removed from the book on the grounds of obscenity, with Baudelaire incurring a fine of 300 (later reduced to 50) francs. The six poems were first republished in Belgium in 1866 in the collection *Les Épaves* ("Wreckage"), and the official ban on them would not be revoked until 1949. Owing largely to these circumstances, *Les Fleurs du mal* became a byword for depravity, morbidity, and obscenity, and the legend of Baudelaire as the doomed dissident and pornographic poet was born.

The failure of *Les Fleurs du mal*, from which he had expected so much, was a bitter blow to Baudelaire, and the remaining years of his life were darkened by a growing sense of despair. Although Baudelaire wrote some of his finest works in these years, few were published in book form. In 1859 Baudelaire produced in rapid succession a series of poetic masterpieces beginning with *Le Voyage* in January and culminating in what is widely regarded as his greatest single poem, *Le Cygne* ("The Swan"), in December. In February 1861 a second, and greatly enlarged and improved, edition of *Les Fleurs du mal* was published.

In 1861 Baudelaire made an ill-advised and unsuccessful attempt to gain election to the French Academy. Abandoning verse poetry as his medium, he now concentrated on writing prose poems, a sequence of 20 of which was published in *La Presse* in 1862. In 1864 he was stricken with paralysis and aphasia from which he would never recover. Baudelaire died at age 46 in the Paris nursing home in which he had been confined for the last year of his life.

At the time of Baudelaire's death, many of his writings were unpublished and those that had been published were out of print. This was soon to change, however. The future leaders of the Symbolist movement who attended his funeral were already describing themselves as his followers, and by the 20th century he was widely recognized as one of the greatest French poets of the 19th century.

FYODOR DOSTOYEVSKY

(b. Nov. 11, 1821, Moscow, Russia—d. Feb. 9, 1881, St. Petersburg)

Fyodor Mikhaylovich Dostoyevsky was a Russian novelist and short-story writer whose psychological penetration into the darkest recesses of the human heart, together with his unsurpassed moments of illumination, had an immense influence on 20th-century fiction.

Unlike many other Russian writers of the first part of the 19th century, Dostoyevsky was not born into the landed gentry. He often stressed the difference between his own background and that of Leo Tolstoy or Ivan Turgenev and the effect of that difference on his work. Dostoyevsky gave up a career as a military engineer (for which he was unsuited) in order to write.

In 1849 he was arrested for belonging to Petrashevsky Circle, a radical discussion group; sentenced to be shot, he was reprieved at the last moment. The mock-execution ceremony was in fact part of the punishment. One of the prisoners went permanently insane on the spot; another went on to write *Crime and Punishment*. Dostoyevsky was sentenced to four years in a Siberian prison labour camp, to be followed by an indefinite term as a soldier.

After his return to Russia 10 years later, he wrote a novel based on his prison camp experiences, *Zapiski iz myortvogo doma* (1861–62; *The House of the Dead*). Gone was the tinge of Romanticism and dreaminess present in his early fiction. The novel describes the horrors that Dostoyevsky actually witnessed: the brutality of the guards who enjoyed cruelty for its own sake, the evil of criminals who could enjoy murdering children, and the existence of decent souls amid filth and degradation—all these themes, warranted by the author's own experience, gave the novel the immense power that readers still experience.

In Siberia Dostoyevsky experienced what he called the "regeneration" of his convictions. He also suffered his first attacks of epilepsy. No less than his accounts of being led to execution, his descriptions of epileptic seizures (especially in *The Idiot*) reveal the heights and depths of the human soul. Later he published and wrote for several periodicals while producing his best novels. These novels are concerned especially with faith, suffering, and the meaning of life; they are famous for their psychological depth and insight and their near-prophetic treatment of issues in philosophy and politics. *Igrok* (1866; *The Gambler*) is based on his own gambling addiction. Among his best known is the novella *Zapiski iz podpolya* (1864; *Notes from the Underground*), in the first part of which an unnamed first-person narrator delivers a brilliant attack on a set of beliefs shared by liberals and radicals.

Then there are the great novels. *Prestupleniye i nakazaniye* (1866; *Crime and Punishment*) describes a young intellectual who is willing to gamble on ideas and decides to solve all his problems at a stroke by murdering an old pawnbroker woman. *Idiot* (1869; *The Idiot*) represents Dostoyevsky's attempt to describe a perfectly good man in a way that is still psychologically convincing, while *Besy* (1872; *The Possessed*) presents savage portraits of intellectuals but expresses great sympathy for workers and other ordinary people ill-served by the radicals who presume to speak in their name. *Bratya Karamazovy* (1879–80; *The Brothers Karamazov*) focuses on the problem of evil, the nature of freedom, and the craving for faith.

In 1876–77 Dostoyevsky devoted his energies to *Dnevnik pisatelya* ("The Diary of a Writer"). A one-man journal, for which Dostoyevsky served as editor, publisher, and sole contributor, the *Diary* represented an attempt to initiate a new literary genre. Issue by monthly issue, it created complex thematic resonances among diverse kinds of material: short stories, plans for possible stories, autobiographical essays, sketches that seem to lie on the boundary between fiction and journalism, psychological analyses of sensational crimes, literary criticism, and political commentary. The *Diary* proved immensely popular and financially rewarding.

In 1880 Dostoyevsky delivered an electrifying speech about the poet Aleksandr Pushkin, which he published in a separate issue of *The Diary of a Writer* (August 1880). After finishing *Karamazov*, he resumed the monthly *Diary* but lived to publish only a single issue (January 1881) before dying of a hemorrhage on January 28 in St. Petersburg. By the end of his life, he had been acclaimed one of his country's greatest writers.

At least two modern literary genres, the prison camp novel and the dystopian novel (works such as Yevgeny Zamyatin's *We*, Aldous Huxley's *Brave New World*, and George Orwell's *1984*), derive from Dostoyevsky's writings. His ideas and formal innovations exercised a profound influence on Friedrich Nietzsche, André Gide, Albert Camus, and Jean-Paul Sartre, to name only a few. Above all, his works continue to enthrall readers by combining suspenseful plots with ultimate questions about faith, suffering, and the meaning of life.

GUSTAVE FLAUBERT

(b. Dec. 12, 1821, Rouen, France—d. May 8, 1880, Croisset)

The novelist Gustave Flaubert is regarded as the prime mover of the realist school of French literature and best known for his masterpiece, *Madame Bovary* (1857), a realistic portrayal of bourgeois life.

In 1841 Flaubert was enrolled as a student at the Faculty of Law in Paris. At age 22, however, he was recognized to be suffering from a nervous disease that was taken to be epilepsy. This made him give up the study of law, with the result that henceforth he could devote all his time to literature. Flaubert then retired to his estate at Croisset, near Rouen, on the Seine. He was to spend nearly all the rest of his life there.

The composition of *La Tentation de Saint Antoine* provides an example of that tenacity in the pursuit of perfection that made Flaubert go back constantly to work on subjects without ever being satisfied with the results. In 1839 he was writing *Smarh*, the first product of his bold ambition to give French literature its *Faust*. He resumed the task in 1846–49, in 1856, and in 1870, and finally published the book as *La Tentation de Saint Antoine* in 1874.

Madame Bovary was another work of long gestation. As early as 1837 he had written "Passion et vertu", a short and pointed story with a heroine, Mazza, resembling Emma Bovary. The novel itself cost the author five years of hard work prior to its appearance, with the subtitle *Moeurs de province* ("Provincial Customs"), in installments in the periodical *Revue* from October 1 to Dec. 15, 1856. For *Madame Bovary* he took a commonplace story of adultery and gave it an unrelenting objectivity—by which Flaubert meant the dispassionate recording of every trait or incident that could illuminate the psychology of his characters and their role in the logical development of his story—that transformed it into a work that represented the beginning of a new age in literature. The French government, however, brought the author to trial on the ground of his novel's alleged immorality, and he narrowly escaped conviction.

To refresh himself after his long application to the dull world of the bourgeoisie in *Madame Bovary*, Flaubert immediately began work on *Salammbô*, a novel about ancient Carthage. Subsequent works include *L'Éducation sentimentale* (1869), which appeared a few months before the outbreak of the Franco-German War of 1870 and was not appreciated by the public; several unsuccessful plays; and *Trois Contes* (1877), a book held to be his masterpiece that contains the three short stories "Un Coeur simple," "La Légende de Saint Julien l'Hospitalier," and "Hérodias." In the 1870s Flaubert sought consolation from financial troubles in his work and in the friendship of George Sand, Ivan Turgenev, and younger novelists—Émile Zola, Alphonse Daudet, and, especially, Guy de Maupassant. Flaubert's long novel *Bouvard et Pécuchet* was left unfinished when he died suddenly of an apoplectic stroke.

HENRIK IBSEN

(b. March 20, 1828, Skien, Nor.—d. May 23, 1906, Kristiania [formerly Christiania; now Oslo])

Henrik Ibsen was a major Norwegian playwright of the late 19th century who introduced to the European stage a new order of moral analysis that was placed against a severely realistic middle-class background and developed with economy of action, penetrating dialogue, and rigorous thought.

At the age of 23 Ibsen got himself appointed director and playwright to a new theatre at Bergen, in which capacity he had to write a new play every year. First at Bergen and then at the Norwegian Theatre in Christiania from 1857 to 1862, Ibsen tried to make palatable dramatic fare out of three incongruous ingredients: the drawing-room drama of the French playwright Eugène Scribe that was then popular; the actors, acting traditions, and language of Denmark; and the medieval Icelandic sagas—Norway's heroic, austere literature of unique magnificence. In addition to writing plays which were uncongenial to him and unacceptable to audiences, he did a lot of directing. In *Kongsemnerne* (1863; *The Pretenders*) he dramatized the mysterious inner authority that makes a man a man, a king, or a great playwright. This one play was in fact the national drama after which Ibsen had been groping so long, and before long it would be recognized as such.

The theatre in Christiania soon went bankrupt, however. In April 1864 he left Norway for Italy. For the next 27 years he lived abroad, mainly in Rome, Dresden, and Munich, returning to Norway only for short visits in 1874 and 1885. For reasons that he sometimes summarized as "small-mindedness," his homeland had left a very bitter taste in his mouth.

With him into exile Ibsen brought the fragments of a long semi-dramatic poem to be named *Brand*. Its central figure is a dynamic rural pastor who takes his religious calling with a blazing sincerity that transcends not only all forms of compromise but all traces of human sympathy and warmth as well. In Norway *Brand* was a tremendous popular success, even though (and in part because) its central meaning was so troubling. Hard on the heels of *Brand* (1866) came *Peer Gynt* (1867), another drama in rhymed couplets presenting an utterly antithetical view of human nature. If Brand is a moral monolith, Peer Gynt is a capering will-o'-the-wisp, a buoyant and self-centred opportunist who is aimless, yielding, and wholly unprincipled, yet who remains a lovable and beloved rascal.

With these two poetic dramas, Ibsen won his battle with the world; he paused now to work out his future. But Ibsen had not yet found his proper voice. When he did, its effect was not to criticize or reform social life but to blow it up. The explosion came with *Et dukkehjem* (1879; *A Doll's House*), about a very ordinary family that disintegrates. Audiences were scandalized at Ibsen's refusal in *A Doll's House* to scrape together (as any other contemporary playwright would have done) a "happy ending," however shoddy or contrived. But that was not Ibsen's way; his play was about knowing oneself and being true to that self.

Ibsen's next play, *Gengangere* (1881; *Ghosts*), created even more dismay and distaste than its predecessor by showing worse consequences of covering up even more ugly truths. Ostensibly the play's theme is congenital venereal disease, but on another level, it deals with the power of ingrained moral contamination to undermine the most determined idealism. The play is a grim study of contamination spreading through a family under cover of the widowed Mrs. Alving's timidly respectable views.

Among his later plays are *Fruen fra havet* (1888; *The Lady from the Sea*), *Hedda Gabler* (1890), *Bygmester Solness* (1892; *The Master Builder*), *Lille Eyolf* (1894; *Little Eyolf*), and *Naar vi døde vaagner* (1899; *When We Dead Awaken*). Two of these plays, *Hedda Gabler* and *The Master Builder*, are vitalized by the presence of a demonically idealistic and totally destructive female. Another obsessive personage in these late plays is an aging artist who is bitterly aware of his failing powers. Personal and confessional feelings infuse many of these last dramas; perhaps these resulted from Ibsen's decision in 1891 to return to Norway, or perhaps from the series of fascinated, fearful dalliances he had with young women in his later years. After his return to Norway, Ibsen continued to write plays until a stroke in 1900 and another a year later reduced him to a bedridden invalid. He died in Kristiania in 1906.

LEO TOLSTOY

(b. Aug. 28 [Sept. 9, New Style], 1828, Yasnaya Polyana, Tula province, Russian Empire—d. Nov. 7 [Nov. 20], 1910, Astapovo, Ryazan province)

Leo Tolstoy, the Russian master of realistic fiction, is one of the world's greatest novelists. The scion of prominent aristocrats, Tolstoy spent much of his life at his family estate of Yasnaya Polyana. Educated at home by tutors, Tolstoy enrolled in the University of Kazan in 1844. His poor record soon forced him to transfer to the less demanding law faculty, where he began to pursue his interests in literature and ethics. He left the university in 1847 without a degree. He served in the army, which included service in the Crimean War (1853–56).

Among his early published works are three sketches about the Siege of Sevastopol: "Sevastopol v dekabre mesyatse" ("Sevastopol in December"), "Sevastopol v maye" ("Sevastopol in May"), and "Sevastopol v avguste 1855 goda" ("Sevastopol in August"; all published 1855–56). Tolstoy was at first hailed by the literary world of St. Petersburg. But his prickly vanity, his refusal to join any intellectual camp, and his insistence on his complete independence soon earned him the dislike of the radical intelligentsia. He was to remain throughout his life an "archaist," opposed to prevailing intellectual trends.

He traveled in Europe before returning home and starting a school for peasant children. His novel *Kazaki* (1863; *The Cossacks*) was among the works from a period during which he experimented with new forms for expressing his moral and philosophical concerns. *Voyna i mir* (1865–69; *War and Peace*) marked the beginning of the period during which Tolstoy reached the height of his creative powers. It contains three kinds of material—a historical account of the Napoleonic wars, the biographies of fictional characters, and a set of essays about the philosophy of history. It examines the lives of a large group of characters, centring on the partly autobiographical figure of the spiritually questing Pierre. Its structure, with its flawless placement of complex characters in a turbulent historical setting, is regarded as one of the great technical achievements in the history of the Western novel.

His other great novel, *Anna Karenina* (1875–77), takes family life as its concern. The novel's first sentence, which indicates its concern with the domestic, is perhaps Tolstoy's most famous: "All happy families resemble each other; each unhappy family is unhappy in its own way." Both *War and Peace* and *Anna Karenina* advance the idea that ethics can never be a matter of timeless rules applied to particular situations. Rather, ethics depends on a sensitivity, developed over a lifetime, to particular people and specific situations. Tolstoy's preference for particularities over abstractions is often described as the hallmark of his thought.

After the publication of *Anna Karenina* Tolstoy underwent a spiritual crisis (described in *Ispoved*, 1884; *My Confession*). Drawn at first to the Russian Orthodox church into which he had been born, he rapidly decided that it, and all other Christian churches, were corrupt institutions that had thoroughly falsified true Christianity. Having discovered what he believed to be Christ's message and having overcome his paralyzing fear of death, Tolstoy devoted the rest of his life to developing and propagating

Leo Tolstoy. The Bettmann Archive

his new faith, which stressed simplicity, nonviolence, and social reform. He was excommunicated from the Russian Orthodox church in 1901.

Among his later works is *Smert Ivana Ilicha* (written 1886; *The Death of Ivan Ilyich*), a novella describing a man's gradual realization that he is dying and that his life has been wasted on trivialities; it is often considered the greatest novella in Russian literature. Tolstoy also wrote a treatise and several essays on art. In *Chto takoye iskusstvo?* (1898; *What Is Art?*), for instance, he argued that true art requires a sensitive appreciation of a particular experience, a highly specific feeling that is communicated to the reader not by propositions but by "infection."

Tolstoy lived humbly on his great estate, practicing a radical asceticism and in constant conflict with his wife. In November 1910, unable to bear his situation any longer, he left his estate incognito, although the international press was soon able to report on his movements. During his flight he contracted pneumonia, and died of heart failure at the railroad station of Astapovo.

EMILY DICKINSON

(b. Dec. 10, 1830, Amherst, Mass., U.S.—d. May 15, 1886, Amherst)

The American lyric poet Emily Dickinson, who lived in seclusion and commanded a singular brilliance of style and integrity of vision, is widely considered to be one of the leading 19th-century American poets.

Early Years

The second of three children, Dickinson grew up in moderate privilege and with strong local and religious attachments. For her first nine years she resided in a mansion built by her paternal grandfather, Samuel Fowler Dickinson, who had helped found Amherst College but then went bankrupt shortly before her birth. Her parents were loving but austere, and she became closely attached to her brother, Austin, and sister, Lavinia. Never marrying, the two sisters remained at home, and when their brother married, he and his wife established their own household next door.

Dickinson attended the coeducational Amherst Academy, where she was recognized by teachers and students alike for her prodigious abilities in composition. She also excelled in other subjects emphasized by the school, most notably Latin and the sciences. When she left home to attend Mount Holyoke Female Seminary (now Mount Holyoke College) in nearby South Hadley, she found the school's institutional tone uncongenial. Mount Holyoke's strict rules and invasive religious practices, along with her own homesickness and growing rebelliousness, help explain why she did not return for a second year.

At home as well as at school and church, the religious faith that ruled the poet's early years was evangelical Calvinism, a faith centred on the belief that humans are born totally depraved and can be saved only if they undergo a life-altering conversion in which they accept the vicarious sacrifice of Jesus Christ. Questioning this tradition soon after leaving Mount Holyoke, Dickinson was to be the only member of her family who did not experience conversion or join Amherst's First Congregational Church. Yet she seems to have retained a belief in the soul's immortality or at least to have transmuted it into a Romantic quest for the transcendent and absolute. One reason her mature religious views elude specification is that she took no interest in creedal or doctrinal definition. In this she was influenced by both the Transcendentalism of Ralph Waldo Emerson and the mid-century tendencies of liberal Protestant orthodoxy.

Development as a Poet

Although Dickinson had begun composing verse by her late teens, few of her early poems are extant. Until she was in her mid-20s, her writing mostly took the form of letters, and a surprising number of those that she wrote from age 11 onward have been preserved. Sent to her brother, Austin, or to friends of her own sex, especially Abiah Root, Jane Humphrey, and Susan Gilbert (who would marry Austin), these generous communications overflow with humour, anecdote, invention, and sombre reflection. In general, Dickinson seems to have given and demanded more from her correspondents than she received. On occasion she interpreted her correspondents' laxity in replying as evidence of neglect or even betrayal. Indeed, the loss of friends, whether through death or cooling interest, became a basic pattern for Dickinson. Much of her writing, both poetic and epistolary, seems premised on a feeling of abandonment and a matching effort to deny, overcome, or reflect on a sense of solitude.

Dickinson's closest friendships usually had a literary flavour. She was introduced to the poetry of Ralph Waldo Emerson by one of her father's law students, Benjamin F. Newton, and to that of Elizabeth Barrett Browning by Susan Gilbert and Henry Vaughan Emmons, a gifted college student. Two of Barrett Browning's works, *A Vision of Poets*, describing the pantheon of poets, and *Aurora Leigh*, on the development of a female poet, seem to have played a formative role for Dickinson, validating the idea of female greatness and stimulating her ambition.

In 1855 Dickinson traveled to Washington, D.C., with her sister and father, who was then ending his term as U.S. representative. On the return trip the sisters made an extended stay in Philadelphia, where it is thought the poet heard the preaching of Charles Wadsworth, a fascinating Presbyterian minister whose pulpit oratory suggested (as a colleague put it) "years of conflict and agony." Seventy years later, Martha Dickinson Bianchi, the poet's niece, claimed that Emily had fallen in love with Wadsworth, who was married, and then grandly renounced him. The story is too highly coloured for its details to be credited; certainly, there is no evidence the minister returned the poet's love. Yet it is true that a correspondence arose between the two and that Wadsworth visited her in Amherst about 1860, and again in 1880.

Always fastidious, Dickinson began to restrict her social activity in her early 20s, staying home from communal functions and cultivating intense epistolary relationships with a reduced number of correspondents. In 1855, leaving the large and much-loved house in which she had lived for 15 years, the 25-year-old woman and her family moved back to the dwelling associated with her first decade: the Dickinson mansion on Main Street in Amherst. She found the return profoundly disturbing, and when her mother became incapacitated by a mysterious illness that lasted from 1855 to 1859, both daughters were compelled to give more of themselves to domestic pursuits.

Mature Career

In summer 1858, Dickinson began assembling her manuscript-books. She made clean copies of her poems on fine quality stationery and then sewed small bundles of these sheets together at the fold. Over the next seven years she created 40 such booklets and several unsewn sheaves, and altogether they contained about 800 poems.

Dickinson sent more poems to her sister-in-law, Susan Gilbert Dickinson, a cultivated reader, than to any other known correspondent. Repeatedly professing eternal allegiance, these poems often imply that there was a certain distance between the two—that the sister-in-law was felt to be haughty, remote, or even incomprehensible. Yet Susan admired the poetry's wit and verve and offered the kind of personally attentive audience Dickinson craved. Susan was an active hostess, and her home was the venue at which Dickinson met a few friends, most importantly Samuel Bowles, publisher and editor of the influential *Springfield Republican*. Gregarious, captivating, and unusually liberal on the question of women's careers, Bowles had a high regard for Dickinson's poems, publishing (without her consent) seven of them during her lifetime—more than appeared in any other outlet.

In those years Dickinson experienced a painful and obscure personal crisis, partly of a romantic nature. The abject and pleading drafts of her second and third letters to the unidentified person she called "Master" are probably related to her many poems about a loved but distant person, usually male. Whoever the person was, Master's failure to return Dickinson's affection—together with Susan's absorption in her first childbirth and Bowles's growing invalidism—contributed to a piercing and ultimate sense of distress. Instead of succumbing to anguish, however, she came to view it as the sign of a special vocation, and it became the basis of an unprecedented creativity.

In April 1862, about the time Wadsworth left the East Coast for a pastorate in San Francisco, Dickinson sought the critical advice of Thomas Wentworth Higginson, whose witty article of advice to writers, *A Letter to a Young Contributor*, had just appeared in *The Atlantic Monthly*. Higginson was known as a writer of delicate nature essays and a crusader for women's rights. Enclosing four poems, Dickinson asked for his opinion of her verse—whether or not it was "alive." The ensuing correspondence lasted for years, with the poet sending her "preceptor," as she called him, many more samples of her work. In addition to seeking an informed critique from a professional but not unsympathetic man of letters, she was reaching out at a time of accentuated loneliness.

Dickinson's last trips from Amherst were in 1864 and 1865, when she shared her cousins Louisa and Frances Norcross's boardinghouse in Cambridge and underwent a course of treatment with the leading Boston ophthalmologist. She described her symptoms as an aching in her eyes and a painful sensitivity to light. In 1869 Higginson invited the poet to Boston to attend a literary salon; she refused the offer. When Higginson visited her the next year, he recorded his vivid first impression of her "plain" features, "exquisitely" neat attire, "childlike" manner, and loquacious and exhausting brilliance. He was "glad not to live near her."

In her last 15 years Dickinson averaged 35 poems a year and conducted her social life mainly through her chiselled and often sibylline written messages. Her father's sudden death in 1874 caused a profound and persisting emotional upheaval yet eventually led to a greater openness, self-possession, and serenity. She repaired an 11-year breach with Samuel Bowles and made friends with Maria Whitney, a teacher of modern languages at Smith College, and Helen Hunt Jackson, poet and author of the novel *Ramona* (1884). Dickinson resumed contact with Wadsworth, and from about age 50 she conducted a passionate romance with Otis Phillips Lord, an elderly judge on the supreme court of Massachusetts. The letters she apparently sent Lord reveal her at her most playful, alternately teasing and confiding. In declining an erotic advance or his proposal of marriage, she asked, "Dont you know you are happiest while I withhold and not confer—dont you know that 'No' is the wildest word we consign to Language?"

After Dickinson's aging mother was incapacitated by a stroke and a broken hip, caring for her at home made large demands on the poet's time and patience. The deaths of Dickinson's friends in her last years left her feeling terminally alone. But the single most shattering death, occurring in 1883, was that of her eight-year-old nephew next door. Her health broken by this culminating tragedy, she ceased seeing almost everyone, apparently including her sister-in-law. The poet died in 1886, when she was 55 years old. The immediate cause of death was a stroke.

Only 10 of Emily Dickinson's nearly 1,800 poems are known to have been published in her lifetime. She habitually worked in verse forms suggestive of hymns and ballads, with lines of three or four stresses. Her unusual off-rhymes have been seen as both experimental and influenced by the 18th-century hymnist Isaac Watts. She freely ignored the usual rules of versification and even of grammar, and in the intellectual content of her work she likewise proved exceptionally bold and original. Her verse is distinguished by its epigrammatic compression, haunting personal voice, enigmatic brilliance, and lack of high polish.

LEWIS CARROLL

(b. Jan. 27, 1832, Daresbury, Cheshire, Eng.—d. Jan. 14, 1898, Guildford, Surrey)

Lewis Carroll, the pseudonym of Charles Lutwidge Dodgson, was a English logician, mathematician, photographer, and novelist who is especially remembered for *Alice's Adventures in Wonderland* (1865) and its sequel, *Through the Looking-Glass* (1871).

Dodgson excelled in his mathematical and classical studies at the Christ Church, Oxford, which he entered as an undergraduate in 1851; he proceeded to a Bachelor of Arts degree in 1854. He was made a "senior student" (called a fellow in other colleges) and appointed lecturer in mathematics in 1855, a post he resigned in 1881. As was the case with all fellowships at that time, the studentship was dependent upon his remaining unmarried, and, by the terms of this particular endowment, proceeding to holy orders. Dodgson was ordained a deacon in the Church of England on Dec. 22, 1861. Had he gone on to become a priest he could have married and would then have been appointed to a parish by the college. But he felt himself unsuited for parish work and decided that he was perfectly content to remain a bachelor.

Dodgson's association with children grew naturally enough out of his position as an eldest son with eight younger brothers and sisters. He also suffered from a bad stammer (which he never wholly overcame) and found that he was able to speak naturally and easily to children. It is therefore not surprising that he should begin to entertain the children of Henry George Liddell, dean of Christ Church. Alice Liddell and her sisters Lorina and Edith were not the first of Dodgson's child friends. They had been preceded or were overlapped by the children of the writer George Macdonald, the sons of the poet Alfred, Lord Tennyson, and various other chance acquaintances. But the Liddell children undoubtedly held an especially high place in his affections—partly because they were the only children in Christ Church, since only heads of houses were free both to marry and to continue in residence.

On July 4, 1862, Dodgson and his friend Robinson Duckworth, fellow of Trinity, rowed the three children up the Thames from Oxford to Godstow, picnicked on the bank, and returned to Christ Church late in the evening: "On which occasion," wrote Dodgson in his diary, "I told them the fairy-tale of *Alice's Adventures Underground*, which I undertook to write out for Alice." Much of the story was based on a picnic a couple of weeks earlier when they had all been caught in the rain; for some reason, this inspired Dodgson to tell so much better a story than usual that both Duckworth and Alice noticed the difference, and Alice went so far as to cry, when they parted at the door of the deanery, "Oh, Mr. Dodgson, I wish you would write out Alice's adventures for me!"

Dodgson was able to write down the story more or less as told and added to it several extra adventures that had been told on other occasions. He illustrated it with his own crude but distinctive drawings and gave the finished product to Alice Liddell, with no thought of hearing of it again. But the novelist Henry Kingsley, while visiting the deanery, chanced to pick it up from the drawing-room table, read it, and urged Mrs. Liddell to persuade the author to publish it. Dodgson, honestly surprised, consulted his friend George Macdonald, author of some of the best children's stories of the period. Macdonald took it home to be read to his children, and his son Greville, aged six, declared that he "wished there were 60,000 volumes of it."

Accordingly, Dodgson revised it for publication. At Duckworth's suggestion he got an introduction to John Tenniel, the *Punch* magazine cartoonist, whom he commissioned to make illustrations to his specification. The book was published as *Alice's Adventures in Wonderland* in 1865. The book was a slow but steadily increasing success, and by the following year Dodgson was already considering a sequel to it. The result was *Through the Looking-Glass and What Alice Found There* (dated 1872; actually published December 1871). By the time of Dodgson's death, *Alice*

(taking the two volumes as a single artistic triumph) had become the most popular children's book in England: by the time of his centenary in 1932 it was one of the most popular and perhaps the most famous in the world.

Before he had told the original tale of *Alice's Adventures*, Dodgson had published a number of humorous items in verse and prose and a few inferior serious poems. The earliest of these appeared anonymously, but in March 1856 a poem called *Solitude* was published under the pseudonym Lewis Carroll. Dodgson arrived at this pen name by taking his own names Charles Lutwidge, translating them into Latin as Carolus Ludovicus, then reversing and retranslating them into English. He used the name afterward for all his nonacademic works. His humorous and other verses were collected in 1869 as *Phantasmagoria and Other Poems* and later separated (with additions) as *Rhyme? and Reason?* (1883) and *Three Sunsets and Other Poems* (published posthumously, 1898). The 1883 volume also contained *The Hunting of the Snark*, a narrative nonsense poem that is rivalled only by the best of Edward Lear.

MARK TWAIN

(b. Nov. 30, 1835, Florida, Mo., U.S.—d. April 21, 1910, Redding, Conn.)

Mark Twain (the pseudonym of Samuel Clemens) was an American humorist, journalist, lecturer, and novelist who acquired international fame for his travel narratives, especially *The Innocents Abroad* (1869), *Roughing It* (1872), and *Life on the Mississippi* (1883), and for his adventure stories of boyhood, especially *The Adventures of Tom Sawyer* (1876) and *Adventures of Huckleberry Finn* (1885). A gifted raconteur, distinctive humorist, and irascible moralist, he transcended the apparent limitations of his origins to become a popular public figure and one of America's best and most beloved writers.

YOUTH AND APPRENTICESHIPS

Samuel Clemens, the sixth child of John Marshall and Jane Moffit Clemens, was born two months prematurely and was in relatively poor health for the first 10 years of his life. It was the diminishing fortunes of the Clemens family that led them in 1839 to move 30 miles (50 km) east from Florida, Mo., to the Mississippi River port town of Hannibal, where there were greater opportunities. John Clemens opened a store and eventually became a justice of the peace, which entitled him to be called "Judge" but not to a great deal more.

In 1848 Clemens became a printer's apprentice for Joseph P. Ament's *Missouri Courier*. He lived sparingly in the Ament household but was allowed to continue his schooling and, from time to time, indulge in boyish amusements. Nevertheless, by the time Clemens was 13, his boyhood had effectively come to an end. He became more than competent as a typesetter while working for his brother, who owned a newspaper, but he also occasionally contributed sketches and articles. Some of those early sketches, such as *The Dandy Frightening the Squatter* (1852), appeared in Eastern newspapers and periodicals.

Having acquired a trade by age 17, Clemens left Hannibal in 1853 with some degree of self-sufficiency. For almost two decades he would be an itinerant labourer, trying many occupations. It was not until he was 37, he once remarked, that he woke up to discover he had become a "literary person." In the meantime, he was intent on seeing the world and exploring his own possibilities. He worked briefly as a typesetter in St. Louis in 1853 before working in New York City, Philadelphia, and Washington, D.C. He continued to write, though without firm literary ambitions.

Still restless and ambitious, he booked passage in 1857 on a steamboat bound for New Orleans, La., planning to find his fortune in South America. Instead, he saw a more immediate opportunity and persuaded the accomplished riverboat captain Horace Bixby to take him on as an apprentice. Clemens studied the Mississippi River and the operation of a riverboat under the masterful instruction of Bixby, with an eye toward obtaining a pilot's license, which he did in 1859. The profession of riverboat pilot was, as he confessed many years later in *Old Times on the Mississippi*, the most congenial one he had ever followed. He continued to write occasional pieces throughout these years and, in one satirical sketch, *River Intelligence* (1859), lampooned the self-important senior pilot Isaiah Sellers, whose observations of the Mississippi were published in a New Orleans newspaper. Clemens and the other "starchy boys," as he once described his fellow riverboat pilots in a letter to his wife, had no particular use for this nonunion man, but Clemens did envy what he later recalled to be Sellers's delicious pen name, Mark Twain.

The Civil War severely curtailed river traffic, and, fearing that he might be pressed into service as a Union gunboat pilot, Clemens brought his years on the river to a halt in 1861. After a sojourn in Hannibal, Clemens accompanied his brother Orion to the Nevada Territory, where Sam had to shift for himself. He submitted several letters to the Virginia City *Territorial Enterprise*, and these attracted the attention of the editor, Joseph Goodman, who offered him a salaried job as a reporter. He again embarked on an apprenticeship, in the hearty company of a group of writers sometimes called the Sagebrush Bohemians, and again he succeeded.

In February 1863 Clemens covered the legislative session in Carson City and wrote three letters for the

Enterprise. He signed them "Mark Twain." Apparently the mistranscription of a telegram misled Clemens to believe that the pilot Isaiah Sellers had died and that his cognomen was up for grabs. Clemens seized it. It would be several years before this pen name would acquire the firmness of a full-fledged literary persona, however. In the meantime, he was discovering by degrees what it meant to be a "literary person." Some of his articles and sketches had appeared in New York papers, and he became the Nevada correspondent for the San Francisco *Morning Call*. A period as a reporter in San Francisco followed.

He then went to the Tuolumne foothills to do some mining. It was there that he heard the story of a jumping frog. The story was widely known, but it was new to Clemens, and he took notes for a literary representation of the tale. When the humorist Artemus Ward invited him to contribute something for a book of humorous sketches, Clemens decided to write up the story. *Jim Smiley and His Jumping Frog* arrived too late to be included in the volume, but it was published in the New York *Saturday Press* in November 1865 and was subsequently reprinted throughout the country. "Mark Twain" had acquired sudden celebrity, and Sam Clemens was following in his wake.

Literary Maturity

The next few years were important for Clemens. It appears that he was committed to making a professional career for himself. He continued to write for newspapers, traveling to Hawaii for the Sacramento *Union* and also writing for New York newspapers, but he apparently wanted to become something more than a journalist. He went on his first lecture tour, speaking mostly on the Sandwich Islands (Hawaii) in 1866. It was a success, and for the rest of his life, though he found touring grueling, he knew he could

Mark Twain. Library of Congress, Washington, D.C. LC-USZ62-112728

take to the lecture platform when he needed money. His first book was *The Celebrated Jumping Frog of Calaveras County and Other Sketches* (1867), but it did not sell well. That same year, he moved to New York City, serving as the traveling correspondent for the San Francisco *Alta California* and for New York newspapers. He had ambitions to enlarge his reputation and his audience, and the announcement of a transatlantic excursion to Europe and the Holy Land provided him with just such an opportunity. The *Alta* paid the substantial fare in exchange for some 50 letters he would write concerning the trip. Eventually his account of the voyage was published as *The Innocents Abroad* (1869). It was a great success.

The trip abroad was fortuitous in another way. He met on the boat a young man named Charlie Langdon, who invited Clemens to dine with his family in New York and introduced him to his sister Olivia; the writer fell in love with her. Clemens's courtship of Olivia Langdon, the daughter of a prosperous businessman from Elmira, N.Y., was an ardent one, conducted mostly through correspondence. They were married in February 1870.

A book about his experiences in the West, *Roughing It*, was published in February 1872 and sold well. *The Gilded Age* (1873), Twain's first attempt at a novel, was remarkably well received and encouraged him to begin writing *Tom Sawyer*, along with his reminiscences about his days as a riverboat pilot. The latter became *Old Times*, which in turn would later become a portion of *Life on the Mississippi*. It described comically, but a bit ruefully too, a way of life that would never return. The highly episodic narrative of *Tom Sawyer* (1876), which recounts the mischievous adventures of a boy growing up along the Mississippi River, was coloured by a nostalgia for childhood and simplicity that would permit Twain to characterize the novel as a "hymn" to childhood.

In the summer of 1876, while staying with his in-laws Susan and Theodore Crane on Quarry Farm overlooking Elmira, Clemens began writing what he called in a letter to his friend William Dean Howells "Huck Finn's Autobiography." Huck had appeared as a character in *Tom Sawyer*, and Clemens decided that the untutored boy had his own story to tell. He soon discovered that it had to be told in Huck's own vernacular voice. *Huckleberry Finn* was written in fits and starts over an extended period and would not be published until 1885. During that interval, Twain often turned his attention to other projects, only to return again and again to the novel's manuscript. What distinguishes *Huckleberry Finn* from the other Huck-and-Tom sequels that Twain wrote is the moral dilemma Huck faces in aiding the runaway slave Jim while at the same time escaping from the unwanted influences of so-called civilization. Through Huck, the novel's narrator, Twain was able to address the shameful legacy of chattel slavery prior to the Civil War and the persistent racial discrimination and violence after.

Clemens's travels at home and abroad resulted in several books published during the 1880s. He embarked on a lecture tour in 1884. All the while, however, he continued to make often ill-advised investments. Clemens eventually assigned his property, including his copyrights, to his wife, announced the failure of his publishing house, and declared personal bankruptcy. In 1894, approaching his 60th year, Samuel Clemens was forced to repair his fortunes and remake his career.

Old Age

Clemens's last years have been described as his "bad mood" period. The description may or may not be apt. His eldest daughter died in 1896, his wife in 1904, and another daughter in 1909. It is true that in his polemical essays and in much of his fiction during this time he was venting powerful moral feelings and commenting freely on the "damn'd human race." But he had always been against sham and corruption, greed, cruelty, and violence. Some of Twain's best work during his late years was not fiction but polemical essays in which his earnestness was not in doubt: an essay against anti-Semitism, *Concerning the Jews* (1899); a denunciation of imperialism, *To the Man Sitting in Darkness* (1901); and an essay on lynching, *The United States of Lyncherdom* (posthumously published in 1923). Yet this was also a period during which he received palpable tokens of public approbation in the form of three honorary degrees—from Yale University in 1901, from the University of Missouri in 1902, and, the one he most coveted, from Oxford University in 1907.

More important, a world lecture tour and the publication of *Following the Equator* (1897), which described that tour, combined with shrewd investments of his money, allowed Clemens to pay his creditors in full. He traveled to Bermuda in January 1910. By early April he was having severe chest pains, and he returned to his home in Connecticut, where he died.

ÉMILE ZOLA

(b. April 2, 1840, Paris, France—d. Sept. 28, 1902, Paris)

Émile Zola, a French critic and political activist, was also the most prominent French novelist of the late 19th century. Raised in straitened circumstances, Zola worked at a Paris publishing house and as a journalist during the 1860s while establishing himself as a fiction writer. Two early novels are *Thérèse Raquin* (1867), a grisly tale of murder and its aftermath, and *Madeleine Férat* (1868), a rather unsuccessful attempt at applying the principles of heredity to the novel.

It was this interest in science that led Zola, in the fall of 1868, to conceive the idea of a large-scale series of novels similar to Honoré de Balzac's *La Comédie humaine* (*The Human Comedy*), which had appeared earlier in the century. Zola's project, originally involving 10 novels, each featuring a different member of the same family, was gradually expanded to comprise the 20 volumes of the *Rougon-Macquart* series. *La Fortune des Rougon* (*The Rougon Family Fortune*), the first novel in the series, began to appear in serial form in 1870, was interrupted by the outbreak of the

Franco-German War in July, and was eventually published in book form in October 1871. Zola went on to produce these 20 novels—most of which are of substantial length—at the rate of nearly one per year, completing the series in 1893. The series thus constitutes a family saga while providing a valuable sociological document of the events, institutions, and ideas that marked the rise of modern industrialism and the cultural changes it entailed.

As the founder and most celebrated member of the naturalist movement, Zola also published several treatises to explain his theories on art, including *Le Roman expérimental* (1880; *The Experimental Novel*) and *Les Romanciers naturalistes* (1881; *The Naturalist Novelists*). Naturalism, as Zola explained, involves the application to literature of two scientific principles: determinism, or the belief that character, temperament, and, ultimately, behaviour are determined by the forces of heredity, environment, and historical moment; and the experimental method, which entails the objective recording of precise data in controlled conditions.

In 1898 Zola intervened in the Dreyfus Affair—that of a Jewish French army officer whose wrongful conviction for treason in 1894 sparked a 12-year controversy that deeply divided French society. At an early stage in the proceedings Zola had decided, rightly, that Alfred Dreyfus was innocent. On Jan. 13, 1898, in the newspaper *L'Aurore*, Zola published a fierce denunciation of the French general staff in an open letter beginning with the words "J'accuse" ("I accuse"). He charged various high-ranking military officers and, indeed, the War Office itself of concealing the truth in the wrongful conviction of Dreyfus for espionage. Zola was prosecuted for libel and found guilty. In July 1899, when his appeal appeared certain to fail, he fled to England. He returned to France the following June when he learned that the Dreyfus case was to be reopened with a possible reversal of the original verdict. Zola's intervention in the controversy helped to undermine anti-Semitism and rabid militarism in France.

Zola died unexpectedly in September 1902, the victim of coal gas asphyxiation resulting from a blocked chimney flue. He had produced some 60 volumes of fiction, theory, and criticism, in addition to numerous pieces of journalism, during his 40-year career. At the time of his death, Zola was recognized not only as one of the greatest novelists in Europe but also as a man of action—a defender of truth and justice, a champion of the poor and the persecuted.

HENRY JAMES

(b. April 15, 1843, New York, N.Y., U.S.—d. Feb. 28, 1916, London, Eng.)

Henry James was an American novelist and, as a naturalized English citizen, a great figure in the transatlantic culture. His fundamental theme was the innocence and exuberance of the New World in clash with the corruption and wisdom of the Old.

He was named for his father, a prominent social theorist and lecturer, and was the younger brother of the pragmatist philosopher William James. They were taken abroad as infants, were schooled by tutors and governesses, and spent their preadolescent years in Manhattan. Returned to Geneva, Paris, and London during their teens, the James children acquired languages and an awareness of Europe few Americans had in their times. When he was 19 years of age Henry enrolled at the Harvard Law School, but he devoted his study time to reading Charles-Augustin Sainte-Beuve, Honoré de Balzac, and Nathaniel Hawthorne. His first story appeared anonymously two years later in the New York *Continental Monthly* and his first book reviews in the *North American*

Review. By his mid-20s James was regarded as one of the most skillful writers of short stories in America.

James began his long expatriation in the 1870s, heralded by publication of the novel *Roderick Hudson* (1875), the story of an American sculptor's struggle by the banks of the Tiber between his art and his passions; *Transatlantic Sketches*, his first collection of travel writings; and a collection of tales. With these three substantial books, he inaugurated a career that saw about 100 volumes through the press during the next 40 years.

In 1878 he achieved international renown with his story of an American flirt in Rome, *Daisy Miller*, and further advanced his reputation with *The Europeans* that same year. James's reputation was founded on his versatile studies of "the American girl," and he ended this first phase of his career by producing his masterpiece, *The Portrait of a Lady* (1881), a study of a young woman from Albany who brings to Europe her narrow provincialism and pretensions but also her sense of her own sovereignty, her "free spirit," her refusal to be treated, in the Victorian world, merely as a marriageable object. As a picture of Americans moving in the expatriate society of England and of Italy, this novel has no equal in the history of modern fiction.

Subsequent works were many. In *The Bostonians* (1886) and *The Princess Casamassima* (1886), his subjects were social reformers and revolutionaries. In *The Spoils of Poynton* (1897), *What Maisie Knew* (1897), and *The Turn of the Screw* (1898), he made use of complex moral and psychological ambiguity. *The Wings of the Dove* (1902), *The Ambassadors* (1903), and *The Golden Bowl* (1904) were the great novels of the final phase of his career, all showing a small group of characters in a tense situation, with a retrospective working out, through multiple angles of vision, of their drama. In these late works James resorted to an increasingly allusive prose style, which became dense and charged with symbolic imagery.

In his later years, James lived in retirement in an 18th-century house at Rye in Sussex, though on completion of *The Golden Bowl* he revisited the United States in 1904–05. James had lived abroad for 20 years, and in the interval America had become a great industrial and political power. On his return to England he wrote *The American Scene* (1907), prophetic in its vision of urban doom, spoliation, and pollution of resources and filled with misgivings over the anomalies of a "melting pot" civilization. He devoted three years to rewriting and revising his principal novels and tales for the highly selective "New York Edition," published in 24 volumes. For this edition James wrote 18 significant prefaces, which contain both reminiscence and exposition of his theories of fiction. Throwing his moral weight into Britain's struggle in World War I, James became a British subject in 1915 and received the Order of Merit from King George V.

AUGUST STRINDBERG

(b. Jan. 22, 1849, Stockholm, Swed.—d. May 14, 1912, Stockholm)

August Strindberg was a Swedish playwright, novelist, and short-story writer who combined psychology and Naturalism in a new kind of European drama that evolved into Expressionist drama.

Strindberg's childhood was marred by emotional insecurity, poverty, his grandmother's religious fanaticism, and neglect. He studied intermittently at the University of Uppsala, preparing in turn for the ministry and a career in medicine but never taking a degree. To earn his living, he worked as a freelance journalist in Stockholm, as well as at other jobs that he almost invariably lost. Meanwhile he struggled to complete his first important work, the historical drama *Mäster Olof* (published in 1872), on the theme of the Swedish Reformation, influenced by Shakespeare and by Henrik Ibsen's *Brand*. The Royal Theatre's rejection of *Mäster Olof* deepened his pessimism and sharpened his contempt for official institutions and traditions. For several years he continued revising the play, later recognized as the first modern Swedish drama.

In 1874 he became a librarian at the Royal Library, and in 1875 he met the Finno-Swedish Siri von Essen, then the unhappy wife of an officer of the guards; two years later they married. Their intense but ultimately disastrous relationship ended in divorce in 1891, when Strindberg, to his great grief, lost the custody of their four children. At first, however, marriage stimulated his writing, and in 1879 he published his first novel, *The Red Room*, a satirical account of abuses and frauds in Stockholm society. This was something new in Swedish fiction and made its author nationally famous.

He also wrote more plays, of which *Lucky Peter's Travels* (1881) contains the most biting social criticism. In 1883 Strindberg left Stockholm with his family and for six years moved restlessly about the Continent. Although he was then approaching a state of complete mental breakdown, he produced a great number of plays, novels, and stories. The publication in 1884 of the first volume of his collected stories, *Married*, led to a prosecution for blasphemy. He was acquitted, but the case affected his mind, and he imagined himself persecuted, even by Siri.

He returned to drama with new intensity, and the conflict between the sexes inspired some of the outstanding works written at this time, such as *The Father* (1887), *Miss Julie* (1888), and *The Creditors* (1888). All of these were written in total revolt against contemporary social conventions. In these bold and concentrated works, he combined the techniques of dramatic Naturalism—including unaffected dialogue, stark rather than luxurious scenery, and the use of stage props as symbols—with his own conception of psychology, thereby inaugurating a new movement in European drama. *The People of Hemsö*, a vigorous novel about the Stockholm skerries (rocky islands), always one of Strindberg's happiest sources of inspiration, was also produced during this intensively creative phase.

The years after his return to Sweden in 1889 were lonely and unhappy. Even though revered as a famous writer who had become the voice of modern Sweden, he was by now an alcoholic unable to find steady employment. In 1892 he went abroad again, to Berlin. His second marriage, to a young Austrian journalist, Frida Uhl, followed in 1893; they finally parted in Paris in 1895.

A period of literary sterility, emotional and physical stress, and considerable mental instability culminated in a kind of religious conversion, the crisis that he described in *Inferno*. During these years Strindberg devoted considerable time to experiments in alchemy and to the study of theosophy. His new faith, coloured by mysticism, re-created him as a writer. The immediate result was a drama in three parts, *To Damascus*, in which he depicts himself as "the Stranger," a wanderer seeking spiritual peace and finding it with another character, "the Lady," who resembles both Siri and Frida.

By this time Strindberg had again returned to Sweden, settling first in Lund and then, in 1899, in Stockholm, where he lived until his death. The summers he often spent among his beloved skerries. His view that life is ruled by the "Powers," punitive but righteous, was reflected in a series of historical plays that he began in 1889. Of these, *Gustav Vasa* is the best, masterly in its firmness of construction, characterization, and its vigorous dialogue. In 1901 he married the young Norwegian actress Harriet

Bosse; in 1904 they parted, and again Strindberg lost the child, his fifth.

Yet his last marriage, this "spring in winter," as he called it, inspired, among other works, the plays *The Dance of Death* and *A Dream Play*, as well as the charming autobiography *Ensam* ("Alone") and some lyrical poems. Renewed bitterness after his parting from his last wife provoked the grotesquely satirical novel *Svarta Fanor* (1907; "Black Banners"), which attacked the vices and follies of Stockholm's literary coteries, as Strindberg saw them. *Kammarspel* ("Chamber Plays"), written for the little Intima Theatre, which Strindberg ran for a time with a young producer, August Falck, embody further developments of his dramatic technique: of these, *The Ghost Sonata* (1907) is the most fantastic, anticipating much in later European drama. His last play, *The Great Highway*, a symbolic presentation of his own life, appeared in 1909. He was ignored in death, as in life, by the Swedish Academy but mourned by his countrymen as their greatest writer. On Swedish life and letters he has exercised a lasting influence.

OSCAR WILDE

(b. Oct. 16, 1854, Dublin, Ire.—d. Nov. 30, 1900, Paris, France)

Oscar Wilde was an Irish wit, poet, and dramatist whose reputation rests on his only novel, *The Picture of Dorian Gray* (1891), and on his comic plays. He was a spokesman for the late 19th-century Aesthetic movement in England, which advocated art for art's sake; and he was the object of celebrated civil and criminal suits involving homosexuality and ending in his imprisonment.

Wilde went, on successive scholarships, to Trinity College, Dublin (1871–74), and Magdalen College, Oxford (1874–78), which awarded him a degree with honours.

Oscar Wilde's plays were filled with bon mots, or clever sayings, regarding marriage and social propriety. But neither his wit nor popularity could keep him from doing hard time in an Irish prison. Library of Congress Prints and Photographs Division

During these four years, he distinguished himself not only as a classical scholar, a poseur, and a wit but also as a poet by winning the coveted Newdigate Prize in 1878 with a long poem, *Ravenna*.

In the early 1880s, when Aestheticism was the rage and despair of literary London, Wilde established himself in social and artistic circles by his wit and flamboyance. Soon the periodical *Punch* made him the satiric object of its antagonism to the Aesthetes for what was considered their unmasculine devotion to art; and in their comic opera *Patience*, Gilbert and Sullivan based the character Bunthorne, a "fleshly poet," partly on Wilde.

In 1884 Wilde married Constance Lloyd, daughter of a prominent Irish barrister; two children, Cyril and Vyvyan, were born, in 1885 and 1886. Meanwhile, Wilde was a reviewer for the *Pall Mall Gazette* and then became editor of *Woman's World* (1887–89).

In the final decade of his life, Wilde wrote and published nearly all of his major works. In his only novel, *The Picture of Dorian Gray* (published in *Lippincott's Magazine*, 1890, and in book form, revised and expanded by six chapters, 1891), Wilde combined the supernatural elements of the Gothic novel with the unspeakable sins of French decadent fiction. Critics charged immorality despite Dorian's self-destruction; Wilde, however, insisted on the amoral nature of art regardless of an apparently moral ending. Several volumes of essays, stories, and fairy tales also were published in 1891.

But Wilde's greatest successes were his society comedies. Within the conventions of the French "well-made play" (with its social intrigues and artificial devices to resolve conflict), he employed his paradoxical, epigrammatic wit to create a form of comedy new to the 19th-century English theatre. His first success, *Lady Windermere's Fan*, demonstrated that this wit could revitalize the rusty machinery of French drama. In the same year, rehearsals of his macabre play *Salomé*, written in French and designed, as he said, to make his audience shudder by its depiction of unnatural passion, were halted by the censor because it contained biblical characters. It was published in 1893, and an English translation appeared in 1894 with Aubrey Beardsley's celebrated illustrations.

A second society comedy, *A Woman of No Importance*, was produced in 1893. In rapid succession, Wilde's final plays, *An Ideal Husband* and *The Importance of Being Earnest*, were produced early in 1895. In the latter, his greatest achievement, the conventional elements of farce are transformed into satiric epigrams—seemingly trivial but mercilessly exposing Victorian hypocrisies:

> *I suppose society is wonderfully delightful. To be in it is merely a bore. But to be out of it simply a tragedy.*
>
> *I never travel without my diary. One should always have something sensational to read in the train.*
>
> *All women become like their mothers. That is their tragedy. No man does. That's his.*

In many of his works, exposure of a secret sin or indiscretion and consequent disgrace is a central design. If life imitated art, as Wilde insisted in his essay "The Decay of Lying" (1889), he was himself approximating the pattern in his reckless pursuit of pleasure. In addition, his close friendship with Lord Alfred Douglas, whom he had met in 1891, infuriated the Marquess of Queensberry, Douglas's father. Accused, finally, by the marquess of being a sodomite, Wilde, urged by Douglas, sued for criminal libel. Wilde's case collapsed, however, when the evidence went against him, and he dropped the suit. Urged to flee to

France by his friends, Wilde refused, unable to believe that his world was at an end. He was arrested and ordered to stand trial.

Wilde testified brilliantly, but the jury failed to reach a verdict. In the retrial he was found guilty and sentenced, in May 1895, to two years at hard labour. Most of his sentence was served at Reading Gaol, where he wrote a long letter to Douglas (published in 1905 in a drastically cut version as *De Profundis*) filled with recriminations against the younger man for encouraging him in dissipation and distracting him from his work. In May 1897 Wilde was released and immediately went to France, hoping to regenerate himself as a writer. His only remaining work, however, was *The Ballad of Reading Gaol* (1898), revealing his concern for inhumane prison conditions. He died suddenly of acute meningitis brought on by an ear infection. In his semiconscious final moments, he was received into the Roman Catholic Church, which he had long admired.

ARTHUR RIMBAUD

(b. Oct. 20, 1854, Charleville, France—d. Nov. 10, 1891, Marseille)

Arthur Rimbaud was a French poet and adventurer who won renown among the Symbolist movement and markedly influenced modern poetry.

The provincial son of an army captain, he had begun by age 16 to write violent, blasphemous poems, and he formulated an aesthetic doctrine stating that a poet must become a seer, break down the restraints and controls on personality, and thus become the instrument for the voice of the eternal. At the end of August 1871, on the advice of a friend, Rimbaud sent to the poet Paul Verlaine samples of his new poetry. Verlaine, impressed by their brilliance, summoned Rimbaud to Paris and sent the money for his fare. In a burst of self-confidence, Rimbaud composed

Le Bateau ivre (written 1871; "The Drunken Boat"), perhaps his finest poem, which displays his astonishing verbal virtuosity and a daring choice of images and metaphors. Once in Paris, he embarked upon a life of drink and debauchery, becoming involved in a homosexual relationship with Verlaine that gave rise to scandal. The two men were soon being seen in public as lovers, and Rimbaud was blamed for breaking up Verlaine's marriage.

In May 1872 Rimbaud was recalled to Paris by Verlaine, who said that he could not live without him. That July Verlaine abandoned his wife and child and fled with Rimbaud to London, where they spent the following winter. During this winter Rimbaud composed a series of 40 prose poems to which he gave the title *Illuminations*. These are his most ambitious attempt to develop new poetic forms from the content of his visions; they try to abolish the distinction between reality and hallucination.

The two poets' relationship was growing so tense and violent that Verlaine became physically ill and mentally disturbed. In April 1873 Rimbaud left him to return to his family, and it was at their farm at Roche, near Charleville, that he began to apply himself to another major work, *Une Saison en enfer* (1873; *A Season in Hell*). A month later Verlaine persuaded Rimbaud to accompany him to London. Rimbaud treated Verlaine with sadistic cruelty, and after more wanderings and quarrels, he rejoined Verlaine in Brussels only to make a last farewell. As he was leaving Verlaine shot him, wounding him in the wrist. Rimbaud was hospitalized, and Verlaine was arrested and sentenced to two years' imprisonment. Rimbaud soon returned to Roche, where he finished *Une Saison en enfer*, which consists of nine fragments of prose and verse. It is a remarkable work of self-confession and psychological examination. In the book's final section, "Adieu" ("Goodbye"), Rimbaud takes a nostalgic backward look at his past life and then moves on; it is a poem sometimes read as Rimbaud's farewell to creative writing.

The rest of Rimbaud's life, from the literary point of view, was silence. In 1875 he set out to see the world, and by 1879 he had crossed the Alps on foot, joined and deserted the Dutch colonial army in the East Indies, visited Egypt, and worked as a labourer in Cyprus, in every instance suffering illness or other hardships. In 1880 he found employment in the service of a coffee trader at Aden (now in Yemen), who sent him to Hārer (now in Ethiopia). He became the first white man to journey into the Ogaden region of Ethiopia, and his report of this expedition was published by France's National Society of Geography in 1884. He made his fortune in Ethiopia, but in early 1891 he returned to France plagued by a tumour on his right knee. The leg was amputated, and cancer was diagnosed; he died several months later.

GEORGE BERNARD SHAW

(b. July 26, 1856, Dublin, Ire.—d. Nov. 2, 1950, Ayot St. Lawrence, Hertfordshire, Eng.)

George Bernard Shaw was an Irish comic dramatist, literary critic, and socialist propagandist and the winner of the Nobel Prize for Literature in 1925.

In 1876 Shaw resolved to become a writer, and he left Ireland to join his mother and elder sister in London. Shaw in his 20s suffered continuous frustration and poverty. He spent his afternoons in the British Museum reading room, writing novels and reading what he had missed at school, and his evenings in search of additional self-education in the lectures and debates that characterized contemporary middle-class London intellectual activities.

His fiction failed utterly. The semiautobiographical and aptly titled *Immaturity* (1879; published 1930) repelled every publisher in London. His next four novels were similarly refused, as were most of the articles he submitted to the press for a decade. Despite his failure as a novelist, Shaw found himself during the 1880s. He became a vegetarian, a socialist, a spellbinding orator, a polemicist, and tentatively a playwright. He became the force behind the newly founded (1884) Fabian Society, a middle-class socialist group that aimed at the transformation of English society not through revolution but through permeation of the country's intellectual and political life. Shaw involved himself in every aspect of its activities, most visibly as editor of one of the classics of British socialism, *Fabian Essays in Socialism* (1889), to which he also contributed two sections.

Eventually, in 1885 the drama critic William Archer found Shaw steady journalistic work. But Shaw truly began to make his mark when he was recruited to the *Saturday Review* as theatre critic (1895–98); in that position he used all his wit and polemical powers in a campaign to displace the artificialities and hypocrisies of the Victorian stage with a theatre of vital ideas. He also began writing his own plays.

In his first play, *Widowers' Houses* (performed 1892), he emphasized social and economic issues instead of romance, adopting the ironic comedic tone that would characterize all his work. He described his first plays as "unpleasant" because they forced the spectator to face unpleasant facts; these plays include *Mrs. Warren's Profession*, which concerns prostitution; it was written in 1893 but barred from performance until 1902. He followed these with several "pleasant" plays in an effort to find the producers and audiences that his mordant comedies had offended. The first of the second group, *Arms and the Man* (performed 1894), has a Balkan setting and makes lighthearted, though sometimes mordant, fun of romantic falsifications of both love and warfare. *Candida* (performed 1897) and *You Never Can Tell* (performed 1899) are other "pleasant" plays.

Shaw soon became established as a major playwright on the Continent by the performance of his plays there, but, curiously, his reputation lagged in England. It was only with the production of *John Bull's Other Island* (performed 1904) in London, with a special performance for Edward VII, that Shaw's stage reputation was belatedly made in England. Other plays of about the same time include *Man and Superman* (performed 1905), *Major Barbara* (performed 1905), and *The Doctor's Dilemma* (performed 1906), the latter two using high comedy for serious purposes. Possibly Shaw's comedic masterpiece, and certainly his funniest and most popular play, is *Pygmalion* (performed 1913). It was claimed by Shaw to be a didactic drama about phonetics, but the play is a humane comedy about love and the English class system.

World War I was a watershed for Shaw. At first he ceased writing plays. But by the 1920s he had returned to drama, most notably with *Saint Joan* (performed 1923), a chronicle play about Joan of Arc. Acclaim for it led to the awarding of the 1925 Nobel Prize for Literature to Shaw (he refused the award).

Impudent, irreverent, and always a showman, Shaw used his buoyant wit to keep himself in the public eye to the end of his 94 years. He was not merely the best comic dramatist of his time but also one of the most significant playwrights in the English language since the 17th century. He was also the most trenchant pamphleteer since Swift; the most readable music critic in English; the best theatre critic of his generation; a prodigious lecturer and essayist on politics, economics, and sociological subjects; and one of the most prolific letter writers in literature.

ANTON CHEKHOV

(b. Jan. 29 [Jan. 17, Old Style], 1860, Taganrog, Russia—d. July 14/15 [July 1/2], 1904, Badenweiler, Ger.)

Anton Pavlovich Chekhov was a major Russian playwright and master of the modern short story. He is regarded as the outstanding representative of the late 19th-century Russian realist school.

Chekhov, the son of a former serf, became a doctor in 1884. He began his writing career as the author of anecdotes for humorous journals, signing his early work pseudonymously. By 1888 he had become widely popular with a "lowbrow" public and had already produced a body of work more voluminous than all his later writings put together. He had also experimented in serious writing, providing studies of human misery and despair at variance with the frenzied facetiousness of his comic work. Gradually this serious vein absorbed him and soon predominated over the comic.

In 1888, Chekhov published his first work in a leading literary review, *Severny vestnik* ("Northern Herald"). With the work in question—a long story entitled "Steppe"—he at last turned his back on comic fiction. "Steppe," an autobiographical work describing a journey in the Ukraine as seen through the eyes of a child, is the first among more than 50 stories published in a variety of journals and selections between 1888 and his death in 1904.

Chekhov also wrote several profoundly tragic studies at this time. The play *Ivanov* (1887–89) culminates in the suicide of a young man nearer to the author's own age. Together with other works of this period, this play belongs to a group among Chekhov's works that have been called clinical studies. They explore the experiences of the mentally or physically ill in a spirit that reminds one that the

author was himself a qualified—and remained a sporadically practicing—doctor.

By the late 1880s many critics had begun to reprimand Chekhov for holding no firm political and social views and for failing to endow his works with a sense of direction. Such expectations irked Chekhov, who was unpolitical and philosophically uncommitted. In early 1890 he suddenly sought relief from the irritations of urban intellectual life by undertaking a one-man sociological expedition to a remote island, Sakhalin.

During the years just before and after his Sakhalin expedition, Chekhov had continued his experiments as a dramatist. His *Wood Demon* (1888–89) is a long-winded and ineptly facetious four-act play, which somehow, by a miracle of art, became converted—largely by cutting—into *Dyadya Vanya* (*Uncle Vanya*), one of his greatest stage masterpieces. The conversion—to a superb study of aimlessness in a rural manor house—took place some time between 1890 and 1896; the play was published in 1897. Other dramatic efforts of the period include several of the uproarious one-act farces known as vaudevilles: *Medved* (*The Bear*), *Predlozheniye* (*The Proposal*), and others.

Chayka (*The Seagull*) was first performed in St. Petersburg in 1896. This four-act drama, misnamed a comedy, was badly received; indeed, it was almost hissed off the stage. Chekhov was greatly distressed and left the auditorium during the second act, having suffered one of the most traumatic experiences of his life and vowing never to write for the stage again. Two years later, however, the play was revived by the newly created Moscow Art Theatre, enjoying considerable success and helping to reestablish Chekhov as a dramatist. *The Seagull* is a study of the clash between the older and younger generations as it affects two actresses and two writers, some of the details having been suggested by episodes in the lives of Chekhov's friends.

In March 1897 Chekhov had suffered a lung hemorrhage caused by tuberculosis, symptoms of which had become apparent considerably earlier. Never a successful financial manager, Chekhov attempted to regularize his literary affairs in 1899 by selling the copyright of all his existing works, excluding plays, to a publisher for 75,000 rubles, an unduly low sum.

Chekhov's two last plays—*Tri sestry* (1901; *Three Sisters*) and *Vishnyovy sad* (1904; *The Cherry Orchard*)—were both written for the Moscow Art Theatre. But much as Chekhov owed to the theatre's two founders, Vladimir Nemirovich-Danchenko and Konstanin Stanislavsky, he remained dissatisfied with such rehearsals and performances of his plays as he was able to witness. In *Three Sisters* Chekhov sensitively portrays the longings of a trio of provincial young women, while in *The Cherry Orchard* he offered a poignant picture of the Russian landowning class in decline, portraying characters who remain comic despite their very poignancy. Less than six months after its first performance Chekhov died of tuberculosis.

RABINDRANATH TAGORE

(b. May 7, 1861, Calcutta, India—d. Aug. 7, 1941, Calcutta)

Rabindranath Tagore, a Bengali poet, short-story writer, song composer, playwright, essayist, and painter, was awarded the Nobel Prize for Literature in 1913. Tagore introduced new prose and verse forms and the use of colloquial language into Bengali literature, thereby freeing it from traditional models based on classical Sanskrit. He was highly influential in introducing the best of Indian culture to the West and vice versa, and he is

Bengali poet and short-story writer Rabindranath Tagore bridged the gap between East and West with groundbreaking, influential prose and verse. E. O. Hoppe/Hulton Archive/Getty Images

generally regarded as the outstanding creative artist of modern India.

The son of the religious reformer Debendranath Tagore, he early began to write verses. After incomplete studies in England in the late 1870s, he returned to India. There he published several books of poetry in the 1880s and completed *Mānasī* (1890), a collection that marks the maturing of his genius. It contains some of his best-known poems, including many in verse forms new to Bengali, as well as some social and political satire that was critical of his fellow Bengalis.

In 1891 Tagore went to East Bengal (now in Bangladesh) to manage his family's estates at Shilaidah and Shazadpur for 10 years. There he often stayed in a houseboat on the Padma River (i.e., the Ganges River), in close contact with village folk, and his sympathy for their poverty and backwardness became the keynote of much of his later writing. Most of his finest short stories, which examine "humble lives and their small miseries," date from the 1890s and have a poignancy, laced with gentle irony, that is unique to him, though admirably captured by the director Satyajit Ray in later film adaptations. Tagore came to love the Bengali countryside, most of all the Padma River, an often-repeated image in his verse. During these years he published several poetry collections, notably *Sonār Tarī* (1894; *The Golden Boat*), and plays, notably *Chitrāngadā* (1892; *Chitra*). Tagore's poems are virtually untranslatable, as are his more than 2,000 songs, which remain extremely popular among all classes of Bengali society.

In 1901 Tagore founded an experimental school in rural West Bengal at *Śantiniketan* ("Abode of Peace"), where he sought to blend the best in the Indian and Western traditions. He settled permanently at the school, which became Viśva-Bhārati University in 1921. Years of sadness arising from the deaths of his wife and two children between 1902 and 1907 are reflected in his later poetry, which was introduced to the West in *Gitanjali, Song Offerings* (1912). This book, containing Tagore's English prose translations of religious poems from several of his Bengali verse collections, including *Gītāñjali* (1910), was hailed by W. B. Yeats and André Gide and won him the Nobel Prize in 1913. Tagore was awarded a knighthood in 1915, but he repudiated it in 1919 as a protest against the Amritsar Massacre.

From 1912 Tagore spent long periods out of India, lecturing and reading from his work in Europe, the Americas, and East Asia and becoming an eloquent spokesperson for the cause of Indian independence. Tagore's novels, though less outstanding than his poems and short stories, are also worthy of attention; the best known are *Gorā* (1910) and *Ghare-Bāire* (1916; *The Home and the World*). In the late 1920s, at nearly 70 years of age, Tagore took up painting and produced works that won him a place among India's foremost contemporary artists.

WILLIAM BUTLER YEATS

(b. June 13, 1865, Sandymount, Dublin, Ire.—d. Jan. 28, 1939, Roquebrune-Cap-Martin, France)

The Irish poet, dramatist, and prose writer William Butler Yeats was one of the greatest English-language poets of the 20th century. He received the Nobel Prize for Literature in 1923.

In 1867, when Yeats was only two, his family moved to London, but he spent much of his boyhood and school holidays in Sligo, in western Ireland, with his grandparents. This country—its scenery, folklore, and supernatural legend—would colour Yeats's work and form the setting of many of his poems. In 1880 his family moved back to Dublin, where he attended the high school. In 1883 he attended the Metropolitan School of Art in Dublin, where the most important part of his education was in meeting other poets and artists.

Meanwhile, Yeats was beginning to write. His first publication, two brief lyrics, appeared in the *Dublin University Review* in 1885. When the family moved back to London in 1887, Yeats took up the life of a professional writer. He joined the Theosophical Society, whose mysticism appealed to him because it was a form of imaginative life far removed from the workaday world. His early poems, collected in *The Wanderings of Oisin, and Other Poems* (1889), are the work of an aesthete, often beautiful but always rarefied, a soul's cry for release from circumstance.

Yeats quickly became involved in the literary life of London. He became friends with William Morris and W. E. Henley, and he was a cofounder of the Rhymers' Club, whose members included his friends Lionel Johnson and Arthur Symons. In 1889 Yeats met Maud Gonne, an Irish beauty, ardent and brilliant. He fell in love with her, but she was not in love with him. Her passion was lavished upon Ireland; she was an Irish patriot, a rebel, and a rhetorician, commanding in voice and in person. When Yeats joined in the Irish nationalist cause, he did so partly from conviction, but mostly for love of Maud. When Yeats's play *Cathleen ni Houlihan* was first performed in Dublin in 1902, she played the title role.

After the rapid decline and death of the controversial Irish leader Charles Stewart Parnell in 1891, Yeats felt that Irish political life lost its significance. The vacuum left by politics might be filled, he felt, by literature, art, poetry, drama, and legend. *The Celtic Twilight* (1893), a volume of essays, was Yeats's first effort toward this end, but progress was slow until 1898, when he met Augusta Lady Gregory, an aristocrat who was to become a playwright and his close friend.

Yeats (along with Lady Gregory and others) was one of the originators of the Irish Literary Theatre, which gave its first performance in Dublin in 1899 with Yeats's play *The Countess Cathleew*. To the end of his life Yeats remained a director of this theatre, which became the Abbey Theatre in 1904. In the crucial period from 1899 to 1907, he managed the theatre's affairs, encouraged its playwrights (notably John Millington Synge), and contributed many of his own plays that became part of the Abbey Theatre's repertoire.

The years from 1909 to 1914 mark a decisive change in his poetry. The otherworldly, ecstatic atmosphere of the early lyrics has cleared, and the poems in *Responsibilities: Poems and a Play* (1914) show a tightening and hardening of his verse line, a more sparse and resonant imagery, and a new directness with which Yeats confronts reality and its imperfections.

In 1917 Yeats published *The Wild Swans at Coole*. From then onward he reached and maintained the height of his achievement—a renewal of inspiration and a perfecting of technique that are almost without parallel in the history of English poetry. *The Tower* (1928), named after the castle he owned and had restored, is the work of a fully accomplished artist; in it, the experience of a lifetime is brought to perfection of form. Still, some of Yeats's greatest verse was written subsequently, appearing in *The Winding Stair* (1929). The poems in both of these works use, as their dominant subjects and symbols, the Easter Rising and the Irish civil war; Yeats's own tower; the Byzantine Empire and its mosaics; Plato, Plotinus, and Porphyry; and the author's interest in contemporary psychical research.

In 1922, on the foundation of the Irish Free State, Yeats accepted an invitation to become a member of the new Irish Senate: he served for six years. In 1923 he was awarded the Nobel Prize for Literature. Now a celebrated figure, he was indisputably one of the most significant modern poets. He died in January 1939 while abroad.

Had Yeats ceased to write at age 40, he would probably now be valued as a minor poet writing in a dying Pre-Raphaelite tradition that had drawn renewed beauty and poignancy for a time from the Celtic revival. There is no precedent in literary history for a poet who produces his greatest work between the ages of 50 and 75. Yeats's work of this period takes its strength from his long and dedicated apprenticeship to poetry; from his experiments in a wide range of forms of poetry, drama, and prose; and from his spiritual growth and his gradual acquisition of personal wisdom, which he incorporated into the framework of his own mythology.

LUIGI PIRANDELLO

(b. June 28, 1867, Agrigento, Sicily, Italy—d. Dec. 10, 1936, Rome)

Luigi Pirandello was an Italian playwright, novelist, and short-story writer who won the 1934 Nobel Prize for Literature. With his invention of the "theatre within the theatre" in the play *Sei personaggi in cerca d'autore* (1921; *Six Characters in Search of an Author*), he became an important innovator in modern drama.

In 1891 Pirandello gained his Doctorate in Philology for a thesis on the dialect of Agrigento. In 1894 his father arranged his marriage to Antonietta Portulano, the daughter of a business associate, a wealthy sulfur merchant. This marriage gave him financial independence, allowing him to live in Rome and to write. He had already published an early volume of verse, *Mal giocondo* (1889), which paid tribute to the poetic fashions set by Giosuè Carducci. This was followed by other volumes of verse. But his first significant works were short stories.

In 1903 a landslide shut down the sulfur mine in which his wife's and his father's capital was invested. Suddenly poor, Pirandello was forced to earn his living not only by writing but also by teaching Italian at a teacher's college in Rome. As a further result of the financial disaster, his wife developed a persecution mania, which manifested itself in a frenzied jealousy of her husband. His torment ended only with her removal to a sanatorium in 1919 (she died in 1959). It was this bitter experience that finally determined the theme of his most characteristic work, already perceptible in his early short stories—the exploration of the tightly closed world of the forever changeable human personality.

Pirandello's early narrative style stems from the *verismo* ("realism") of two Italian novelists of the late 19th century—Luigi Capuana and Giovanni Verga. Success came with his third novel, often acclaimed as his best, *Il fu Mattia Pascal* (1904; *The Late Mattia Pascal*). Although the theme is not typically "Pirandellian," since the obstacles confronting its hero result from external circumstances, it already shows the acute psychological observation that was later to be directed toward the exploration of his characters' subconscious. Other novels, notably *I vecchi e i giovani* (1913; *The Old and The Young*) and *Uno, nessuno e centomila* (1925–26; *One, None, and a Hundred Thousand*), followed.

Pirandello also wrote over 50 plays. He had first turned to the theatre in 1898 with *L'epilogo*, but the accidents that prevented its production until 1910 (when it was retitled *La morsa*) kept him from other than sporadic attempts at drama until the success of *Così è (se vi pare)* in 1917. This delay may have been fortunate for the development of his dramatic powers. *L'epilogo* does not greatly differ from other drama of its period, but *Così è (se vi pare)* began the series of plays that were to make him world famous in the

1920s. Its title can be translated as *Right You Are (If You Think You Are)*. A demonstration, in dramatic terms, of the relativity of truth, and a rejection of the idea of any objective reality not at the mercy of individual vision, it anticipates Pirandello's two great plays, *Six Characters in Search of an Author* (1921) and *Enrico IV* (1922; *Henry IV*).

Six Characters is the most arresting presentation of the typical Pirandellian contrast between art, which is unchanging, and life, which is an inconstant flux. Characters that have been rejected by their author materialize on stage, throbbing with a more intense vitality than the real actors, who, inevitably, distort their drama as they attempt its presentation. And in *Henry IV* the theme is madness, which lies just under the skin of ordinary life and is, perhaps, superior to ordinary life in its construction of a satisfying reality. The play finds dramatic strength in its hero's choice of retirement into unreality in preference to life in the uncertain world. The production of *Six Characters* in Paris in 1923 made Pirandello widely known, and his work became one of the central influences on the French theatre.

The universal acclaim that followed *Six Characters* and *Henry IV* sent Pirandello touring the world (1925–27) with his own company, the Teatro d'Arte in Rome. It also emboldened him to disfigure some of his later plays (e.g., *Ciascuno a suo modo* [1924]) by calling attention to himself, just as in some of the later short stories it is the surrealistic and fantastic elements that are accentuated.

After the dissolution, because of financial losses, of the Teatro d'Arte in 1928, Pirandello spent his remaining years in frequent and extensive travel. In his will he requested that there should be no public ceremony marking his death—only "a hearse of the poor, the horse and the coachman."

MARCEL PROUST

(b. July 10, 1871, Auteuil, near Paris, France—d. Nov. 18, 1922, Paris)

Marcel Proust was a French novelist and is best known as the author of *À la recherche du temps perdu* (1913–27; *In Search of Lost Time*), a seven-volume novel based on Proust's life told psychologically and allegorically.

Proust was the son of an eminent physician of provincial French Catholic descent and the daughter of a wealthy Jewish family. After a first attack in 1880, he suffered from asthma throughout his life. In 1896 he published *Les Plaisirs et les jours* (*Pleasures and Days*), a collection of short stories at once precious and profound, most of which had appeared during 1892–93 in the magazines *Le Banquet* and *La Revue Blanche*. From 1895 to 1899 he wrote *Jean Santeuil*, an autobiographical novel that showed awakening genius. A gradual disengagement from social life coincided with growing ill health and with his active involvement in the Dreyfus affair of 1897–99, when French politics and society were split by the movement to liberate the Jewish army officer Alfred Dreyfus, unjustly imprisoned on Devil's Island as a spy. Proust helped to organize petitions and assisted Dreyfus's lawyer Labori, courageously defying the risk of social ostracism.

The death of Proust's father in 1903 and of his mother in 1905 left him grief stricken and alone but financially independent and free to attempt his great novel. At least one early version was written in 1905–06. Another, begun in 1907, was laid aside in October 1908. This had itself been interrupted by a series of brilliant parodies—of Balzac, Flaubert, Renan, Saint-Simon, and others of Proust's favourite French authors—called "L'Affaire Lemoine" (published in *Le Figaro*), through which he endeavoured to purge his style of extraneous influences.

In January 1909 occurred the real-life incident of an involuntary revival of a childhood memory through the taste of tea and a rusk biscuit (which in his novel became madeleine cake); in July he began *À la recherche du temps perdu*.

He thought of marrying "a very young and delightful girl" whom he met at Cabourg, a seaside resort in Normandy that became the Balbec of his novel, where he spent summer holidays from 1907 to 1914. Instead, he retired from the world to write his novel, finishing the first draft in September 1912. The first volume, *Du côté de chez Swann* (*Swann's Way*), was refused by the best-selling publishers Fasquelle and Ollendorff and even by the intellectual *La Nouvelle Revue Française*, under the direction of the novelist André Gide, but was finally issued at the author's expense in November 1913 by the progressive young publisher Bernard Grasset and met with some success. Proust then planned only two further volumes, the premature appearance of which was fortunately thwarted by his anguish at the flight and death of his secretary Alfred Agostinelli and by the outbreak of World War I.

During the war he revised the remainder of his novel, enriching and deepening its feeling, texture, and construction, increasing the realistic and satirical elements, and tripling its length. In this majestic process he transformed a work that in its earlier state was still below the level of his highest powers into one of the greatest achievements of the modern novel. In June 1919 *À l'ombre des jeunes filles en fleurs* (*Within a Budding Grove*) was published simultaneously with a reprint of *Swann* and with *Pastiches et mélanges*, a miscellaneous volume containing "L'Affaire Lemoine" and other works. In December 1919, through Léon Daudet's recommendation, *À l'ombre* received the Prix Goncourt, and Proust suddenly became world famous. Three more installments appeared in his lifetime, with the benefit of his final revision, comprising *Le Côté de*

Guermantes (1920–21; *The Guermantes Way*) and *Sodome et Gomorrhe* (1921–22; *Sodom and Gomorrah*).

Proust died in Paris of pneumonia, succumbing to a weakness of the lungs that many had mistaken for a form of hypochondria and struggling to the last with the revision of *La Prisonnière* (*The Captive*). The last three parts of *À la recherche* were published posthumously, in an advanced but not final stage of revision: *La Prisonnière* (1923), *Albertine disparue* (1925; *The Fugitive*), and *Le Temps retrouvé* (1927; *Time Regained*). The novel remains one of the supreme achievements of modern fiction.

ROBERT FROST

(b. March 26, 1874, San Francisco, Calif., U.S.—d. Jan. 29, 1963, Boston, Mass.)

The American poet Robert Frost was much admired for his depictions of the rural life of New England, his command of American colloquial speech, and his realistic verse portraying ordinary people in everyday situations.

Frost attended Dartmouth College and continued to labour on the poetic career he had begun in a small way during high school; he first achieved professional publication in 1894 when *The Independent*, a weekly literary journal, printed his poem *My Butterfly: An Elegy*. Impatient with academic routine, Frost left Dartmouth after less than a year and married. The young poet supported his wife, Elinor, by teaching school and farming, neither with notable success. Frost resumed his college education at Harvard University in 1897 but left after two years' study there. From 1900 to 1909 the family raised poultry on a farm near Derry, New Hampshire, and for a time Frost also taught. He became an enthusiastic botanist and acquired his poetic persona of a New England rural sage during the years he and his family spent at Derry. All this while he was writing poems, but publishing outlets showed little interest in them.

By 1911 Frost was fighting against discouragement. Poetry had always been considered a young person's game, but Frost, who was nearly 40 years old, had not published a single book of poems and had seen just a handful appear in magazines. In 1911 ownership of the Derry farm passed to Frost. A momentous decision was made: to sell the farm and use the proceeds to make a radical new start in London, where publishers were perceived to be more receptive to new talent. Accordingly, in August 1912 the Frost family sailed across the Atlantic to England. Frost carried with him sheaves of verses he had written but not gotten into print. English publishers in London did indeed prove more receptive to innovative verse, and, through his own vigorous efforts and those of the expatriate American poet Ezra Pound, Frost within a year had published *A Boy's Will* (1913). From this first book, such poems as *Storm Fear*, *Mowing*, and *The Tuft of Flowers* have remained standard anthology pieces.

A Boy's Will was followed in 1914 by a second collection, *North of Boston*, that introduced some of the most popular poems in all of Frost's work, among them *Mending Wall*, *The Death of the Hired Man*, *Home Burial*, and *After Apple-Picking*. In London, Frost's name was frequently mentioned by those who followed the course of modern literature, and soon American visitors were returning home with news of this unknown poet who was causing a sensation abroad.

The outbreak of World War I brought the Frosts back to the United States in 1915. By then the Boston poet Amy Lowell's review had already appeared in *The New Republic*, and writers and publishers throughout the Northeast were aware that a writer of unusual abilities stood in their midst. The American publishing house of Henry Holt had brought out its edition of *North of Boston* in 1914. It became a best-seller, and, by the time the Frost family landed in Boston, Holt was adding the American edition of *A Boy's Will*. Frost soon found himself besieged by magazines seeking to publish his poems. Never before had an American poet achieved such rapid fame after such a disheartening delay. From this moment his career rose on an ascending curve.

Frost bought a small farm at Franconia, New Hampshire, in 1915, but his income from both poetry and farming proved inadequate to support his family, and so he lectured and taught part-time at Amherst College and at the University of Michigan from 1916 to 1938. Any remaining doubt about his poetic abilities was dispelled by the collection *Mountain Interval* (1916), which continued the high level established by his first books. His reputation was further enhanced by *New Hampshire* (1923), which received the Pulitzer Prize. That prize was also awarded to Frost's *Collected Poems* (1930) and to the collections *A Further Range* (1936) and *A Witness Tree* (1942). Frost served as a poet-in-residence at Harvard (1939–43), Dartmouth (1943–49), and Amherst College (1949–63), and in his old age he gathered honours and awards from every quarter. He was the poetry consultant to the Library of Congress (1958–59), and he recited his poem *The Gift Outright* at the inauguration of President John F. Kennedy in 1961.

THOMAS MANN

(b. June 6, 1875, Lübeck, Ger.—d. Aug. 12, 1955, near Zürich, Switz.)

Thomas Mann was a German novelist and essayist whose early novels—*Buddenbrooks* (1900), *Der Tod in Venedig* (1912; *Death in Venice*), and *Der Zauberberg* (1924; *The Magic Mountain*)—earned him the Nobel Prize for Literature in 1929.

After perfunctory work in Munich in an insurance office and on the editorial staff of *Simplicissimus*, a satirical weekly, Mann devoted himself to writing. His early tales, collected as *Der kleine Herr Friedemann* (1898), reflect the aestheticism of the 1890s but are given depth by the influence of the philosophers Schopenhauer and Nietzsche and the composer Wagner, to all of whom Mann was always to acknowledge a deep, if ambiguous, debt.

In his first novel, *Buddenbrooks*, Mann built the story of the family and its business house over four generations, showing how an artistic streak not only unfits the family's later members for the practicalities of business life but undermines their vitality as well. But, almost against his will, Mann also wrote a tender elegy for the old bourgeois virtues.

The outbreak of World War I evoked Mann's ardent patriotism and awoke, too, an awareness of the artist's social commitment. In 1918 he published a large political treatise, *Reflections of an Unpolitical Man*, in which all his ingenuity of mind was summoned to justify the authoritarian state as against democracy, creative irrationalism as against "flat" rationalism, and inward culture as against moralistic civilization. This work belongs to the tradition of "revolutionary conservatism" that leads from the 19th-century German nationalistic and antidemocratic thinkers Paul Anton de Lagarde and Houston Stewart Chamberlain, the apostle of the superiority of the "Germanic" race, toward National Socialism; and Mann later was to repudiate these ideas.

With the establishment of the German (Weimar) Republic in 1919, Mann slowly revised his outlook. His new position was clarified in the novel *The Magic Mountain*. Its theme grows out of an earlier motif: a young engineer, Hans Castorp, visiting a cousin in a sanatorium in Davos, abandons practical life to submit to the rich seductions of disease, inwardness, and death. But the sanatorium comes to be the spiritual reflection of the possibilities and dangers of the actual world. In the end, somewhat skeptically but humanely, Castorp decides for life and service to his people.

From this time onward Mann's imaginative effort was directed to the novel. His literary and cultural essays began to play an ever-growing part in elucidating and communicating his awareness of the fragility of humaneness, tolerance, and reason in the face of political crisis. In 1930 he gave a courageous address in Berlin, "Ein Appell an die Vernunft" ("An Appeal to Reason"), appealing for the formation of a common front of the cultured bourgeoisie and the socialist working class against the inhuman fanaticism of the National Socialists. In essays and on lecture tours in Germany, to Paris, Vienna, Warsaw, Amsterdam, and elsewhere during the 1930s, Mann, while steadfastly attacking Nazi policy, often expressed sympathy with socialist and communist principles in the very general sense that they were the guarantee of humanism and freedom.

When Hitler became chancellor early in 1933, Mann and his wife, on holiday in Switzerland, were warned by their son and daughter in Munich not to return. For some years his home was in Switzerland, near Zürich, but he traveled widely, visiting the United States on lecture tours and finally, in 1938, settling there. In 1936 he was deprived of his German citizenship; in the same year the University of Bonn took away the honorary doctorate it had bestowed in 1919 (it was restored in 1949). From 1936 to 1944 Mann was a citizen of Czechoslovakia. In 1944 he became a U.S. citizen. After the war, he refused to return to Germany to live. In 1952 he settled again near Zürich.

The novels on which Mann was working throughout this period of exile reflect variously the cultural crisis of his times. In *Doktor Faustus*, begun in 1943 at the darkest period of the war, Mann wrote the most directly political of his novels. It is the life story of a German composer, Adrian Leverkühn, born in 1885, who dies in 1940 after 10 years of mental alienation. A solitary, estranged figure, he "speaks" the experience of his times in his music, and the story of Leverkühn's compositions is that of German culture in the two decades before 1930—more specifically of the collapse of traditional humanism and the victory of the mixture of sophisticated nihilism and barbaric primitivism that undermine it.

The composition of the novel was fully documented by Mann in 1949 in *The Genesis of a Novel. Doktor Faustus* exhausted him as no other work of his had done, and *The Holy Sinner* and *The Black Swan*, published in 1951 and 1953, respectively, show a relaxation of intensity in spite of their accomplished, even virtuoso style.

Mann's style is finely wrought and full of resources, enriched by humour, irony, and parody; his composition is subtle and many-layered, brilliantly realistic on one level and yet reaching to deeper levels of symbolism.

LU XUN

(b. Sept. 25, 1881, Shaoxing, Zhejiang province, China—d. Oct. 19, 1936, Shanghai)

Lu Xun, which is the pen name of Zhou Shuren, was a Chinese writer commonly considered the greatest in 20th-century Chinese literature. He was also an important critic known for his sharp and unique essays on the historical traditions and modern conditions of China.

Born to a family that was traditional, wealthy, and esteemed (his grandfather had been a government official in Beijing), Zhou Shuren had a happy childhood. In 1893, however, his grandfather was sentenced to prison for examination fraud, and his father became bedridden. The family's reputation declined, and they were treated with disdain by their community and relatives. This experience is thought to have had a great influence on his writing, which was marked by sensitivity and pessimism.

Zhou Shuren left his hometown in 1899 and attended a mining school in Nanjing; there he developed an interest in Darwin's theory of evolution, which became an important influence in his work. Chinese intellectuals of the time understood Darwin's theory to encourage the struggle for social reform, to privilege the new and fresh over the old and traditional. In 1902 he traveled to Japan to study Japanese and medical science, and while there he became a supporter of the Chinese revolutionaries who gathered there. In 1903 he began to write articles for radical magazines edited by Chinese students in Japan. In 1905 he entered an arranged marriage against his will. In 1909 he published, with his younger brother Zhou Zuoren, a two-volume translation of 19th-century European stories, in the hope that it would inspire readers to revolution, but the project failed to attract interest. Disillusioned, Lu Xun returned to China later that year.

After working for several years as a teacher in his hometown and then as a low-level government official in Beijing, Lu Xun returned to writing and became associated with the nascent Chinese literary movement in 1918. That year, at the urging of friends, he published his now-famous short story *Kuangren riji* ("Diary of a Madman"). Modeled on the Russian realist Nikolay Gogol's tale of the same title, the story is a condemnation of traditional Confucian culture, which the madman narrator sees as a "man-eating" society. The first published Western-style story written wholly in vernacular Chinese, it was a tour de force that attracted immediate attention and helped gain acceptance for the short-story form as an effective literary vehicle.

Another representative work is the novelette *A-Q zhengzhuan* (1921; *The True Story of Ah Q*). A mixture of humour and pathos, it is a repudiation of the old order; it added "Ah Q-ism" to the modern Chinese language as a term characterizing the Chinese penchant for rationalizing defeat as a "spiritual victory." These stories, which were collected in *Nahan* (1923; *Call to Arms*), established Lu Xun's reputation as the leading Chinese writer. Three years later the collection *Panghuang* (1926; *Wandering*) was published. His various symbolic prose poems, which were published in the collection *Yecao* (1927; *Wild Grass*), as well as his reminiscences and retold classical tales, all reveal a modern sensibility informed by sardonic humour and biting satire.

In the 1920s Lu Xun worked at various universities in Beijing as a part-time professor of Chinese script and literature. His academic study *Zhongguo xiaoshuo shilue* (1923–24; *A Brief History of Chinese Fiction*) and companion compilations of classical fiction remain standard works. His translations, especially those of Russian works, are also considered significant.

Despite his success, Lu Xun continued to struggle with his increasingly pessimistic view of Chinese society, which was aggravated by conflicts in his personal and professional life. In addition to marital troubles and mounting pressures from the government, his disagreements with Zhou Zuoren (who had also become one of the leading intellectuals in Beijing) led to a rift between the two brothers in 1926. Such depressing conditions led Lu Xun to formulate the idea that one could resist social darkness only when he was pessimistic about the society. His famous phrase "resistance of despair" is commonly considered a core concept of his thought.

Forced by these political and personal circumstances to flee Beijing in 1926, Lu Xun traveled to Xiamen and

Guangzhou, finally settling in Shanghai in 1927. There he began to live with Xu Guangping, his former student; they had a son in 1929. Lu Xun stopped writing fiction and devoted himself to writing satiric critical essays (*zawen*), which he used as a form of political protest. In 1930 he became the nominal leader of the League of Left-Wing Writers. During the following decade he began to see the Chinese communists as the only salvation for his country. Although he himself refused to join the Chinese Communist Party, he considered himself a *tongluren* (fellow traveler), recruiting many writers and countrymen to the communist cause through his Chinese translations of Marxist literary theories, as well as through his own political writing.

During the last several years of Lu Xun's life, the government prohibited the publication of most of his work, so he published the majority of his new articles under various pseudonyms. He criticized the Shanghai communist literary circles for their embrace of propaganda, and he was politically attacked by many of their members. In 1934 he described his political position as *hengzhan* ("horizontal stand"), meaning he was struggling simultaneously against both the right and the left, against both cultural conservatism and mechanical evolution. *Hengzhan*, the most important idea in Lu Xun's later thought, indicates the complex and tragic predicament of an intellectual in modern society.

The Chinese communist movement adopted Lu Xun posthumously as the exemplar of Socialist Realism. Many of his fiction and prose works have been incorporated into school textbooks. In 1951 the Lu Xun Museum opened in Shanghai; it contains letters, manuscripts, photographs, and other memorabilia. English translations of Lu Xun's works include *Silent China: Selected Writings of Lu Xun* (1973), *Lu Hsun: Complete Poems* (1988), and *Diary of a Madman and Other Stories* (1990).

VIRGINIA WOOLF

(b. Jan. 25, 1882, London, Eng.—d. March 28, 1941, near Rodmell, Sussex)

Virginia Woolf was an English writer whose novels, through their nonlinear approaches to narrative, exerted a major influence on the genre. While she is best known for her novels, especially *Mrs. Dalloway* (1925) and *To the Lighthouse* (1927), Woolf also wrote pioneering essays on artistic theory, literary history, women's writing, and the politics of power.

Early Life and Influences

Born Virginia Stephen, she was the child of ideal Victorian parents. Her father, Leslie Stephen, was an eminent literary figure and the first editor (1882–91) of the *Dictionary of National Biography*. Her mother, Julia Jackson, possessed great beauty and a reputation for saintly self-sacrifice. Both Julia Jackson's first husband, Herbert Duckworth, and Leslie's first wife, a daughter of the novelist William Makepeace Thackeray, had died unexpectedly, leaving her three children and him one. Julia Jackson Duckworth and Leslie Stephen married in 1878, and four children followed: Vanessa (born 1879), Thoby (born 1880), Virginia (born 1882), and Adrian (born 1883).

The Stephen family made summer migrations from London to the rugged Cornwall coast. That annual relocation cleanly structured Woolf's childhood world. Her neatly divided, predictable world ended, however, when her mother died in 1895 at age 49. Woolf was just emerging from depression when, in 1897, her half sister Stella Duckworth died at age 28. Then in 1904, after her father died, she had a nervous breakdown.

Virginia Woolf. George C. Beresford/Hulton Archive/Getty Images

While she was recovering, Vanessa supervised the Stephen children's move to the bohemian Bloomsbury section of London. Leonard Woolf dined with them in November 1904, just before sailing to Ceylon (now Sri Lanka) to become a colonial administrator. Soon the Stephens hosted weekly gatherings of radical young people. Then, after a family excursion to Greece in 1906, Thoby died of typhoid fever. Virginia Woolf grieved but did not slip into depression. She overcame the loss of Thoby and the "loss" of Vanessa, who became engaged to Clive Bell just after Thoby's death, through writing. Vanessa's marriage (and perhaps Thoby's absence) helped transform conversation at the avant-garde gatherings of what came to be known as the Bloomsbury group into irreverent repartee that inspired Woolf to exercise her wit publicly, even while privately she was writing her poignant *Reminiscences*—about her childhood and her lost mother—which was published in 1908.

Early Fiction

Woolf determined in 1908 to "re-form" the novel. While writing anonymous reviews for the *Times Literary Supplement* and other journals, she experimented with such a novel, which she called *Melymbrosia*. In the summer of 1911, Leonard Woolf returned from the East. After he resigned from the colonial service, Leonard and Virginia married in August 1912.

Between 1910 and 1915, Virginia Woolf's mental health was precarious. Nevertheless, she completely recast *Melymbrosia* as *The Voyage Out* in 1913. Rachel Vinrace, the novel's central character, is a sheltered young woman who, on an excursion to South America, is introduced to freedom and sexuality. After an excursion up the Amazon,

Rachel contracts a terrible illness that plunges her into delirium and then death. The book endorses no explanation for her death. That indeterminacy set the book at odds with the certainties of the Victorian era and especially the conventions of realism.

Woolf's manic-depressive worries provoked a suicide attempt in September 1913. Publication of *The Voyage Out* was delayed until early 1915. That April, she sank into a distressed state in which she was often delirious. Later that year she overcame the "vile imaginations" that had threatened her sanity. She kept the demons of mania and depression mostly at bay for the rest of her life.

In 1917 the Woolfs bought a printing press and founded the Hogarth Press, named for Hogarth House, their home in the London suburbs. The Woolfs themselves (she was the compositor while he worked the press) published their own *Two Stories* in the summer of 1917. It consisted of Leonard's *Three Jews* and Virginia's *The Mark on the Wall*, the latter about contemplation itself.

Proving that she could master the traditional form of the novel before breaking it, Woolf plotted her next novel in two romantic triangles, with its protagonist Katharine in both. *Night and Day* (1919) focuses on the very sort of details that Woolf had deleted from *The Voyage Out*: credible dialogue, realistic descriptions of early 20th-century settings, and investigations of issues such as class, politics, and suffrage.

Woolf was writing nearly a review a week for the *Times Literary Supplement* in 1918. Her essay *Modern Novels* (1919; revised in 1925 as *Modern Fiction*) attacked the "materialists" who wrote about superficial rather than spiritual or "luminous" experiences. The Woolfs also printed by hand, with Vanessa Bell's illustrations, Virginia's *Kew Gardens* (1919), a story organized, like a Post-Impressionistic painting, by pattern. With the Hogarth Press's emergence as a major publishing house, the Woolfs gradually ceased being their own printers. In 1919 they bought a cottage in Rodmell village called Monk's House, which looked out over the Sussex Downs and the meadows where the River Ouse wound down to the English Channel. Three years later Woolf published *Jacob's Room*, in which she transformed personal grief over the death of Thoby Stephen into a "spiritual shape." Though *Jacob's Room* is an antiwar novel, Woolf feared that she had ventured too far beyond representation.

Major Period

At the beginning of 1924, the Woolfs moved their city residence from the suburbs back to Bloomsbury, where they were less isolated from London society. Soon the aristocratic Vita Sackville-West began to court Woolf, a relationship that would blossom into a lesbian affair.

Having already written a story about a Mrs. Dalloway, Woolf thought of a foiling device that would pair that highly sensitive woman with a shell-shocked war victim, a Mr. Smith, so that "the sane and the insane" would exist "side by side." Her aim was to "tunnel" into these two characters until Clarissa Dalloway's affirmations meet Septimus Smith's negations. In *Mrs. Dalloway* (1925), the boorish doctors presume to understand personality, but its essence evades them. This novel is as patterned as a Post-Impressionist painting but is also so accurately representational that the reader can trace Clarissa's and Septimus's movements through the streets of London on a single day in June 1923. At the end of the day, Clarissa gives a grand party and Septimus commits suicide. Their lives come together when the doctor who was treating (or, rather, mistreating) Septimus arrives at Clarissa's party with news of the death. The main characters are connected by motifs and, finally, by Clarissa's intuiting why Septimus threw his life away.

Woolf wished to build on her achievement in *Mrs. Dalloway* by merging the novelistic and elegiac forms. As an elegy, *To the Lighthouse*—published on May 5, 1927, the 32nd anniversary of Julia Stephen's death—evoked her childhood summers. As a novel, it broke narrative continuity into a tripartite structure and thereby melded into its structure questions about creativity and the nature and function of art.

Dust jacket designed by Vanessa Bell for the first edition of Virginia Woolf's To the Lighthouse, *published by the Hogarth Press in 1927.* Between the Covers Rare Books, Merchantville, N.J.

Their relationship having cooled by 1927, Woolf sought to reclaim Sackville-West through a "biography" that would include Sackville family history. She solved biographical, historical, and personal dilemmas with the story of Orlando, who lives from Elizabethan times through the entire 18th century; he then becomes female, experiences debilitating gender constraints, and lives into the 20th century. Woolf herself writes in mock-heroic imitation of biographical styles that change over the same period of time. Thus, *Orlando: A Biography* (1928) exposes the artificiality of both gender and genre prescriptions.

In 1921 John Maynard Keynes had told Woolf that one of her memoirs represented her best writing. Afterward she was increasingly angered by masculine condescension to female talent. In *A Room of One's Own* (1929), Woolf blamed women's absence from history not on their lack of brains and talent but on their poverty. For her 1931 talk *Professions for Women*, Woolf studied the history of women's education and employment and argued that unequal opportunities for women negatively affect all of society.

Having praised a 1930 exhibit of Vanessa Bell's paintings for their wordlessness, Woolf planned a mystical novel that would be similarly impersonal and abstract. In *The Waves* (1931), poetic interludes describe the sea and sky from dawn to dusk. *The Waves* offers a six-sided shape that illustrates how each individual experiences events uniquely. Through *To the Lighthouse* and *The Waves*, Woolf became, with James Joyce and William Faulkner, one of the three major English-language Modernist experimenters in stream-of-consciousness writing.

Late Work

Even before finishing *The Waves*, she began compiling a scrapbook of clippings illustrating the horrors of war, the threat of fascism, and the oppression of women. The discrimination against women that Woolf had discussed in *A Room of One's Own* and *Professions for Women* inspired her to plan a book that would trace the story of a fictional family named Pargiter and explain the social conditions affecting family members over a period of time. In *The Pargiters: A Novel-Essay* she would alternate between sections of fiction and of fact. The task of doing so, however, was daunting.

Woolf took a holiday from *The Pargiters* to write a mock biography of Flush, the dog of poet Elizabeth Barrett Browning. *Flush* (1933) remains both a biographical satire and a lighthearted exploration of perception, in this case a dog's. But she feared she would never finish *The Pargiters*. She solved this dilemma by jettisoning the essay sections, keeping the family narrative, and renaming her book *The Years*. She narrated 50 years of family history through the decline of class and patriarchal systems, the rise of feminism, and the threat of another war. Though (or perhaps because) Woolf's trimming muted the book's radicalism, *The Years* (1937) became a best-seller.

Woolf's chief anodyne against Adolf Hitler, World War II, and her own despair was writing. During the bombing of London in 1940 and 1941, she worked on *Between the Acts*. In her novel, war threatens art and humanity itself. Despite *Between the Acts*' affirmation of the value of art, Woolf worried that this novel was "too slight" and indeed that all writing was irrelevant when England seemed on the verge of invasion and civilization about to slide over a precipice. Facing such horrors, a depressed Woolf found herself unable to write. On March 28, 1941, she walked behind Monk's House and down to the River Ouse, put stones in her pockets, and drowned herself. *Between the Acts* was published posthumously later that year.

JAMES JOYCE

(b. Feb. 2, 1882, Dublin, Ire.—d. Jan. 13, 1941, Zürich, Switz.)

James Joyce was an Irish novelist noted for his experimental use of language and exploration of new literary methods in such large works of fiction as *Ulysses* (1922) and *Finnegans Wake* (1939).

Joyce was educated at University College, Dublin, which was then staffed by Jesuit priests. There he studied languages and reserved his energies for extracurricular activities, reading widely—particularly in books not recommended by the Jesuits—and taking an active part in the college's Literary and Historical Society. Early success in publishing a theatre review confirmed Joyce in his resolution to become a writer and persuaded his family, friends, and teachers that the resolution was justified. He received a B.A. in 1902. To support himself while writing, he decided to become a doctor, but, after attending a few lectures in Dublin, he borrowed what money he could and went to Paris, where he abandoned the idea of medical studies, wrote some book reviews, and studied in the Sainte-Geneviève Library.

By 1903 he had begun writing a lengthy naturalistic novel, *Stephen Hero*, based on the events of his own life, when in 1904 George Russell offered £1 each for some simple short stories with an Irish background to appear in a farmers' magazine, *The Irish Homestead*. In response Joyce began writing the stories published as *Dubliners* (1914). Three stories, *The Sisters*, *Eveline*, and *After the Race*, had appeared under the pseudonym Stephen Dedalus before the editor decided that Joyce's work was not suitable for his readers. Meanwhile Joyce had met a girl named Nora Barnacle, with whom he fell in love on June 16, the day that he chose as what is known as "Bloomsday" (the day of his novel *Ulysses*). Eventually he persuaded her to leave Ireland with him, although he refused, on principle, to go through a ceremony of marriage.

Joyce and Barnacle left Dublin together in October 1904. Joyce obtained a position in the Berlitz School, Pola, Austria-Hungary, working in his spare time at his novel and short stories. In 1905 they moved to Trieste. In

1906–07, for eight months, he worked at a bank in Rome, disliking almost everything he saw. His studies in European literature had interested him in both the Symbolists and the Realists; his work began to show a synthesis of these two rival movements. He decided that *Stephen Hero* lacked artistic control and form and rewrote it as "a work in five chapters" under a title—*A Portrait of the Artist as a Young Man*—intended to direct attention to its focus upon the central figure.

After the outbreak of World War I, Joyce's financial difficulties were great. He was helped by a large grant from Edith Rockefeller McCormick and finally by a series of grants from Harriet Shaw Weaver, editor of the *Egoist* magazine, which by 1930 had amounted to more than £23,000. Her generosity resulted partly from her admiration for his work and partly from her sympathy with his difficulties, for, as well as poverty, he had to contend with eye diseases that never really left him. From February 1917 until 1930 he endured a series of 25 operations for iritis, glaucoma, and cataracts, sometimes being for short intervals totally blind. Despite this he kept up his spirits and continued working, some of his most joyful passages being composed when his health was at its worst.

Unable to find an English printer willing to set up *A Portrait of the Artist as a Young Man* for book publication, Weaver published it herself, having the sheets printed in the United States, where it was also published in 1916. Encouraged by the acclaim given to this, in March 1918, the American *Little Review* began to publish episodes from *Ulysses*, continuing until the work was banned in December 1920. An autobiographical novel, *A Portrait of the Artist* traces the intellectual and emotional development of a young man named Stephen Dedalus and ends with his decision to leave Dublin for Paris to devote his life to art.

After World War I, Joyce returned for a few months to Trieste, and then, at the invitation of Ezra Pound, he went to Paris in July 1920. His novel *Ulysses* was published there on Feb. 2, 1922, by Sylvia Beach, proprietor of a bookshop called Shakespeare and Company. Already well known because of the censorship troubles, it became immediately famous upon publication. *Ulysses* is constructed as a modern parallel to Homer's *Odyssey*. All of the action of the novel takes place in Dublin on a single day (June 16, 1904). The three central characters—Stephen Dedalus (the hero of Joyce's earlier *Portrait of the Artist*); Leopold Bloom, a Jewish advertising canvasser; and his wife, Molly Bloom—are intended to be modern counterparts of Telemachus, Ulysses, and Penelope. By the use of interior monologue Joyce reveals the innermost thoughts and feelings of these characters as they live hour by hour, passing from a public bath to a funeral, library, maternity hospital, and brothel.

In Paris Joyce worked on *Finnegans Wake*, the title of which was kept secret, the novel being known simply as "Work in Progress" until it was published in its entirety in May 1939. In addition to his chronic eye troubles, Joyce suffered great and prolonged anxiety over his daughter's mental health. What had seemed her slight eccentricity grew into unmistakable and sometimes violent mental disorder that Joyce tried by every possible means to cure, but it became necessary finally to place her in a mental hospital near Paris. In 1931 he and Barnacle visited London, where they were married, his scruples on this point having yielded to his daughter's complaints.

Meanwhile he wrote and rewrote sections of *Finnegans Wake*; often a passage was revised more than a dozen times before he was satisfied. Basically the book is, in one sense, the story of a publican in Chapelizod, near Dublin, his wife, and their three children; but Mr. Humphrey Chimpden

Earwicker (often designated by variations on his initials, HCE, one form of which is "Here Comes Everybody"), Mrs. Anna Livia Plurabelle, Kevin, Jerry, and Isabel are every family of mankind, the archetypal family about whom all humanity is dreaming. It is thousands of dreams in one. Languages merge: Anna Livia has "vlossyhair"—*włosy* being Polish for "hair"; "a bad of wind" blows, *bâd* being Turkish for "wind." Characters from literature and history appear and merge and disappear as "the intermisunderstanding minds of the anticollaborators" dream on. And throughout the book Joyce himself is present, joking, mocking his critics, defending his theories, remembering his father, enjoying himself.

After the fall of France in World War II (1940), Joyce took his family back to Zürich, where he died, still disappointed with the reception given to his last book.

FRANZ KAFKA

(b. July 3, 1883, Prague, Bohemia, Austria-Hungary [now in Czech Republic]—d. June 3, 1924, Kierling, near Vienna, Austria)

Franz Kafka was a German-language writer of visionary fiction, whose posthumously published novels—especially *Der Prozess* (1925; *The Trial*) and *Das Schloss* (1926; *The Castle*)—express the anxieties and alienation of 20th-century humankind.

The son of an assimilated Jew who held only perfunctorily to the religious practices and social formalities of the Jewish community, Kafka was German both in language and culture. He was a timid, guilt-ridden, and obedient child who did well in elementary school and in the Altstädter Staatsgymnasium, an exacting high school for the academic elite. He was respected and liked by his teachers. Inwardly, however, he rebelled against the authoritarian institution and the dehumanized humanistic curriculum, with its emphasis on rote learning and classical languages.

Kafka's opposition to established society became apparent when, as an adolescent, he declared himself a socialist as well as an atheist. Throughout his adult life he expressed qualified sympathies for the socialists, he attended meetings of the Czech Anarchists (before World War I), and in his later years he showed marked interest and sympathy for a socialized Zionism. Even then he was essentially passive and politically unengaged. As a Jew, Kafka was isolated from the German community in Prague, but, as a modern intellectual, he was also alienated from his own Jewish heritage. He was sympathetic to Czech political and cultural aspirations, but his identification with German culture kept even these sympathies subdued. Thus, social isolation and rootlessness contributed to Kafka's lifelong personal unhappiness. Kafka did, however, become friendly with some German-Jewish intellectuals and literati in Prague, and in 1902 he met Max Brod; this minor literary artist became the most intimate and solicitous of Kafka's friends, and eventually he emerged as the promoter, saviour, and interpreter of Kafka's writings and as his most influential biographer.

The two men became acquainted while Kafka was studying law at the University of Prague. He received his doctorate in 1906, and in 1907 he took up regular employment with an insurance company. The long hours and exacting requirements of the Assicurazioni Generali, however, did not permit Kafka to devote himself to writing. In 1908 he found in Prague a job in the seminationalized Workers' Accident Insurance Institute for the Kingdom of Bohemia. There he remained until 1917, when tuberculosis forced him to take intermittent sick leaves and, finally, to retire (with a pension) in 1922, about two years before he died. In his job he was considered tireless and ambitious; he soon became the right hand of his boss, and he was esteemed and liked by all who worked with him.

Generally speaking, Kafka was a charming, intelligent, and humorous individual, but he found his routine office job and the exhausting double life into which it forced him (for his nights were frequently consumed in writing) to be excruciating torture, and his deeper personal relationships were neurotically disturbed. The conflicting inclinations of his complex and ambivalent personality found expression in his sexual relationships. His health was poor and office work exhausted him. In 1917 he was diagnosed as having tuberculosis, and from then onward he spent frequent periods in sanatoriums.

In 1923 Kafka went to Berlin to devote himself to writing. During a vacation on the Baltic coast later that year, he met Dora Dymant (Diamant), a young Jewish socialist. The couple lived in Berlin until Kafka's health significantly worsened during the spring of 1924. After a brief final stay in Prague, where Dymant joined him, he died of tuberculosis in a clinic near Vienna.

Sought out by leading avant-garde publishers, Kafka reluctantly published a few of his writings during his lifetime. These publications include, among others, works representative of Kafka's maturity as an artist—*The Judgment*, a long story written in 1912; two further long stories, *Die Verwandlung* (1915; *Metamorphosis*) and *In der Strafkolonie* (1919; *In the Penal Colony*); and a collection of short prose, *Ein Landarzt* (1919; *A Country Doctor*). *Ein Hungerkünstler* (1924; *A Hunger Artist*), four stories exhibiting the concision and lucidity characteristic of Kafka's late style, had been prepared by the author but did not appear until after his death.

In fact, misgivings about his work caused Kafka before his death to request that all of his unpublished manuscripts be destroyed; his literary executor, Max Brod, disregarded his instructions. Brod published the novels *The Trial*, *The Castle*, and *Amerika* in 1925, 1926, and 1927, respectively, and a collection of shorter pieces, *Beim Bau der chinesischen Mauer* (*The Great Wall of China*), in 1931.

Many of Kafka's fables contain an inscrutable, baffling mixture of the normal and the fantastic, though occasionally the strangeness may be understood as the outcome of a literary or verbal device, as when the delusions of a pathological state are given the status of reality or when the metaphor of a common figure of speech is taken literally. Thus in *The Judgment* a son unquestioningly commits suicide at the behest of his aged father. In *The Metamorphosis* the son wakes up to find himself transformed into a monstrous and repulsive insect; he slowly dies, not only because of his family's shame and its neglect of him but because of his own guilty despair.

Many of the tales are even more unfathomable. *In the Penal Colony* presents an officer who demonstrates his devotion to duty by submitting himself to the appalling (and clinically described) mutilations of his own instrument of torture. This theme, the ambiguity of a task's value and the horror of devotion to it—one of Kafka's constant preoccupations—appears again in *A Hunger Artist*. Many of the motifs in the short fables also recur in the novels.

Kafka's stories and novels have provoked a wealth of interpretations. Brod and Kafka's foremost English translators, Willa and Edwin Muir, viewed the novels as allegories of divine grace. Existentialists have seen Kafka's environment of guilt and despair as the ground upon which to construct an authentic existence. Some have seen his neurotic involvement with his father as the heart of his work; others have emphasized the social criticism, the inhumanity of the powerful and their agents, the violence and barbarity that lurk beneath normal routine. Some have found an imaginative anticipation of totalitarianism in the random and faceless bureaucratic terror of *The Trial*. There is evidence in both the works and the diaries for each of these interpretations, but Kafka's work as a whole transcends them all.

T. S. ELIOT

(b. Sept. 26, 1888, St. Louis, Mo., U.S.—d. Jan. 4, 1965, London, Eng.)

Thomas Sterns Eliot was an American-English poet, playwright, literary critic, and editor who was a leader of the Modernist movement in poetry in such works as *The Waste Land* (1922) and *Four Quartets* (1943). His experiments in diction, style, and versification revitalized English poetry, and in a series of critical essays he shattered old orthodoxies and erected new ones. In 1948 he was awarded both the Order of Merit and the Nobel Prize for Literature.

Eliot entered Harvard in 1906 and received a B.A. in 1909. He spent the year 1910–11 in France, attending Henri Bergson's lectures in philosophy at the Sorbonne and reading poetry with Alain-Fournier. From 1911 to 1914 he was back at Harvard reading Indian philosophy and studying Sanskrit. By 1916 he had finished, in Europe, a dissertation entitled *Knowledge and Experience in the Philosophy of F.H. Bradley*. But World War I had intervened, and he never returned to Harvard to take the final oral examination for the Ph.D. degree.

Eliot was to pursue four careers: editor, dramatist, literary critic, and philosophical poet. His first important publication, and the first masterpiece of "Modernism" in English, was *The Love Song of J. Alfred Prufrock*. It represented a break with the immediate past as radical as that of Samuel Taylor Coleridge and William Wordsworth in *Lyrical Ballads* (1798). From the appearance of Eliot's first volume, *Prufrock and Other Observations*, in 1917, one may conveniently date the maturity of the 20th-century poetic revolution.

For a year Eliot taught French and Latin at the Highgate School; in 1917 he began his brief career as a bank clerk in Lloyds Bank Ltd. Meanwhile he was also a prolific reviewer and essayist in both literary criticism and technical philosophy. In 1919 he published *Poems*, which contained the poem *Gerontion*, a meditative interior monologue in blank verse: nothing like this poem had appeared in English.

With the publication in 1922 of his poem *The Waste Land*, Eliot won an international reputation. *The Waste Land* expresses with great power the disenchantment, disillusionment, and disgust of the period after World War I. In a series of vignettes, loosely linked by the legend of the search for the Grail, it portrays a sterile world of panicky fears and barren lusts, and of human beings waiting for some sign or promise of redemption. *The Waste Land* showed him to be, in addition, a metrist of great virtuosity, capable of astonishing modulations ranging from the sublime to the conversational.

Consciously intended or not, Eliot's criticism created an atmosphere in which his own poetry could be better understood and appreciated than if it had to appear in a literary milieu dominated by the standards of the preceding age. In the essay *Tradition and the Individual Talent*, appearing in his first critical volume, *The Sacred Wood* (1920), Eliot asserts that tradition, as used by the poet, is not a mere repetition of the work of the immediate past; rather, it comprises the whole of European literature from Homer to the present. The poet writing in English may therefore make his own tradition by using materials from any past period, in any language.

Two other essays almost complete the Eliot critical canon: *The Metaphysical Poets* and *Andrew Marvell*, published in *Selected Essays, 1917–32* (1932). In these essays he effects a new historical perspective on the hierarchy of English poetry, putting at the top Donne and other Metaphysical poets of the 17th century and lowering poets of the 18th and 19th centuries.

Eliot was confirmed in the Church of England (1927); in that year he also became a British subject. The first long poem after his conversion was *Ash Wednesday* (1930), a religious meditation in a style entirely different from that of any of the earlier poems. This and subsequent poems were written in a more relaxed, musical, and meditative style than his earlier works.

Eliot's masterpiece is *Four Quartets*, which was issued as a book in 1943. This work made a deep impression on the reading public, and even those who were unable to accept the poems' Christian beliefs recognized the intellectual integrity with which Eliot pursued his high theme, the originality of the form he had devised, and the technical mastery of his verse. This work led to the award to Eliot, in 1948, of the Nobel Prize for Literature.

Eliot's plays, which begin with *Sweeney Agonistes* (published 1926; first performed in 1934) and end with *The Elder Statesman* (first performed 1958; published 1959), are, with the exception of *Murder in the Cathedral* (published and performed 1935), inferior to the lyric and meditative poetry. All his plays are in a blank verse of his own invention; thus he brought "poetic drama" back to the popular stage. *The Family Reunion* (1939) and *Murder in the Cathedral* are Christian tragedies, the former a tragedy of revenge, the latter of the sin of pride. *Murder in the Cathedral* is a modern miracle play on the martyrdom of Thomas Becket.

After World War II, Eliot returned to writing plays with several comedies derived from Greek drama. Eliot's career as editor was ancillary to his main interests, but his quarterly review, *The Criterion* (1922–39), was the most distinguished international critical journal of the period. He was a "director," or working editor, of the publishing firm of Faber & Faber Ltd. from the early 1920s until his death.

From the 1920s onward, Eliot's influence as a poet and as a critic—in both Great Britain and the United States—was immense. Since his death, interpreters have been markedly more critical, focusing on his complex relationship to his American origins, his elitist cultural and social views, and his exclusivist notions of tradition and of race.

EUGENE O'NEILL

(b. Oct. 16, 1888, New York, N.Y., U.S.—d. Nov. 27, 1953, Boston, Mass.)

Eugene O'Neill was a foremost American dramatist of the 20th century and the winner of the Nobel Prize for Literature in 1936.

O'Neill, who was born in a hotel and whose father was a touring actor, spent his early childhood in hotel rooms, on trains, and backstage. He was educated at boarding schools, and he attended Princeton University for one year (1906–07), after which he left school to begin what he later regarded as his real education in "life experience." He shipped to sea, lived a derelict's existence on the waterfronts of Buenos Aires, Liverpool, and New York City, submerged himself in alcohol, and attempted suicide. Recovering briefly at the age of 24, he held a job for a few months as a reporter and contributor to the poetry column of the *New London Telegraph* but soon came down with tuberculosis. Confined to the Gaylord Farm Sanitarium in Wallingford, Conn., for six months (1912–13), he confronted himself soberly and nakedly for the first time and seized the chance for what he later called his "rebirth." He began to write plays.

O'Neill's first appearance as a playwright came in the summer of 1916, in the quiet fishing village of Provincetown, Mass., where a group of young writers and painters had launched an experimental theatre. In their tiny, ramshackle playhouse on a wharf, they produced his one-act sea play *Bound East for Cardiff.* The talent inherent in the play was immediately evident to the group, which that fall formed the Playwrights' Theater in Greenwich Village. Their first bill, on Nov. 3, 1916, included *Bound East for Cardiff*—O'Neill's New York debut. Although he was only one of several writers whose plays were produced by the Playwrights' Theater, his contribution within the next few years made the group's reputation. By the time his first full-length play, *Beyond the Horizon*, was produced on Broadway, Feb. 2, 1920, at the Morosco Theater, the young playwright already had a small reputation.

Beyond the Horizon impressed the critics with its tragic realism, won for O'Neill the first of four Pulitzer prizes in drama—others were for *Anna Christie*, *Strange Interlude*, and *Long Day's Journey into Night*—and brought him to the attention of a wider theatre public. For the next 20 years his reputation grew steadily, both in the United States and abroad; after Shakespeare and Shaw, O'Neill became the most widely translated and produced dramatist.

O'Neill's capacity for and commitment to work were staggering. Between 1920 and 1943 he completed 20 long plays—several of them double and triple length—and a number of shorter ones. He wrote and rewrote many of his manuscripts half a dozen times before he was satisfied. His most-distinguished short plays include the four early sea plays, *Bound East for Cardiff*, *In the Zone*, *The Long Voyage Home*, and *The Moon of the Caribbees*, which were written between 1913 and 1917 and produced in 1924 under the overall title *S.S. Glencairn*; *The Emperor Jones* (1920; about the disintegration of a Pullman porter turned tropical-island dictator); and *The Hairy Ape* (1922; about the disintegration of a displaced steamship coal stoker). *Desire Under the Elms* (1924), *The Great God Brown* (1926), *Strange Interlude* (1928), *Mourning Becomes Electra* (1931), and *The Iceman Cometh* (1946) are among his important long plays. *Ah, Wilderness!* (1933) was his only comedy.

O'Neill's plays were written from an intensely personal point of view, deriving directly from the scarring effects of his family's tragic relationships—his mother and father, who loved and tormented each other; his older brother, who loved and corrupted him and died of alcoholism in middle age; and O'Neill himself, caught and torn between love for and rage at all three.

O'Neill's final years were spent in grim frustration. Unable to work, he longed for his death and sat waiting for it in a Boston hotel, seeing no one except his doctor, a nurse, and his third wife. O'Neill died as broken and tragic a figure as any he had created for the stage. He was the first American dramatist to regard the stage as a literary medium and the only American playwright ever to receive the Nobel Prize for Literature. Through his efforts, the American theatre grew up during the 1920s, developing into a cultural medium that could take its place with the best in American fiction, painting, and music.

ANNA AKHMATOVA

(b. June 11 [June 23, New Style], 1889, Bolshoy Fontan, near Odessa, Ukraine, Russian Empire—d. March 5, 1966, Domodedovo, near Moscow, Russia, U.S.S.R.)

The Russian poet Anna Akhmatova (the pseudonym of Anna Andreyevna Gorenko) was recognized at her death as the greatest woman poet in Russian literature.

Akhmatova began writing verse at age 11 and at 21 joined a group of St. Petersburg poets, the Acmeists. To

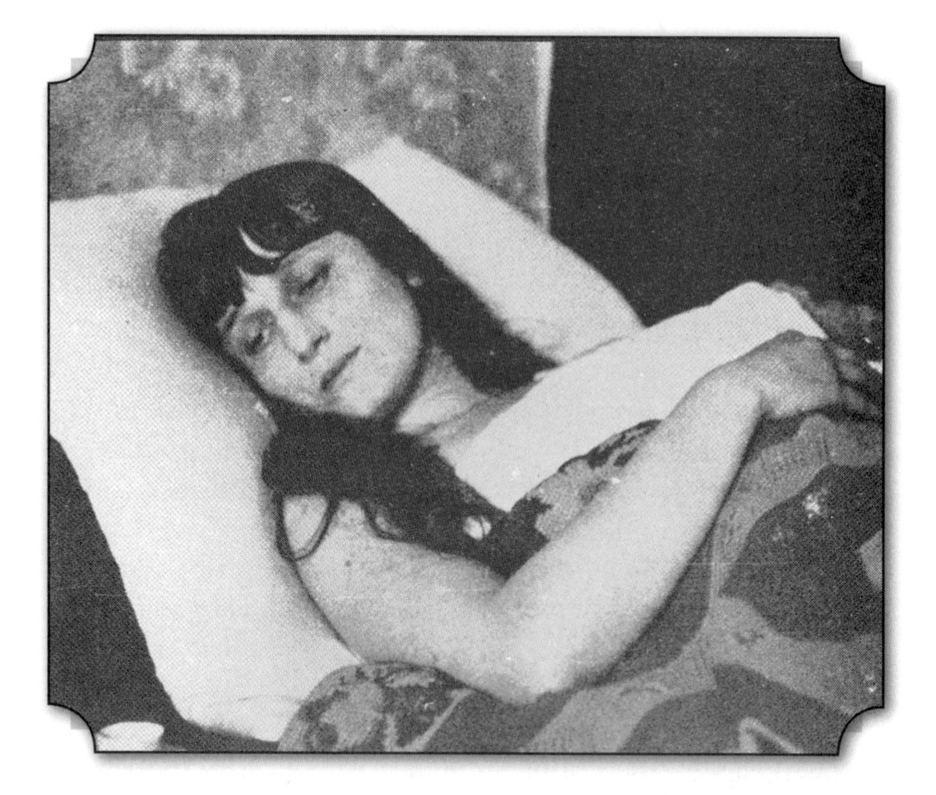

Though her work often angered Communist Party officials in the former Soviet Union, Anna Akhmatova's poetry served as an inspiration to many. Hulton Archive/Getty Images

their program of concrete representation and precise form and meaning Akhmatova added her own stamp of elegant colloquialism and the psychological sophistication of a young cosmopolitan woman, fully in control of the subtle verbal and gestural vocabulary of modern intimacies and romance. Her first collections, *Vecher* (1912; "Evening") and *Chyotki* (1914; "Rosary"), especially the latter, brought her fame and made her poetic voice emblematic of the experience of her generation.

During World War I and following the Revolution of 1917, she added to her main theme some civic, patriotic, and religious motifs but did not sacrifice her personal intensity or artistic conscience. Her artistry and increasing control of her medium were particularly prominent in her next collections: *Belaya staya* (1917; "The White Flock"), *Podorozhnik* (1921; "Plantain"), and *Anno Domini MCMXXI* (1921). The broadening of her thematic range, however, did not prevent the communist cultural watchdogs from proclaiming her "bourgeois and aristocratic" and condemning her poetry for its narrow preoccupation with love and God. In 1923 she entered a period of almost complete poetic silence and literary ostracism, and no volume of her poetry appeared in the Soviet Union until 1940. In September 1941, following the German invasion, Akhmatova was permitted to deliver an inspiring radio address to the women of Leningrad (St. Petersburg). Evacuated to Tashkent, Uzbekistan, soon thereafter, she read her poems to hospitalized soldiers and published a number of war-inspired poems; a small volume of selected poetry appeared in Tashkent in 1943. At the end of the war she returned to Leningrad, where her poems began to appear in local magazines and newspapers. She gave poetic readings, and plans were made for publication of a large edition of her works.

In August 1946, however, she was harshly denounced by the Central Committee of the Communist Party for her "eroticism, mysticism, and political indifference." She was expelled from the Union of Soviet Writers; an unreleased book of her poems, already in print, was destroyed; and none of her work appeared in print for three years.

Then, in 1950, a number of her poems eulogizing Stalin and Soviet communism were printed in several issues of the illustrated weekly magazine *Ogonyok* ("The Little Light") under the title *Iz tsikla "Slava miru"* ("From the Cycle 'Glory to Peace'"). This uncharacteristic capitulation to the Soviet dictator was motivated by Akhmatova's desire to propitiate Stalin and win the freedom of her son, who had been arrested in 1949 and exiled to Siberia. The tone of these poems (those glorifying Stalin were omitted from Soviet editions of Akhmatova's works published after his death) is far different from the moving and universalized lyrical cycle, *Rekviem* ("Requiem"), composed between 1935 and 1940 and occasioned by Akhmatova's grief over an earlier arrest and imprisonment of her son in 1938. This masterpiece—a poetic monument to the sufferings of the Soviet people during Stalin's terror—was published in Russia for the first time in 1989.

Akhmatova's longest work and perhaps her masterpiece, *Poema bez geroya* ("Poem Without a Hero"), on which she worked from 1940 to 1962, was not published in the Soviet Union until 1976. This difficult and complex work, in which the life of St. Petersburg bohemia in pre–World War I years is "double-exposed" onto the tragedies and suffering of the post-1917 decades, is a powerful lyric summation of Akhmatova's philosophy and her own definitive statement on the meaning of her life and poetic achievement.

In 1964 she was awarded the Etna-Taormina prize, an international poetry prize awarded in Italy, and in 1965 she received an honorary doctoral degree from the University of Oxford. Her journeys to Sicily and England to receive these honours were her first travel outside her homeland since 1912.

WILLIAM FAULKNER

(b. Sept. 25, 1897, New Albany, Miss., U.S.—d. July 6, 1962, Byhalia, Miss.)

William Faulkner was an American novelist and short-story writer who was awarded the 1949 Nobel Prize for Literature.

A reluctant student, Faulkner left high school in Oxford, Miss., without graduating but devoted himself to "undirected reading." In July 1918, impelled by dreams of martial glory and by despair at a broken love affair, Faulkner joined the British Royal Air Force (RAF) as a cadet pilot under training in Canada, although the November 1918 armistice intervened before he could finish ground school, let alone fly or reach Europe. After returning home, he enrolled for a few university courses, published poems and drawings in campus newspapers, and acted out a self-dramatizing role as a poet who had seen wartime service.

His first novel, *Soldiers' Pay* (1926), given a Southern though not a Mississippian setting, was an impressive achievement, stylistically ambitious and strongly evocative of the sense of alienation experienced by soldiers returning from World War I to a civilian world of which they seemed no longer a part. Back in Oxford—with occasional visits to Pascagoula on the Gulf Coast—Faulkner again worked at a series of temporary jobs but was chiefly concerned with proving himself as a professional writer. None of his short stories was accepted, however, and he was especially shaken by his difficulty in finding a publisher for *Flags in the Dust* (published posthumously, 1973), a long, leisurely novel, drawing extensively on local observation and his own family history, that he had confidently counted upon to establish his reputation and career. When the novel eventually did appear, severely truncated, as *Sartoris* in 1929, it created in print for the first time that densely imagined world of Jefferson and Yoknapatawpha County—based partly on Ripley but chiefly on Oxford and Lafayette county and characterized by frequent recurrences of the same characters, places, and themes—which Faulkner was to use as the setting for so many subsequent novels and stories.

In *The Sound and the Fury* (1929), his first major novel, he combined a Yoknapatawpha setting with radical technical experimentation. In successive "stream-of-consciousness" monologues the three brothers of Candace (Caddy) Compson—Benjy the idiot, Quentin the disturbed Harvard undergraduate, and Jason the embittered local businessman—expose their differing obsessions with their sister and their loveless relationships with their parents. A fourth section, narrated as if authorially, provides new perspectives on some of the central characters, including Dilsey, the Compsons' black servant, and moves toward a powerful yet essentially unresolved conclusion. Faulkner's next novel, the brilliant tragicomedy called *As I Lay Dying* (1930), is centred upon the conflicts within the "poor white" Bundren family as it makes its slow and difficult way to Jefferson to bury its matriarch's malodorously decaying corpse. Entirely narrated by the various Bundrens and people encountered on their journey, it is the most systematically multi-voiced of Faulkner's novels and marks the culmination of his early post-Joycean experimentalism.

Absalom, Absalom! (1936) was Faulkner's next major novel. Because this profoundly Southern story is constructed—speculatively, conflictingly, and inconclusively—by a series of narrators with sharply divergent self-interested perspectives, *Absalom, Absalom!* is often seen, in its infinite open-endedness, as Faulkner's supreme "modernist" fiction, focused above all on the processes of its own telling.

Other novels followed in the late 1930s and early 1940s, but Faulkner's American reputation—which had always lagged well behind his reputation in Europe—was boosted by *The Portable Faulkner* (1946), an anthology skillfully edited by Malcolm Cowley in accordance with the arresting if questionable thesis that Faulkner was deliberately constructing a historically based "legend" of the South.

Faulkner's *Collected Stories* (1950), impressive in both quantity and quality, was also well received, and later in 1950 the award of the Nobel Prize for Literature catapulted the author instantly to the peak of world fame and enabled him to affirm, in a famous acceptance speech, his belief in the survival of the human race, even in an atomic age, and in the importance of the artist to that survival.

The Nobel Prize had a major impact on Faulkner's private life. Confident now of his reputation and future sales, he became less consistently "driven" as a writer than in earlier years and allowed himself more personal freedom, drinking heavily at times and indulging in a number of extramarital affairs—his opportunities in these directions being considerably enhanced by several overseas trips (most notably to Japan in 1955) undertaken on behalf of the U.S. State Department. He took his "ambassadorial" duties seriously, speaking frequently in public and to interviewers, and also became politically active at home, taking positions on major racial issues in the vain hope of finding middle ground between entrenched Southern conservatives and interventionist Northern liberals.

The quality of Faulkner's writing is often said to have declined in the wake of the Nobel Prize, although *Requiem for a Nun* (1951) and *A Fable* (1954) suggest otherwise. He died of a heart attack in July 1962, at the age of 64, his health undermined by his drinking and by too many falls from horses too big for him.

VLADIMIR NABOKOV

(b. April 22, 1899, St. Petersburg, Russia—d. July 2, 1977, Montreux, Switz.)

Vladimir Vladimirovich Nabokov was a Russian-born American novelist and critic, the foremost of the post-1917 émigré authors. He wrote in both Russian and English, and his best works, including *Lolita* (1955), feature stylish, intricate literary effects.

Nabokov was born into an old aristocratic family. In 1922, after the family had settled in Berlin, Nabokov's father was assassinated by a reactionary rightist while shielding another man at a public meeting. Nabokov published two collections of verse, *Poems* (1916) and *Two Paths* (1918), before leaving Russia in 1919. He and his family eventually made their way to England, and he attended Trinity College, Cambridge, on a scholarship provided for the sons of prominent Russians in exile. While at Cambridge he first studied zoology but soon switched to French and Russian literature; he graduated with first-class honours in 1922. While still in England he continued to write poetry, mainly in Russian but also in English, and two collections of his Russian poetry, *The Cluster* and *The Empyrean Path*, appeared in 1923.

Between 1922 and 1940, Nabokov lived in Germany and France. By 1925 he settled upon prose as his main genre. His first short story had already been published in Berlin in 1924. His first novel, the autobiographical *Mashenka* (*Mary*), appeared in 1926; his second novel, *King, Queen, Knave*, which appeared in 1928, marked his turn to a highly stylized form that characterized his art thereafter.

During his years of European emigration, Nabokov lived in a state of happy and continual semipenury. All of his Russian novels were published in very small editions in Berlin and Paris. His first two novels had German translations, and the money he obtained for them he used for butterfly-hunting expeditions (he eventually published 18 scientific papers on entomology). But until his best-seller *Lolita*, no book he wrote in Russian or English produced more than a few hundred dollars. During the period in which he wrote his first eight novels, he made his living in Berlin and later in Paris by giving lessons in tennis, Russian, and English and from occasional walk-on parts in films. Even after great wealth came to him with the success of *Lolita* and the subsequent interest in his previous work, Nabokov and his family (he and his wife had one son, Dmitri) chose to live (from 1959) in genteelly shabby quarters in a Swiss hotel.

The subject matter of Nabokov's novels is principally the problem of art itself presented in various figurative disguises. The same may be said of his plays, *Sobytiye* ("The Event"), published in 1938, and *The Waltz Invention*. The problem of art again appears in Nabokov's best novel in Russian, *The Gift*, the story of a young artist's development in the spectral world of post–World War I Berlin. This novel, with its reliance on literary parody, was a turning point. Serious use of parody thereafter became a key device in Nabokov's art. His first novels in English, *The Real Life of Sebastian Knight* (1941) and *Bend Sinister* (1947), do not rank with his best Russian work. *Pale Fire* (1962), however, a novel consisting of a long poem and a commentary on it by a mad literary pedant, extends and completes Nabokov's mastery of unorthodox structure, first shown in *The Gift* and present also in *Solus Rex*, a Russian novel that began to appear serially in 1940 but was never completed. *Lolita* (1955), with its antihero, Humbert Humbert, who is possessed by an overpowering desire for very young girls, is yet another of Nabokov's subtle allegories: love examined in the light of its seeming opposite, lechery. *Ada* (1969), Nabokov's 17th and longest novel, is a parody of the family chronicle form. All of his earlier themes come into play in the novel, and, because the work is a medley of Russian, French, and English, it is his most difficult work.

Nabokov's major critical works are an irreverent book about Nikolay Gogol (1944) and a monumental four-volume translation of, and commentary on, Pushkin's *Eugene Onegin* (1964). What he called the "present, final version" of the autobiographical *Speak, Memory*, concerning his European years, was published in 1967, after which he began work on a sequel, *Speak On, Memory*, concerning the American years.

As Nabokov's reputation grew in the 1930s so did the ferocity of the attacks made upon him. His idiosyncratic, somewhat aloof style and unusual novelistic concerns were interpreted as snobbery by his detractors—although his best Russian critic, Vladislav Khodasevich, insisted that Nabokov's aristocratic view was appropriate to his subject matters: problems of art masked by allegory.

ERNEST HEMINGWAY

(b. July 21, 1899, Cicero [now in Oak Park], Ill., U.S.—d. July 2, 1961, Ketchum, Idaho)

Ernest Hemingway, an American novelist and short-story writer, was awarded the Nobel Prize for Literature in 1954. He was noted both for the intense masculinity of his writing and for his adventurous and widely publicized life. His succinct and lucid prose style exerted a powerful influence on American and British fiction in the 20th century.

Hemingway entered World War I as an ambulance driver for the American Red Cross. On July 8, 1918, not yet 19 years old, he was injured on the Austro-Italian front at Fossalta di Piave. He was decorated for heroism.

After recuperating at home, Hemingway sailed for France as a foreign correspondent for the *Toronto Star*. Advised and encouraged by other American writers in Paris—F. Scott Fitzgerald, Gertrude Stein, Ezra Pound—he began to see his nonjournalistic work appear in print there, and in 1925 his first important book, a collection of

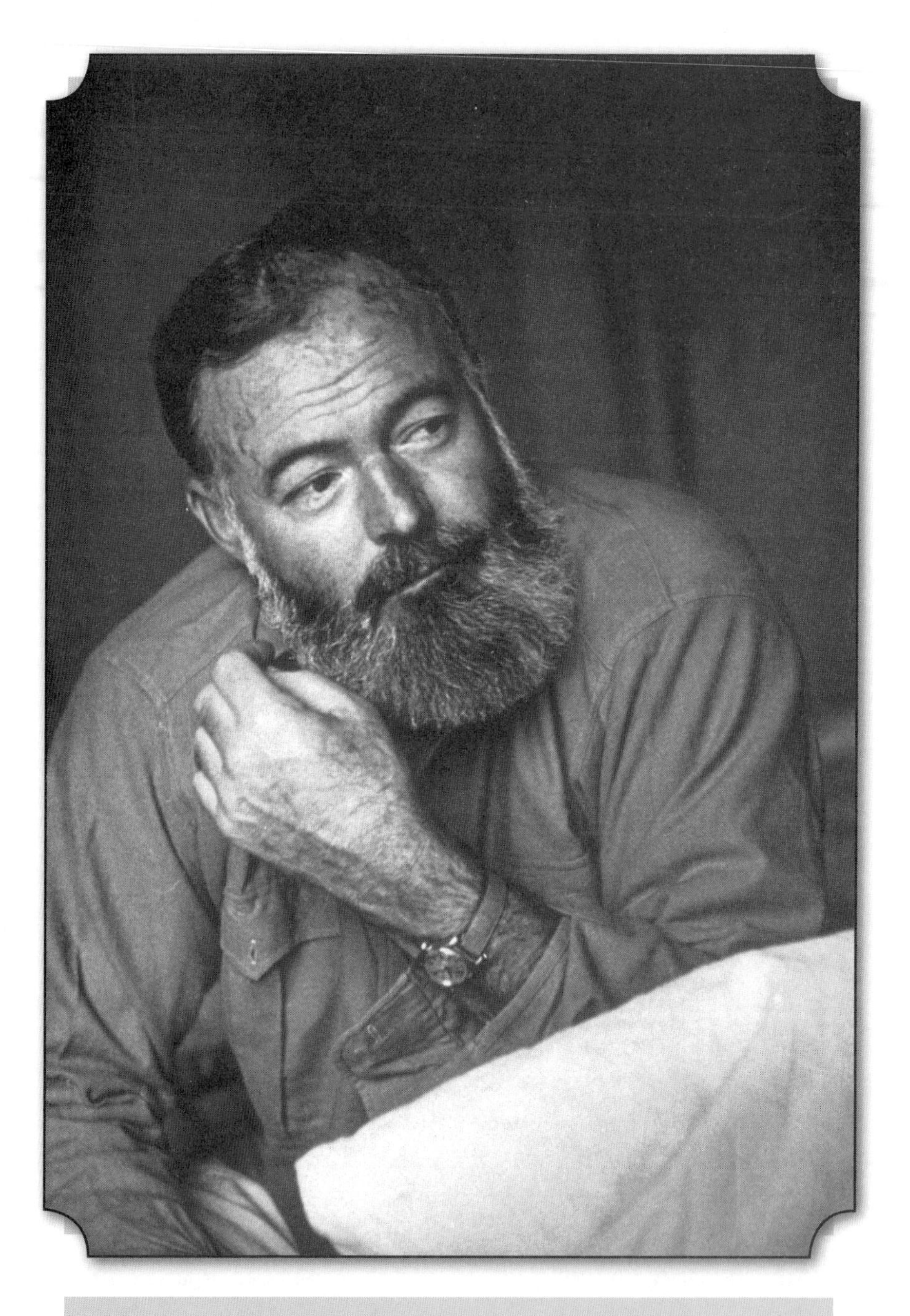

The sparse yet pointed style of writing evidenced in Ernest Hemingway's novels may have been a holdover from the author's days as a journalist and war correspondent. Kurt Hutton/Picture Post/Hulton Archive/Getty Images

stories called *In Our Time*, was published in New York City; it was originally released in Paris in 1924. In 1926 he published *The Sun Also Rises*, a novel with which he scored his first solid success.

The writing of books occupied Hemingway for most of the postwar years. He remained based in Paris, but he traveled widely for the skiing, bullfighting, fishing, and hunting that by then had become part of his life and formed the background for much of his writing. His position as a master of short fiction had been advanced by *Men Without Women* in 1927 and thoroughly established with the stories in *Winner Take Nothing* in 1933. At least in the public view, however, the novel *A Farewell to Arms* (1929) overshadowed such works. Reaching back to his experience as a young soldier in Italy, Hemingway developed a grim but lyrical novel of great power, fusing love story with war story.

Hemingway's love of Spain and his passion for bullfighting resulted in *Death in the Afternoon* (1932), a learned study of a spectacle he saw more as tragic ceremony than as sport. A minor novel of 1937 called *To Have and Have Not* is about a Caribbean desperado and is set against a background of lower-class violence and upper-class decadence in Key West during the Great Depression.

By now Spain was in the midst of civil war. Still deeply attached to that country, Hemingway made four trips there, once more a correspondent. He also raised money for the Republicans in their struggle against the Nationalists under General Francisco Franco. The harvest of Hemingway's considerable experience of Spain in war and peace was the novel *For Whom the Bell Tolls* (1940), a substantial and impressive work that some critics consider his finest novel. It was also the most successful of all his books as measured in sales. Set during the Spanish Civil War, it tells of Robert Jordan, an American volunteer who is sent to join a guerrilla band behind the Nationalist lines in the Guadarrama Mountains. Through dialogue, flashbacks, and stories, Hemingway offers telling and vivid profiles of the Spanish character and unsparingly depicts the cruelty and inhumanity stirred up by the civil war.

Following World War II in Europe, which he experienced firsthand as a journalist, Hemingway returned to his home in Cuba and began to work seriously again. He also traveled widely, and, on a trip to Africa, he was injured in a plane crash. Soon after (in 1953), he received the Pulitzer Prize in fiction for *The Old Man and the Sea* (1952), a short heroic novel about an old Cuban fisherman who, after an extended struggle, hooks and boats a giant marlin only to have it eaten by voracious sharks during the long voyage home. This book, which played a role in gaining for Hemingway the Nobel Prize for Literature in 1954, was enthusiastically praised.

By 1960 Fidel Castro's revolution had driven Hemingway from Cuba. He settled in Ketchum, Idaho, and tried to lead his life and do his work as before. For a while he succeeded, but, anxiety-ridden and depressed, he was twice hospitalized at the Mayo Clinic in Rochester, Minnesota, where he received electroshock treatments. Two days after his return to the house in Ketchum, he took his life with a shotgun.

Hemingway's prose style was probably the most widely imitated of any in the 20th century. In striving to be as objective and honest as possible, Hemingway hit upon the device of describing a series of actions by using short, simple sentences from which all comment or emotional rhetoric has been eliminated. The resulting terse, concentrated prose is concrete and unemotional yet is often resonant and capable of conveying great irony through understatement.

JOHN STEINBECK

(b. Feb. 27, 1902, Salinas, Calif., U.S.—d. Dec. 20, 1968, New York, N.Y.)

The American novelist John Steinbeck is best known for *The Grapes of Wrath* (1939), which summed up the bitterness of the Great Depression decade and aroused widespread sympathy for the plight of migratory farm workers. He received the Nobel Prize for Literature for 1962.

Steinbeck attended Stanford University in California intermittently between 1920 and 1926, but did not take a degree. Before his books attained success, he spent considerable time supporting himself as a manual labourer while writing, and his experiences lent authenticity to his depictions of the lives of the workers in his stories. He spent much of his life in Monterey County, Calif., which later was the setting of some of his fiction.

Steinbeck's first novel, *Cup of Gold* (1929), was followed by *The Pastures of Heaven* (1932) and *To a God Unknown* (1933), none of which were successful. He first achieved popularity with *Tortilla Flat* (1935), an affectionately told story of Mexican-Americans. The mood of gentle humour turned to one of unrelenting grimness in his next novel, *In Dubious Battle* (1936), a classic account of a strike by agricultural labourers and a pair of Marxist labour organizers who engineer it. The novella *Of Mice and Men* (1937), which also appeared in play and film versions, is a tragic story about the strange, complex bond between two migrant labourers.

The Grapes of Wrath won a Pulitzer Prize and a National Book Award and was made into a notable film in 1940. The novel is about the migration of a dispossessed family from the Oklahoma Dust Bowl to California and describes their subsequent exploitation by a ruthless system of agricultural economics. A protest novel punctuated by prose-poem interludes, *The Grapes of Wrath* tells of the Joad family's almost biblical journey, during which they learn the necessity for collective action among the poor and downtrodden to prevent them from being destroyed individually.

After the best-selling success of *The Grapes of Wrath*, Steinbeck went to Mexico to collect marine life with the freelance biologist Edward F. Ricketts, and the two men collaborated in writing *Sea of Cortez* (1941), a study of the fauna of the Gulf of California. During World War II Steinbeck wrote some effective pieces of government propaganda, among them *The Moon Is Down* (1942), a novel of Norwegians under the Nazis. He also served as a war correspondent. His immediate postwar work—*Cannery Row* (1945), *The Pearl* (1947), and *The Wayward Bus* (1947)—contained the familiar elements of his social criticism but were more relaxed in approach and sentimental in tone.

Steinbeck's later writings were comparatively slight works of entertainment and journalism interspersed with three conscientious attempts to reassert his stature as a major novelist: *Burning Bright* (1950), *East of Eden* (1952), and *The Winter of Our Discontent* (1961). In critical opinion, none equaled his earlier achievement. *East of Eden*, an ambitious epic about the moral relations between a California farmer and his two sons, was made into a film in 1955. Steinbeck himself wrote the scripts for the film versions of his stories *The Pearl* (1948) and *The Red Pony* (1949). Outstanding among the scripts he wrote directly for motion pictures were *Forgotten Village* (1941) and *Viva Zapata!* (1952).

Steinbeck's reputation rests mostly on the naturalistic novels with proletarian themes he wrote in the 1930s. It is in these works that his building of rich symbolic structures and his attempts at conveying mythopoeic and archetypal qualities in his characters are most effective.

GEORGE ORWELL

(b. 1903, Motīhāri, Bengal, India—d. Jan. 21, 1950, London, Eng.)

Eric Arthur Blair, better known by his pseudonym George Orwell, was an English novelist, essayist, and critic famous for his novels *Animal Farm* (1945) and *1984* (1949), the latter a profound anti-Utopian novel that examines the dangers of totalitarian rule.

Orwell was born in Bengal, into the class of sahibs. His father was a minor British official in the Indian civil service; his mother, of French extraction, was the daughter of an unsuccessful teak merchant in Burma. He won scholarships to two of England's leading schools, Winchester and Eton, and chose the latter. He stayed from 1917 to 1921. Instead of accepting a scholarship to a university, Orwell decided to follow family tradition and, in 1922, went to Burma as assistant district superintendent in the Indian Imperial Police. When he realized how much against their will the Burmese were ruled by the British, he felt increasingly ashamed of his role as a colonial police officer. Later he was to recount his experiences and his reactions to imperial rule in his novel *Burmese Days* and in two brilliant autobiographical sketches, "Shooting an Elephant" and "A Hanging," classics of expository prose.

In 1927 Orwell, on leave to England, decided not to return to Burma, and on Jan. 1, 1928, he took the decisive step of resigning from the imperial police. Having felt guilty that the barriers of race and caste had prevented his mingling with the Burmese, he thought he could expiate some of his guilt by immersing himself in the life of the poor and outcast people of Europe. Donning ragged clothes, he went into the East End of London to live in cheap lodging houses among labourers and beggars. He spent a period in the slums of Paris and worked as a dishwasher in French hotels and restaurants, and tramped the roads of England with professional vagrants and joined the people of the London slums in their annual exodus to work in the Kentish hopfields. These experiences gave Orwell the material for *Down and Out in Paris and London* (1933), in which actual incidents are rearranged into something like fiction. The book's publication in 1933 earned him some initial literary recognition. Orwell's first novel, *Burmese Days* (1934), established the pattern of his subsequent fiction in its portrayal of a sensitive, conscientious, and emotionally isolated individual who is at odds with an oppressive or dishonest social environment.

Orwell's revulsion against imperialism led not only to his personal rejection of the bourgeois life-style but to a political reorientation as well. Immediately after returning from Burma he called himself an anarchist and continued to do so for several years; during the 1930s, however, he began to consider himself a socialist. Orwell's first socialist book was an original and unorthodox political treatise entitled *The Road to Wigan Pier* (1937). It begins by describing his experiences when he went to live among the destitute and unemployed miners of northern England, sharing and observing their lives; it ends in a series of sharp criticisms of existing socialist movements. It combines mordant reporting with a tone of generous anger that was to characterize Orwell's subsequent writing.

In the 1940s Orwell was a prolific journalist, writing many newspaper articles and reviews, together with serious criticism, that combined patriotic sentiment with the advocacy of a libertarian, decentralist socialism. In 1944 Orwell finished *Animal Farm*, a political fable based on the story of the Russian Revolution and its betrayal by Joseph Stalin. In this book a group of barnyard animals overthrow and chase off their exploitative human masters and set up an egalitarian society of their own. When it appeared in 1945 *Animal Farm* made him famous and, for the first time, prosperous.

Orwell's last book, *1984* (1949), is a novel he wrote as a warning after years of brooding on the twin menaces of Nazism and Stalinism. The novel is set in an imaginary future in which the world is dominated by three perpetually warring totalitarian police states. Orwell's warning of the potential dangers of totalitarianism made a deep impression on his contemporaries and upon subsequent readers, and the book's title and many of its coined words and phrases ("Big Brother is watching you," "newspeak," "doublethink") became bywords for modern political abuses.

Orwell wrote the last pages of *1984* in a remote house on the Hebridean island of Jura, which he had bought from the proceeds of *Animal Farm*. He worked between bouts of hospitalization for tuberculosis, of which he died in a London hospital in January 1950.

PABLO NERUDA

(b. July 12, 1904, Parral, Chile—d. Sept. 23, 1973, Santiago)

Pablo Neruda, a Chilean poet, diplomat, and politician, was awarded the Nobel Prize for Literature in 1971. He was perhaps the most important Latin American poet of the 20th century.

Born Neftalí Ricardo Reyes Basoalto, Neruda began to write poetry at age 10. His father tried to discourage him from writing, which was probably why the young poet began to publish under the pseudonym Pablo Neruda, which he was legally to adopt in 1946. Neruda first published his poems in the local newspapers and later in magazines published in the Chilean capital, Santiago. In 1921 he moved to Santiago to continue his studies and become a French teacher. His first book of poems, *Crepusculario*, was published in 1923. His second book, *Veinte poemas de amor y una canción desesperada* (1924; *Twenty Love Poems and a Song of Despair*), was inspired by an unhappy love affair. It became an instant success and is still one of Neruda's most popular books. The verse in *Twenty Love Poems* is vigorous, poignant, and direct, yet subtle and very original in its imagery and metaphors. The poems express young, passionate, unhappy love perhaps better than any book of poetry in the long Romantic tradition.

More collections followed, but his poetry was not a steady source of income. He managed to get himself appointed honorary consul to Rangoon in Burma (now Yangôn, Myanmar), and for the next five years he represented his country in Asia. He continued to live in abject poverty, however, since as honorary consul he received no salary, and he was tormented by loneliness.

From Rangoon Neruda moved to Colombo in Ceylon (now Sri Lanka). He increasingly came to identify with the South Asian masses, who were heirs to ancient cultures but were downtrodden by poverty, colonial rule, and political oppression. It was during these years in Asia that he wrote *Residencia en la tierra, 1925–1931* (1933; *Residence on Earth*). In this book Neruda moves beyond the lucid, conventional lyricism of *Twenty Love Poems*, abandoning normal syntax, rhyme, and stanzaic organization to create a highly personalized poetic technique. His personal and collective anguish gives rise to nightmarish visions of disintegration, chaos, decay, and death that he recorded in a cryptic, difficult style inspired by Surrealism.

In 1930 Neruda was named consul in Batavia (modern Jakarta), which was then the capital of the Dutch East Indies (now Indonesia). In 1932 Neruda returned to

Chile, but he still could not earn a living from his poetry. In 1933 he was appointed Chilean consul in Buenos Aires, Argentina.

In 1934 Neruda took up an appointment as consul in Barcelona, Spain, and soon he was transferred to the consulate in Madrid, where he moved ever closer to communism.

A second, enlarged edition of the *Residencia* poems entitled *Residencia en la tierra, 1925–35* was published in two volumes in 1935. In this edition, Neruda begins to move away from the highly personal, often hermetic poetry of the first *Residencia* volume, adopting a more extroverted outlook and a clearer, more accessible style in order to better communicate his new social concerns to the reader.

After supporting the Republicans in the Spanish Civil War, Neruda returned to Chile in 1937 and entered his country's political life, giving lectures and poetry readings while also defending Republican Spain and Chile's new centre-left government. In 1939 he was appointed special consul in Paris, where he supervised the migration to Chile of many defeated Spanish Republicans who had escaped to France. In 1940 he took up a post as Chile's consul general in Mexico. He also began work on a long poem, *Canto general* (1950; "General Song," Eng. trans. *Canto general*), that he would complete only after being driven into exile from Chile, after the government he had supported as a member of the Communist Party turned toward the right. Resonant with historical and epic overtones, this epic poem celebrates Latin America—its flora, its fauna, and its history, particularly the wars of liberation from Spanish rule and the continuing struggle of its peoples to obtain freedom and social justice. It also, however, celebrates Joseph Stalin, the bloody Soviet dictator in power at the time. The poem would become one of his key works.

In 1952 the political situation in Chile once again became favourable, and Neruda was able to return home. By that time his works had been translated into many languages, and he was rich and famous. One of his major works, *Odas elementales* (*Elemental Odes*), was published in 1954. Its verse was written in a new poetic style—simple, direct, precise, and humorous—and it contained descriptions of everyday objects, situations, and beings (e.g., *Ode to the Onion* and *Ode to the Cat*). Neruda's poetic output during these years was stimulated by his international fame and personal happiness; 20 books of his appeared between 1958 and his death in 1973, and 8 more were published posthumously. While already ill with cancer in France, Neruda in 1971 learned that he had been awarded the Nobel Prize for Literature. After traveling to Stockholm to receive his prize, he returned to Chile bedridden and terminally ill.

SAMUEL BECKETT

(b. April 13?, 1906, Foxrock, County Dublin, Ire.—d. Dec. 22, 1989, Paris, France)

Author, critic, and playwright Samuel Beckett was the winner of the Nobel Prize for Literature in 1969. He wrote in both French and English and is perhaps best known for his plays, especially *En attendant Godot* (1952; *Waiting for Godot*).

Beckett was born in a suburb of Dublin. Like his fellow Irish writers George Bernard Shaw, Oscar Wilde, and William Butler Yeats, he came from a Protestant, Anglo-Irish background. At the age of 14 he went to the Portora Royal School, in what became Northern Ireland, a school that catered to the Anglo-Irish middle classes.

From 1923 to 1927, he studied Romance languages at Trinity College, Dublin, where he received his bachelor's degree. After a brief spell of teaching in Belfast, he became a reader in English at the École Normale Supérieure in Paris in 1928. There he met the self-exiled Irish writer James Joyce, the author of the controversial and seminally modern novel *Ulysses*, and joined his circle. Contrary to often-repeated reports, however, he never served as Joyce's secretary. He returned to Ireland in 1930 to take up a post as lecturer in French at Trinity College, but after only four terms he resigned, in December 1931, and embarked upon a period of restless travel in London, France, Germany, and Italy.

In 1937 Beckett decided to settle in Paris. As a citizen of a country that was neutral in World War II, he was able to remain there even after the occupation of Paris by the Germans, but he joined an underground resistance group in 1941. When, in 1942, he received news that members of his group had been arrested by the Gestapo, he immediately went into hiding and eventually moved to the unoccupied zone of France. Until the liberation of the country, he supported himself as an agricultural labourer. In 1945 he returned to Ireland but volunteered for the Irish Red Cross and went back to France as an interpreter in a military hospital in Saint-Lô, Normandy. In the winter of 1945, he finally returned to Paris and was awarded the Croix de Guerre for his resistance work.

There followed a period of intense creativity, the most concentratedly fruitful period of Beckett's life. His relatively few prewar publications included two essays on Joyce and the French novelist Marcel Proust. The volume *More Pricks Than Kicks* (1934) contained 10 stories describing episodes in the life of a Dublin intellectual, Belacqua Shuah, and the novel *Murphy* (1938) concerns an Irishman in London who escapes from a girl he is about to marry to a life of contemplation as a male nurse in a mental institution. His two slim volumes of poetry were *Whoroscope* (1930), a poem on the French philosopher René Descartes, and the collection *Echo's Bones* (1935). A number of short stories and poems were scattered in various periodicals. He wrote the novel *Dream of Fair to Middling Women* in the mid-1930s, but it remained incomplete and was not published until 1992.

During his years in hiding in unoccupied France, Beckett also completed another novel, *Watt*, which was not published until 1953. After his return to Paris, between 1946 and 1949, Beckett produced a number of stories, the major prose narratives *Molloy* (1951), *Malone meurt* (1951; *Malone Dies*), and *L'Innommable* (1953; *The Unnamable*), and two plays, the unpublished three-act *Eleutheria* and *Waiting for Godot*.

It was not until 1951, however, that these works saw the light of day. After many refusals, Suzanne Deschevaux-Dumesnil (later Mme Beckett), Beckett's lifelong companion, finally succeeded in finding a publisher for *Molloy*. When this book not only proved a modest commercial success but also was received with enthusiasm by the French critics, the same publisher brought out the two other novels and *Waiting for Godot*. It was with the amazing success of *Waiting for Godot* at the small Théâtre de Babylone in Paris, in January 1953, that Beckett's rise to world fame began. Beckett continued writing, but more slowly than in the immediate postwar years. Plays for the stage and radio and a number of prose works occupied much of his attention.

Beckett continued to live in Paris, but most of his writing was done in a small house secluded in the Marne valley, a short drive from Paris. His total dedication to his art extended to his complete avoidance of all personal publicity, of appearances on radio or television, and of all journalistic interviews. When, in 1969, he received the Nobel Prize for Literature, he accepted the award but declined the trip to Stockholm to avoid the public speech at the ceremonies.

In spite of Beckett's courageous tackling of the ultimate mystery and despair of human existence, he was essentially a comic writer. Far from being gloomy and depressing, the ultimate effect of seeing or reading Beckett is one of cathartic release, an objective as old as theatre itself.

RICHARD WRIGHT

(b. Sept. 4, 1908, near Natchez, Miss., U.S.—d. Nov. 28, 1960, Paris, France)

The novelist and short-story writer Richard Wright was among the first black American writers to protest white treatment of blacks, notably in his novel *Native Son* (1940) and his autobiography, *Black Boy* (1945). He inaugurated the tradition of protest explored by other black writers after World War II.

Wright's grandparents had been slaves. His father left home when he was five, and the boy, who grew up in poverty, was often shifted from one relative to another. He worked at a number of jobs before joining the northward migration, first to Memphis, Tenn., and then to Chicago. There, after working in unskilled jobs, he got an opportunity to write through the Federal Writers' Project. In 1932 he became a member of the Communist Party, and in 1937 he went to New York City, where he became Harlem editor of the Communist *Daily Worker*.

Wright first came to the general public's attention with a volume of novellas, *Uncle Tom's Children* (1938), based on

Protest writers—authors who examine social injustices through their work—owe a debt of gratitude to Richard Wright. His Native Son *and* Black Boy *have been hailed as landmark protest novels.* Hulton Archive/Getty Images

the question: How may a black man live in a country that denies his humanity? In each story but one the hero's quest ends in death. His fictional scene shifted to Chicago in *Native Son*. Its protagonist, a poor black youth named Bigger Thomas, accidentally kills a white girl, and in the course of his ensuing flight his hitherto meaningless awareness of antagonism from a white world becomes intelligible. The book was a best-seller and was staged successfully as a play on Broadway (1941) by Orson Welles. Wright himself played Bigger Thomas in a motion-picture version made in Argentina in 1951.

In 1944 Wright left the Communist Party because of political and personal differences. *Black Boy*, written a year later, is a moving account of his childhood and young manhood in the South. The book chronicles the extreme poverty of his childhood, his experience of white prejudice and violence against blacks, and his growing awareness of his interest in literature.

After World War II, Wright settled in Paris as a permanent expatriate. *The Outsider* (1953), acclaimed as the first American existential novel, warned that the black man had awakened in a disintegrating society not ready to include him. Three later novels were not well-received. Among his polemical writings of that period was *White Man, Listen!* (1957), which was originally a series of lectures given in Europe. *Eight Men*, a collection of short stories, appeared in 1961.

The autobiographical *American Hunger*, which narrates Wright's experiences after moving to the North, was published posthumously in 1977. Some of the more candid passages dealing with race, sex, and politics in Wright's books had been cut or omitted before original publication. Unexpurgated versions of *Native Son*, *Black Boy*, and his other works were published in 1991, however.

EUDORA WELTY

(b. April 13, 1909, Jackson, Miss., U.S.—d. July 23, 2001, Jackson)

Eudora Welty was an American short-story writer and novelist whose work is mainly focused with great precision on the regional manners of people inhabiting a small Mississippi town that resembles her own birthplace and the Delta country.

Welty attended Mississippi State College for Women before transferring to the University of Wisconsin, from which she graduated in 1929. During the Great Depression she was a photographer on the Works Progress Administration's Guide to Mississippi, and photography remained a lifelong interest. *Photographs* (1989) is a collection of many of the photographs she took for the WPA. She also worked as a writer for a radio station and newspaper in her native Jackson, Mississippi, before her fiction won popular and critical acclaim.

Welty's first short story was published in 1936, and thereafter her work began to appear regularly, first in little magazines such as the *Southern Review* and later in major periodicals such as *The Atlantic Monthly* and *The New Yorker*. Her readership grew steadily after the publication of *A Curtain of Green* (1941; enlarged 1979), a volume of short stories that contains two of her most anthologized stories, "The Petrified Man" and "Why I Live at the P.O." In 1942 her short novel *The Robber Bridegroom* was issued, and in 1946 her first full-length novel, *Delta Wedding*. Her later novels include *The Ponder Heart* (1954), *Losing Battles* (1970), and *The Optimist's Daughter* (1972), which won a Pulitzer Prize. *The Wide Net and Other Stories* (1943), *The Golden Apples* (1949), and *The Bride of Innisfallen and Other Stories* (1955) are collections of short stories, and *The Eye of the Story* (1978) is a volume of essays. *The Collected Stories of Eudora Welty* was published in 1980.

Known as the First Lady of Southern literature, Eudora Welty brought a humorous, hopeful outlook to her writing. MPI/Hulton Archive/ Getty Images

Welty's main subject is the intricacies of human relationships, particularly as revealed through her characters' interactions in intimate social encounters. Among her themes are the subjectivity and ambiguity of people's perception of character and the presence of virtue hidden beneath an obscuring surface of convention, insensitivity, and social prejudice. Welty's outlook is hopeful, and love is viewed as a redeeming presence in the midst of isolation and indifference. Her works combine humour and psychological acuity with a sharp ear for regional speech patterns.

One Writer's Beginnings, an autobiographical work, was published in 1984. Originating in a series of three lectures given at Harvard, it beautifully evoked what Welty styled her "sheltered life" in Jackson and how her early fiction grew out of it.

NAGUIB MAHFOUZ

(b. Dec. 11, 1911, Cairo, Egypt—d. Aug. 30, 2006, Cairo)

The Egyptian novelist and screenplay writer Naguid Mahfouz was awarded the Nobel Prize for Literature in 1988, the first Arabic writer to be so honoured.

Mahfouz was the son of a civil servant and grew up in Cairo's Al-Jamāliyyah district. He attended Fu'ād I University (now Cairo University), where in 1934 he received a degree in philosophy. He worked in the Egyptian civil service in a variety of positions from 1934 until his retirement in 1971.

Mahfouz's earliest published works were short stories. His early novels, such as *Rādūbīs* (1943; "Radobis"), were set in ancient Egypt, but he had turned to describing modern Egyptian society by the time he began his major work, *Al-Thulāthiyyah* (1956–57), known as *The Cairo Trilogy*. Its three novels—*Bayn al-qasrayn* (1956; *Palace Walk*), *Qaṣr al-shawq* (1957; *Palace of Desire*), and *Al-Sukkariyyah* (1957; *Sugar Street*)—depict the lives of three generations of different families in Cairo from World War I until after the 1952 military coup that overthrew King Farouk. The trilogy provides a penetrating overview of 20th-century Egyptian thought, attitudes, and social change.

In subsequent works Mahfouz offered critical views of the old Egyptian monarchy, British colonialism, and contemporary Egypt. Several of his more notable novels deal with social issues involving women and political prisoners. His novel *Awlād ḥāratinā* (1959; *Children of the Alley*) was banned in Egypt for a time because of its controversial treatment of religion and its use of characters based on Muhammad, Moses, and other figures. Islamic militants, partly because of their outrage over the work, later called for his death, and in 1994 Mahfouz was stabbed in the neck.

Mahfouz's other novels include *Al-Liṣṣ wa-al-kilāb* (1961; *The Thief and the Dogs*), *Al-Shaḥḥādh* (1965; *The Beggar*), and *Mīrāmār* (1967; *Miramar*), all of which consider Egyptian society under Gamal Abdel Nasser's regime; *Afrāḥ al-qubba* (1981; *Wedding Song*), set among several characters associated with a Cairo theatre company; and the structurally experimental *Ḥadīth al-ṣabāḥ wa-al-masā'* (1987; *Morning and Evening Talk*), which strings together in alphabetical order dozens of character sketches. Together, his novels, which were among the first to gain widespread acceptance in the Arabic-speaking world, brought the genre to maturity within Arabic literature.

Mahfouz's achievements as a short-story writer are demonstrated in such collections as *Dunyā Allāh* (1963; *God's World*). *The Time and the Place, and Other Stories* (1991) and *The Seventh Heaven* (2005) are collections of his stories in English translation. Mahfouz wrote more than 45 novels and short-story collections, as well as some 30 screenplays and several plays. *Asdā' al-sīrah al-dhātiyyah* (1996; *Echoes of an Autobiography*) is a collection of parables and his sayings. In 1996 the Naguib Mahfouz Medal for Literature was established to honour Arabic writers.

ALBERT CAMUS

(b. Nov. 7, 1913, Mondovi, Alg.—d. Jan. 4, 1960, near Sens, France)

The French novelist, essayist, and playwright Albert Camus was best known for such novels as *L'Étranger* (1942; *The Stranger*), *La Peste* (1947; *The Plague*), and *La Chute* (1956; *The Fall*) and for his work in leftist causes. He received the 1957 Nobel Prize for Literature.

While attending the University of Algiers, Camus was particularly influenced by one of his teachers, Jean Grenier, who helped him to develop his literary and philosophical ideas. He obtained a *diplôme d'études supérieures* in 1936 for a thesis on the relationship between Greek and Christian thought in the philosophical writings of Plotinus and St. Augustine. His candidature for the *agrégation* (a qualification that would have enabled him to take up a university career) was cut short, however, by an attack of tuberculosis. To regain his health he went to a resort in the French Alps—his first visit to Europe—and eventually returned to Algiers via Florence, Pisa, and Genoa.

Throughout the 1930s, Camus broadened his interests. He read the French classics as well as the writers of the day—among them André Gide, Henry de Montherlant, André Malraux—and was a prominent figure among the young left-wing intellectuals of Algiers. For a short period in 1934–35 he was also a member of the Algerian Communist Party. In addition, he wrote, produced, adapted, and acted for the Théâtre du Travail (Workers' Theatre, later named the Théâtre de l'Équipe), which aimed to bring outstanding plays to working-class audiences. He maintained a deep love of the theatre until his death. Ironically, his plays are the least-admired part of his literary output, although *Le Malentendu* (*Cross Purpose*) and *Caligula*, first produced in 1944 and 1945, respectively, remain landmarks in the Theatre of the Absurd.

In the two years before the outbreak of World War II, Camus served his apprenticeship as a journalist with *Alger-Républicain* in many capacities. He reviewed some of Jean-Paul Sartre's early literary works and wrote an important series of articles analyzing social conditions among the Muslims of the Kabylie region. These articles, reprinted in abridged form in *Actuelles III* (1958), drew attention (15 years in advance) to many of the injustices that led to the outbreak of the Algerian War in 1954.

He enjoyed the most influence as a journalist during the final years of the occupation of France and the immediate post-Liberation period. As editor of the Parisian daily *Combat*, the successor of a Resistance newssheet run largely by Camus, he held an independent left-wing position based on the ideals of justice and truth and the belief that all political action must have a solid moral basis.

By now Camus had become a leading literary figure. *L'Étranger* (*The Stranger*), a brilliant first novel begun before the war and published in 1942, is a study of 20th-century alienation with a portrait of an "outsider" condemned to death less for shooting an Arab than for the fact that he never says more than he genuinely feels and refuses to conform to society's demands. The same year saw the publication of an influential philosophical essay, *Le Mythe de Sisyphe* (*The Myth of Sisyphus*), in which Camus, with considerable sympathy, analyzed contemporary nihilism and a sense of the "absurd." He was already seeking a way of overcoming nihilism, and his second novel, *La Peste* (1947;

The Plague), is a symbolical account of the fight against an epidemic in Oran by characters whose importance lies less in the (doubtful) success with which they oppose the epidemic than in their determined assertion of human dignity and fraternity. His other major literary works are the technically brilliant novel *La Chute* (1956) and a collection of short stories, *L'Exil et le royaume* (1957; *Exile and the Kingdom*). *La Chute* reveals a preoccupation with Christian symbolism and contains an ironical and witty exposure of the more complacent forms of secular humanist morality.

In 1957, at the early age of 44, Camus received the Nobel Prize for Literature. With characteristic modesty he declared that had he been a member of the awarding committee, his vote would certainly have gone to André Malraux. Less than three years later Camus was killed in an automobile accident.

As novelist and playwright, moralist, and political theorist, Albert Camus after World War II became the spokesman of his own generation and the mentor of the next, not only in France but also in Europe and eventually the world. His writings, which addressed themselves mainly to the isolation of man in an alien universe, the estrangement of the individual from himself, the problem of evil, and the pressing finality of death, accurately reflected the alienation and disillusionment of the postwar intellectual. He is remembered, with Sartre, as a leading practitioner of the existential novel.

ALEKSANDR SOLZHENITSYN

(b. Dec. 11, 1918, Kislovodsk, Russia—d. Aug. 3, 2008, Troitse-Lykovo, near Moscow)

Aleksandr Isayevich Solzhenitsyn, a Russian novelist and historian, was awarded the Nobel Prize for Literature in 1970.

Dissident author Aleksandr Solzhenitsyn resorted to subterfuge, and suffered imprisonment, in order to publish his work. Exiled from the Soviet Union, he eventually returned to Russia and become an honoured citizen. AFP/Getty Images

Solzhenitsyn fought in World War II, achieving the rank of captain of artillery; in 1945, however, he was arrested for writing a letter in which he criticized Joseph Stalin and spent eight years in prisons and labour camps, after which he spent three more years in enforced exile. Rehabilitated in 1956, he was allowed to settle in Ryazan, in central Russia, where he became a mathematics teacher and began to write.

Encouraged by the loosening of government restraints on cultural life that was a hallmark of the de-Stalinizing policies of the early 1960s, Solzhenitsyn submitted his short novel *Odin den iz zhizni Ivana Denisovicha* (1962; *One Day in the Life of Ivan Denisovich*) to the leading Soviet literary periodical *Novy Mir* ("New World"). The novel quickly appeared in that journal's pages and met with immediate popularity, Solzhenitsyn becoming an instant celebrity. *Ivan Denisovich*, based on Solzhenitsyn's own experiences, described a typical day in the life of an inmate of a forced-labour camp during the Stalin era. The book produced a political sensation both abroad and in the Soviet Union, where it inspired a number of other writers to produce accounts of their imprisonment under Stalin's regime.

Solzhenitsyn's period of official favour proved to be short-lived, however. Ideological strictures on cultural activity in the Soviet Union tightened with Nikita Khrushchev's fall from power in 1964, and Solzhenitsyn met first with increasing criticism and then with overt harassment from the authorities when he emerged as an eloquent opponent of repressive government policies. After the publication of a collection of his short stories in 1963, he was denied further official publication of his work, and he resorted to circulating them in the form of *samizdat* ("self-published") literature—i.e., as illegal literature circulated clandestinely—as well as publishing them abroad.

The following years were marked by the foreign publication of several ambitious novels that secured Solzhenitsyn's international literary reputation, among them *V kruge pervom* (1968; *The First Circle*), which traces the varying responses of scientists at work on research for the secret police as they must decide whether to cooperate with the authorities and thus remain within the research prison or to refuse their services and be thrust back into the brutal conditions of the labour camps.

In 1970 Solzhenitsyn was awarded the Nobel Prize for Literature, but he declined to go to Stockholm to receive the prize for fear he would not be readmitted to the Soviet Union by the government upon his return.

In December 1973 the first parts of *Arkhipelag Gulag* (*The Gulag Archipelago*) were published in Paris after a copy of the manuscript had been seized in the Soviet Union by the KGB. (*Gulag* is an acronym formed from the official Soviet designation of its system of prisons and labour camps.) *The Gulag Archipelago* is Solzhenitsyn's attempt to compile a literary-historical record of the vast system of prisons and labour camps that came into being shortly after the Bolsheviks seized power in Russia (1917) and that underwent an enormous expansion during the rule of Stalin (1924–53). Various sections of the work describe the arrest, interrogation, conviction, transportation, and imprisonment of the Gulag's victims as practiced by Soviet authorities over four decades. The work mingles historical exposition and Solzhenitsyn's own autobiographical accounts with the voluminous personal testimony of other inmates that he collected and committed to memory during his imprisonment.

Upon publication of the first volume of *The Gulag Archipelago*, Solzhenitsyn was immediately attacked in the Soviet press. Despite the intense interest in his fate that was shown in the West, he was arrested and charged with treason on Feb. 12, 1974. Solzhenitsyn was exiled from the Soviet Union on the following day, and in December he took possession of his Nobel Prize. The second and third volumes of *The Gulag Archipelago* were published in 1974–75. Solzhenitsyn traveled to the United States, where he eventually settled on a secluded estate in Cavendish, Vt.

In presenting alternatives to the Soviet regime, Solzhenitsyn tended to reject Western emphases on democracy and individual freedom and instead favoured the formation of a benevolent authoritarian regime that would draw upon the resources of Russia's traditional

Christian values. The introduction of *glasnost* ("openness") in the late 1980s brought renewed access to Solzhenitsyn's work in the Soviet Union. In 1989 the Soviet literary magazine *Novy Mir* published the first officially approved excerpts from *The Gulag Archipelago*. Solzhenitsyn's Soviet citizenship was officially restored in 1990.

Solzhenitsyn ended his exile and returned to Russia in 1994. He subsequently made several public appearances and even met privately with Russian Pres. Boris Yeltsin. Installments of his autobiography, *Ugodilo zernyshko promezh dvukh zhernovov: ocherki izgnaniia* ("The Little Grain Managed to Land Between Two Millstones: Sketches of Exile"), were published from 1998 to 2003. In 2007 Solzhenitsyn was awarded Russia's prestigious State Prize for his contribution to humanitarian causes.

JACK KEROUAC

(b. March 12, 1922, Lowell, Mass., U.S.—d. Oct. 21, 1969, St. Petersburg, Fla.)

Jack Kerouac, an American novelist and poet and the leader of the Beat movement, is best known for his book *On the Road* (1957), which captured the spirit of its time as no other work of the 20th century did.

Kerouac, who spoke joual (a Canadian dialect of French), attended a French Canadian school in Lowell, Mass., in the morning and continued his studies in English in the afternoon. He subsequently went to the Horace Mann School, a preparatory school in New York City, on a football scholarship. In 1940 Kerouac enrolled at Columbia University, where he met two writers who would become lifelong friends: Allen Ginsberg and William S. Burroughs. Together with Kerouac they are the seminal figures of the Beat movement.

By the time Kerouac and Burroughs met, in 1944, Kerouac had already written a million words. His boyhood ambition had been to write the "great American novel." His first novel, *The Town & the City* (1950), received favourable reviews but was considered derivative of the novels of Thomas Wolfe, whose *Time and the River* (1935) and *You Can't Go Home Again* (1940) were then popular. Yet Kerouac was unhappy with the pace of his prose. The music of bebop jazz artists Thelonious Monk and Charlie Parker began to drive Kerouac toward his "spontaneous bop prosody," as Ginsberg later called it, which took shape in the late 1940s through various drafts of his second novel, *On the Road*. The original manuscript, a scroll written in a three-week blast in 1951, is legendary: composed of approximately 120 feet (37 metres) of paper taped together and fed into a manual typewriter, the scroll allowed Kerouac the fast pace he was hoping to achieve. Rejected for publication at first, it finally was printed in 1957. Kerouac found himself a national sensation after *On the Road* received a rave review from *The New York Times*.

Readers often confused Kerouac with Sal Paradise, the amoral hipster at the centre of his novel. The critic Norman Podhoretz famously wrote that Beat writing was an assault against the intellect and against decency. This misreading dominated negative reactions to *On the Road*. Through the novel's characterization of hipsters and their nonconformist celebration of sex, jazz, and endless movement, Kerouac wanted to achieve in his writing that which he could find neither in the promise of America nor in the empty spirituality of Roman Catholicism; he strived instead for the serenity that he had discovered in his adopted Buddhism. Kerouac felt that the Beat label marginalized him and prevented him from being treated as he wanted to be treated, as a man of letters in the American tradition of Herman Melville and Walt Whitman.

As he continued to experiment with his prose style, Kerouac also bolstered his standing among the Beat writers as a poet supreme. With his sonnets and odes he ranged across Western poetic traditions. He also experimented with the idioms of blues and jazz in such works as *Mexico City Blues* (1959), a sequential poem comprising 242 choruses. After he met the poet Gary Snyder in 1955, Kerouac's poetry, as well as that of Ginsberg and fellow Beats Philip Whalen and Lew Welch, began to show the influence of the haiku, a genre mostly unknown to Americans at that time.

Kerouac turned to Buddhist study and practice from 1953 to 1956, after his "road" period and in the lull between composing *On the Road* in 1951 and its publication in 1957. In the fall of 1953 he finished *The Subterraneans* (it would be published in 1958). Fed up with the world after the failed love affair upon which the book was based, he read Henry David Thoreau and fantasized a life outside civilization. He immersed himself in the study of Zen.

By the 1960s Kerouac had finished most of the writing for which he is best known. In 1961 he wrote *Big Sur* in 10 days while living in the cabin of Lawrence Ferlinghetti, a fellow Beat poet, in California's Big Sur region. Another important autobiographical book, *Vanity of Duluoz* (1968), recounts stories of his childhood, his schooling, and the dramatic scandals that defined early Beat legend.

In 1969 Kerouac was broke, and many of his books were out of print. An alcoholic, he was living with his third wife and his mother in St. Petersburg, Fla., where he spent his time in local bars. A week after he had been beaten by fellow drinkers whom he had antagonized, he died of internal hemorrhaging while sitting in front of his television.

FLANNERY O'CONNOR

(b. March 25, 1925, Savannah, Ga., U.S.—d. Aug. 3, 1964, Milledgeville, Ga.)

Flannery O'Connor was an American novelist and short-story writer whose works, usually set in the rural American South and often treating alienation, are concerned with the relationship between the individual and God.

O'Connor grew up in a prominent Roman Catholic family in her native Georgia. She lived in Savannah until her adolescence, but the worsening of her father's lupus erythematosus forced the family to relocate in 1938 to the home in rural Milledgeville where her mother had been raised. After graduating from Georgia State College for Women (now Georgia College & State University) in 1945, she studied creative writing at the University of Iowa Writers' Workshop.

Her first published work, a short story, appeared in the magazine *Accent* in 1946. Her first novel, *Wise Blood* (1952; film 1979), explored, in O'Connor's own words, the "religious consciousness without a religion." *Wise Blood* consists of a series of near-independent chapters—many of which originated in previously published short stories—that tell the tale of Hazel Motes, a man who returns home from military service and founds the Church Without Christ, which leads to a series of interactions with the grotesque inhabitants of his hometown. The work combines the keen ear for common speech, caustic religious imagination, and flair for the absurd that were to characterize her subsequent work. With the publication of further short stories, first collected in *A Good Man Is Hard to Find and Other Stories* (1955), she came to be regarded as a master of the form. The collection's eponymous story has become possibly her best-known work. In it O'Connor creates an unexpected agent of salvation in the character of an escaped convict called The Misfit, who kills a quarreling family on vacation in the Deep South.

Her other works of fiction are a novel, *The Violent Bear It Away* (1960), and the short-story collection *Everything That Rises Must Converge* (1965). A collection of occasional prose pieces, *Mystery and Manners*, appeared in 1969. *The Complete Stories*, published posthumously in 1971, contained several stories that had not previously appeared in book form; it won a National Book Award in 1972.

Disabled for more than a decade by the lupus erythematosus she inherited from her father, which eventually proved fatal, O'Connor lived modestly, writing and raising peafowl on her mother's farm at Milledgeville. The posthumous publication of her letters, under the title *The Habit of Being* (1979), and her book reviews and correspondence with local diocesan newspapers, published as *The Presence of Grace and Other Book Reviews* (1983), provided valuable insight into the life and mind of a writer whose works defy conventional categorization. O'Connor's corpus is notable for the seeming incongruity of a devout Catholic whose darkly comic works commonly feature startling acts of violence and unsympathetic, often depraved, characters. She explained the prevalence of brutality in her stories by noting that violence "is strangely capable of returning my characters to reality and preparing them to accept their moment of grace." It is this divine stripping of man's comforts and hubris, along with the attendant degradation of the corporeal, that stands as the most salient feature of O'Connor's work.

TONI MORRISON

(b. Feb. 18, 1931, Lorain, Ohio, U.S.)

Toni Morrison is an American writer noted for her examination of the black experience, particularly black female experience. She received the Nobel Prize for Literature in 1993.

Morrison, born Chloe Anthony Wofford, grew up in the American Midwest in a family that possessed an intense love of and appreciation for black culture. Storytelling, songs, and folktales were a deeply formative part of her childhood. She attended Howard University (B.A., 1953) and Cornell

Toni Morrison has given elegant voice to the black female experience. Her novels have won critical and popular acclaim. Brad Barket/Getty Images

University (M.A., 1955). After teaching at Texas Southern University for two years, she taught at Howard from 1957 to 1964. In 1965 she became a fiction editor. From 1984 she taught writing at the State University of New York at Albany, leaving in 1989 to join the faculty of Princeton University.

Morrison's first book, *The Bluest Eye* (1970), is a novel of initiation concerning a victimized adolescent black girl who is obsessed by white standards of beauty and longs to have blue eyes. In 1973 a second novel, *Sula*, was published; it examines (among other issues) the dynamics of friendship and the expectations for conformity within the community. *Song of Solomon* (1977) is told by a male narrator in search of his identity; its publication brought Morrison to national attention. *Tar Baby* (1981), set on a Caribbean island, explores conflicts of race, class, and sex. The critically acclaimed *Beloved* (1987), which won a Pulitzer Prize for fiction, is based on the true story of a runaway slave who, at the point of recapture, kills her infant daughter in order to spare her a life of slavery. *Jazz* (1992) is a story of violence and passion set in New York City's Harlem during the 1920s. Subsequent novels are *Paradise* (1998), a richly detailed portrait of a black utopian community in Oklahoma, and *Love* (2003), an intricate family story that reveals the myriad facets of love and its ostensible opposite. *A Mercy* (2008) deals with slavery in 17th-century America.

A work of criticism, *Playing in the Dark: Whiteness and the Literary Imagination*, was published in 1992. Many of her essays and speeches were collected in *What Moves at the Margin: Selected Nonfiction* (edited by Carolyn C. Denard), published in 2008. Additionally, Morrison released several children's books, including *Who's Got Game?: The Ant or the Grasshopper?* and *Who's Got Game?: The Lion or the Mouse?*, both written with her son and published in 2003. *Remember* (2004) chronicles the hardships of black students during the integration of the American public school system; aimed at children, it uses archival photographs juxtaposed with captions speculating on the thoughts of their subjects. She also wrote the libretto for *Margaret Garner* (2005), an opera about the same story that inspired *Beloved*.

The central theme of Morrison's novels is the black American experience. In an unjust society, her characters struggle to find themselves and their cultural identity. Her use of fantasy, her sinuous poetic style, and her rich interweaving of the mythic gave her stories great strength and texture.

WOLE SOYINKA

(b. July 13, 1934, Abeokuta, Nigeria)

Wole Soyinka is a Nigerian playwright and political activist who received the Nobel Prize for Literature in 1986. He sometimes wrote of modern West Africa in a satirical style, but his serious intent and his belief in the evils inherent in the exercise of power usually was evident in his work as well.

A member of the Yoruba people, Soyinka attended Government College and University College in Ibadan before graduating in 1958 with a degree in English from the University of Leeds in England. Upon his return to Nigeria, he founded an acting company and wrote his first important play, *A Dance of the Forests* (produced 1960; published 1963), for the Nigerian independence celebrations. The play satirizes the fledgling nation by stripping it of romantic legend and by showing that the present is no more a golden age than was the past.

He wrote several plays in a lighter vein, making fun of pompous, Westernized schoolteachers in *The Lion and the Jewel* (first performed in Ibadan, 1959; published 1963) and mocking the clever preachers of upstart prayer-churches who grow fat on the credulity of their parishioners in *The Trials of Brother Jero* (performed 1960; published 1963) and *Jero's Metamorphosis* (1973). But his more serious plays, such as *The Strong Breed* (1963), *Kongi's Harvest* (opened the first Festival of Negro Arts in Dakar, 1966; published 1967), *The Road* (1965), *From Zia, with Love* (1992), and even the parody *King Baabu* (performed 2001; published 2002), reveal his disregard for African authoritarian leadership and his disillusionment with Nigerian society as a whole.

Other notable plays include *Madmen and Specialists* (performed 1970; published 1971), *Death and the King's Horseman* (1975), and *The Beatification of Area Boy* (1995). In these and Soyinka's other dramas, Western elements are skillfully fused with subject matter and dramatic techniques deeply rooted in Yoruba folklore and religion. Symbolism, flashback, and ingenious plotting contribute to a rich dramatic structure. His best works exhibit humour and fine poetic style as well as a gift for irony and satire and for accurately matching the language of his complex characters to their social position and moral qualities.

From 1960 to 1964, Soyinka was coeditor of *Black Orpheus*, an important literary journal. From 1960 onward he taught literature and drama and headed theatre groups at various Nigerian universities, including those of Ibadan, Ife, and Lagos. After winning the Nobel Prize, he also was sought after as a lecturer, and many of his lectures were published—notably the Reith Lectures of 2004, as *Climate of Fear* (2004).

Though he considered himself primarily a playwright, Soyinka also wrote novels—*The Interpreters* (1965) and *Season of Anomy* (1973)—and several volumes of poetry. The latter include *Idanre, and Other Poems* (1967) and *Poems from Prison* (1969; republished as *A Shuttle in the Crypt*, 1972), published together as *Early Poems* (1998); *Mandela's Earth and Other Poems* (1988); and *Samarkand and Other Markets I Have Known* (2002). His verse is characterized by a precise command of language and a mastery of lyric, dramatic, and meditative poetic forms. He wrote a good deal of *Poems from Prison* while he was jailed in 1967–69 for speaking out against the war brought on by the attempted secession of Biafra from Nigeria. *The Man Died* (1972) is his prose account of his arrest and 22-month imprisonment. Soyinka's principal critical work is *Myth, Literature, and the African World* (1976), a collection of essays in which he examines the role of the artist in the light of Yoruba mythology and symbolism. *Art, Dialogue, and Outrage* (1988) is a work on similar themes of art, culture, and society. He continued to address Africa's ills and Western responsibility in *The Open Sore of a Continent* (1996) and *The Burden of Memory, the Muse of Forgiveness* (1999).

Soyinka was the first black African to be awarded the Nobel Prize for Literature. An autobiography, *Aké: The Years of Childhood*, was published in 1981 and followed by the companion pieces *Ìsarà: A Voyage Around Essay* (1989) and *Ibadan: The Penkelemes Years: A Memoir, 1946–1965* (1994). In 2006 he published another memoir, *You Must Set Forth at Dawn*. In 2005–06 Soyinka served on the Encyclopædia Britannica Editorial Board of Advisors.

SIR SALMAN RUSHDIE

(b. June 19, 1947, Bombay [now Mumbai], India)

Sir Salman Rushdie remains best known as the Anglo-Indian novelist who was condemned to death by leading Iranian Muslim clerics in 1989 for allegedly having blasphemed Islam in his novel *The Satanic Verses*. His case became the focus of an international controversy.

Rushdie was the son of a prosperous Muslim businessman in India. He was educated at Rugby School and the University of Cambridge, receiving an M.A. degree in history in 1968. Throughout most of the 1970s he worked in London as an advertising copywriter, and his first published novel, *Grimus*, appeared in 1975. His next novel, *Midnight's Children* (1981), an allegory about modern India, was an unexpected critical and popular success that won him international recognition. Like Rushdie's subsequent fiction, *Midnight's Children* is an allegorical fable that examines historical and philosophical issues by means of surreal characters, brooding humour, and an effusive and melodramatic prose style.

The novel *Shame* (1983), based on contemporary politics in Pakistan, was also popular, but Rushdie's fourth novel, *The Satanic Verses*, encountered a different reception. Some of the adventures in this book depict a character modeled on the Prophet Muhammad and portray both him and his transcription of the Qur'ān in a manner that, after the novel's publication in the summer of 1988, drew criticism from Muslim community leaders in Britain, who denounced the novel as blasphemous. Public demonstrations against the book spread to Pakistan in January 1989. On February 14 the spiritual leader of revolutionary Iran, Ayatollah Ruhollah Khomeini, publicly condemned the book and issued a fatwa (legal opinion) against Rushdie; a bounty was offered to anyone who would execute him. He went into hiding under the protection of Scotland Yard, and—although he occasionally emerged unexpectedly, sometimes in other countries—he was compelled to restrict his movements.

Despite the standing death threat, Rushdie continued to write, producing *Imaginary Homelands* (1991), a collection of essays and criticism; the children's novel *Haroun and the Sea of Stories* (1990); the short-story collection *East, West* (1994); and the novel *The Moor's Last Sigh* (1995). In 1998, after nearly a decade, the Iranian government announced it would no longer seek to enforce its fatwa against Rushdie.

Rushdie's subsequent novels include *The Ground Beneath Her Feet* (1999) and *Fury* (2001). *Step Across This Line* (2002) is a collection of essays he wrote between 1992 and 2002 on subjects from the September 11 attacks to *The Wizard of Oz*. *Shalimar the Clown* (2005), a novel set primarily in the disputed Kashmir region of the Indian subcontinent, examines the nature of terrorism. *The Enchantress of Florence* (2008) is based on a fictionalized account of the Mughal emperor Akbar.

Rushdie received the Booker Prize in 1981 for *Midnight's Children*. He subsequently won the Booker of Bookers (1993) and the Best of the Booker (2008). These special prizes were voted on by the public in honour of the prize's 25th and 40th anniversaries, respectively. Rushdie was knighted in 2007, an honour criticized by the Iranian government and Pakistan's parliament.

J. K. ROWLING

(b. July 31, 1965, Chipping Sodbury, near Bristol, Eng.)

The British author J. K. Rowling is the creator of the popular and critically acclaimed Harry Potter series, about a young sorcerer in training.

After graduating from the University of Exeter in 1986, Rowling began working for Amnesty International in London, where she started to write the Harry Potter adventures. In the early 1990s she traveled to Portugal to teach English as a foreign language, but, after a brief marriage and the birth of her daughter, she returned to the

J. K. Rowling is widely credited for getting modern-day children back into reading. Her Harry Potter series of books is also popular with adults around the globe. Dan Kitwood/Getty Images

United Kingdom, settling in Edinburgh. Living on public assistance between stints as a French teacher, she continued to write.

Rowling's first book in the series, *Harry Potter and the Philosopher's Stone* (1997; also published as *Harry Potter and the Sorcerer's Stone*), was an immediate success, appealing to both children (its intended audience) and adults. Featuring vivid descriptions and an imaginative story line, it followed the adventures of the unlikely hero Harry Potter, a lonely orphan who discovers that he is actually a wizard and enrolls in the Hogwarts School of Witchcraft and Wizardry. The book received numerous awards, including the British Book Award. Succeeding volumes—*Harry Potter and the Chamber of Secrets* (1998), *Harry Potter and the Prisoner of Azkaban* (1999), *Harry Potter and the Goblet of Fire* (2000), *Harry Potter and the Order of the Phoenix* (2003), and *Harry Potter and the Half-Blood Prince* (2005)—also were best-sellers, available in more than 200 countries and some 60 languages. The seventh and final installment in the series, *Harry Potter and the Deathly Hallows*, was released in 2007. Other works include the companion books *Fantastic Beasts & Where to Find Them* and *Quidditch Through the Ages*, both of which were published in 2001, with proceeds going to charity.

The Harry Potter series sparked great enthusiasm among children and was credited with generating a new interest in reading. A film version of the first Harry Potter book was released in 2001 and became one of the top-grossing movies in the world. Other volumes were also made into highly successful films. In 2008 Rowling followed her successful Harry Potter series with *The Tales of Beedle the Bard*, a collection of fairy tales.

Rowling was appointed OBE (Officer of the British Empire) in March 2001. In 2009 she was named a chevalier of the French Legion of Honour.

Glossary

allegory The use of fictional figures and actions to symbolize truths or generalizations about human existence.

anecdotal Based on unscientific reports and observations; describes a scene that depicts a story.

anodyne An activity or method that calms or relieves pain and tension.

chorus Describes a group of actors who, in the ancient Greek tradition, respond to and comment on the main action of a play with song, dance, and recitation.

didactic A story written or told in such a way that it teaches the reader/listener a moral.

docti Scholarly poets.

dramaturgy Theatre arts, or the act of writing plays.

dream-vision form A style of narrative poetry in which the main character falls asleep and, in his or her dream, experiences events having representational, instructive, or moral significance.

epic poem Long and highly stylized poetry that details the heroic achievements of the main protagonist.

episodic Made up of a series of episodes; when a larger story is told through several smaller stories in sequence.

extant Still in existence.

heroic A type of verse form in which, according to literary critics, poetry of a certain language and age should be written.

martial Having to do with war or military life.
metre The rhythmic arrangement of syllables in verse.
motif A dominant or recurrent theme.
novellas Short narratives with their origins in medieval Italy.
panegyric A formal, public compliment, often offered after the honoree's death.
paean Choral chant to a god.
phraseology The way in which phrases are used to create a writer's style.
picaresque Describes a story that involves a rogue or adventurer surviving mainly by his or her wits in a treacherous society.
polemic Describes a controversial opinion that attacks another more popular opinion or doctrine.
protagonist The main character in a work of literature or drama.
qaṣīdah Classical Arabic ode.
recitation Speaking several lines of written material before an audience.
sabi Love of the old, the faded, and the unobtrusive.
set piece A work of art with a formal theme, created mainly to show the artist's or writer's skill.

For Further Reading

Andronik, Catherine M. *Wildly Romantic: The English Romantic Poets—The Mad, the Bad, and the Dangerous*. New York, NY: Henry Holt and Co., 2007.

Bentley, Eric, and George Bernard Shaw. *Bernard Shaw*. New York, NY: Applause Theatre & Cinema Books, 2002.

Binding, Paul. *The Still Moment: Eudora Welty, Portrait of a Writer*. London, UK: Faber Finds, 2009.

Briggs, Julia. *Virginia Woolf: An Inner Life*. Fort Washington, PA: Harvest Books, 2006.

Cooper Lambdin, Laura. *A Companion to Jane Austen Studies*. Santa Barbara, CA: Greenwood Press, 2000.

Dalby, Andrew. *Rediscovering Homer: Inside the Origins of the Epic*. New York, NY: W.W. Norton & Company, 2007.

De Jong, Mary, and Earl Yarington. *Popular Nineteenth-Century American Women Writers and the Literary Marketplace*. New Castle, UK: Cambridge Scholars Publishing, 2007.

Denard, Carolyn C. *Toni Morrison: Conversations*. Jackson, MS: University of Mississippi Press, 2008.

Deresiewicz, William. *Jane Austen and the Romantic Poets*. New York, NY: Columbia University Press, 2004.

Gandal, Keith. *The Gun and the Pen: Hemingway, Fitzgerald, Faulkner, and the Fiction of Mobilization*. New York, NY: Oxford University Press, 2008.

Granger, John. *Unlocking Harry Potter: Five Keys for the Serious Reader*. Wayne, PA: Zossima Press, 2007

Gurnah, Abdulrazak. *The Cambridge Companion to Salman Rushdie*. Cambridge, UK: Cambridge University Press, 2007.

Holland, Merlin, ed. *Oscar Wilde: A Life in Letters*. New York, NY: Carroll & Graf Publishers, 2007.

Logan, Andrew. *Shakespeare's Marlowe*. Burlington, VT: Ashgate Publishing Company, 2007.

Pearce, Joseph. *Solzhenitsyn: A Soul in Exile*. Grand Rapids, MI: Baker Books, 2001.

Racevskis, Roland. *Tragic Passages: Jean Racine's Art of the Threshold*. Lewisburg, PA: Bucknell University Press, 2007.

Rowley, Hazel. *Richard Wright: The Life and Times*. Chicago, IL: University of Chicago Press, 2008.

Shan Chou, Eva. *Reconsidering Tu Fu: Literary Greatness and Cultural Context*. Cambridge, UK: Cambridge University Press, 2006.

Smiley, Jane. *Charles Dickens*. New York, NY: Viking/Penguin, 2002.

Soyinka, Wole. *You Must Set Forth at Dawn: A Memoir*. New York, NY: Random House, 2007.

Steinbeck, John. *The Harvest Gypsies: On the Road to the Grapes of Wrath*. Berkeley, CA: Heyday Books, 2002.

Thaden, Barbara Z. *Student Companion to Charlotte and Emily Brontë*. Santa Barbara, CA: Greenwood Press, 2001.

Index

A

Abdelazer, 99
Absalom, Absalom!, 285
Ada, 288
Adam Bede, 190
Adventures of Huckleberry Finn, 215, 220–221
Adventures of Tom Sawyer, The, 215, 220
Aeneid, 17, 33, 35–36, 38
Aeschylus, 9, 22–25, 27, 28
Aesthetic movement, 229, 231, 254
Afrāḥ al-qubba (*Wedding Song*), 309
After Apple-Picking, 252
After the Race, 268
Ah, Wilderness!, 280
Aké: The Years of Childhood, 325
Akhmatova, Anna (Anna Andreyevna Gorenko), 280–283
Al Aaraaf, Tamerlane, and Minor Poems, 162
À la recherche du temps perdu (*In Search of Lost Time*), 249, 250, 251
Albertine disparue (*The Fugitive*), 251
Alcott, Bronson, 158
Alexander le grand (*Alexander the Great*), 97
Alice's Adventures in Wonderland, 212, 214–215
Allegro, L', 93
All's Well That Ends Well, 88
All the Year Round, 166
À l'ombre des jeunes filles en fleurs (*Within a Budding Grove*), 250
Amasie, 97
Ambassadors, The, 225
Amelia, 116
American Hunger, 305
American Scene, The, 226
Amerika, 274
Amoretti, 75
Amorous Prince, The, 99
Andrew Marvell, 276–277
Andromaque, 98
Animal Farm, 295, 296–297
Anna Christie, 279
Anna Karenina, 204
Anniversaries, 91
Anno Domini MCMXXI, 282

Antiquary, The, 134
Antony and Cleopatra, 88
A-Q zhengzhuan (*The True Story of Ah Q*), 258
Areopagitica, 95
Aristophanes, 9, 29–31
Aristotle, 25, 28, 57
Arkhipelag Gulag (*The Gulag Archipelago*), 315
Arms and the Man, 236–237
Art, Dialogue, and Outrage, 325
Asdā' al-sīrah al-dhātiyyah (*Echoes of an Autobiography*), 310
Ash Wednesday, 277
As I Lay Dying, 285
As You Like It, 87
Athalie, 99
Ausgabe letzter Hand ("Edition of the Last Hand"), 124
Austen, Jane, 11, 138–142
Awlād ḥāratinā (*Children of the Alley*), 309

B

Bajazet, 98
Ballad of Reading Gaol, The, 233
Balloon-Hoax, The, 163
Balzac, Honoré de, 222, 224, 249
Barnaby Rudge, 165
Barrett Browning, Elizabeth, 208
Bashō (Matsuo Bashō), 100–102
Bateau ivre, Le ("The Drunken Boat"), 234
Baudelaire, Charles, 192–196
Bayn al-qaṣrayn (*Palace Walk*), 308
Beat Generation, 10, 316, 317, 318
Beautification of Area Boy, The, 324
Beckett, Samuel, 300–303
Behn, Aphra, 99–100
Beim Bau der chinesischen Mauer (*The Great Wall of China*), 274
Belaya staya ("The White Flock"), 282
Bells and Pomegranates, 168
Beloved, 11, 322, 323
Bend Sinister, 288
Beppo, 144
Bérénice, 98
Bernardo, 72
Besy (*The Possessed*), 197–198
Between the Acts, 267
Beyond the Horizon, 279
Big Sur, 318
Billy Budd, 187
Bingqu xing (*The Ballad of the Army Carts*), 40
Biographia Literaria, 136, 138
Black Boy, 12, 303, 305
Black Dwarf, The, 134
Black Swan, The, 256
Bleak House, 166
Blot in the 'Scutcheon, A, 168
Bluest Eye, The, 322
Boccaccio, Giovanni, 55, 59, 72
Book of the Duchess, 58, 59
Boris Godunov, 152–153
Bostonians, The, 225
Bound East for Cardiff, 279
Bouvard et Pécuchet, 200
Boy's Will, A, 252, 253
Brand, 201, 227
Bride of Innisfallen and Other Stories, The, 306
Bride of Lammermoor, The, 134

Britannicus, 98
Brontë, Anne, 172, 173, 174, 178–179
Brontë, Charlotte, 171–174, 178–179
Brontë, Emily, 10, 172, 173, 174, 177–179
Brothers, The, 131
Brothers Karamazov, The (*Bratya Karamazovy*), 198
Browning, Robert, 168–171
Buddenbrooks, 253, 254
Burbage, Richard, 85
Burden of Memory, the Muse of Forgiveness, The, 325
Burmese Days, 295, 296
Burning Bright, 294
Burns, Robert, 125–128
Burroughs, William S., 316, 317
Bygmester Solness (*The Master Builder*), 202
Byron, Lord (George Gordon), 142–145, 146, 147, 162

C

Cairo Trilogy, The, 308–309
Caligula, 311
Camões, Luís de, 62–64
Camus, Albert, 198, 310–312
Candida, 237
Candide, 113–114
Cannery Row, 294
Canterbury Tales, The, 58, 60–61
Canto general, 299
Carroll, Lewis, 212–215
casamiento engañoso, El ("The Deceitful Marriage"), 72
Castle, The, 271, 274
Cathleen ni Houlihan, 244
Catullus, Gaius Valerius, 31–33
Celebrated Jumping Frog of Calaveras County and Other Sketches, 219
Celtic Twilight, The, 244
Cenci, The, 147
Cervantes, Miguel de, 67–73, 77, 78
Chase, and William and Helen, The, 132
Châtiments, Les (*The Punishments*), 157
Chaucer, Geoffrey, 58–61
Chayka (*The Seagull*), 239–240
Chekhov, Anton, 238–240
Cherry Orchard, The, 240
Chevelure, La ("The Head of Hair"), 194
Childe Harolde's Pilgrimage, 143, 144
Chitrāngadā, 242
chorus, 24, 25, 27
Christmas Carol, A, 167
Chute, La (*The Fall*), 310, 312
Chyotki ("Rosary"), 281
Ciascuno a suo modo, 248
"Civil Disobedience," 175, 177
Classical age, 17, 55, 56, 57, 81, 96, 104, 125, 156
Clemens, Samuel (Mark Twain), 215–222
Climate of Fear, 324
Cluster, The, 287
Coleridge, Samuel Taylor, 129–130, 131, 135–138, 162, 275
Collected Poems (Frost), 253
Collected Stories (Faulkner), 286

Collected Stories of Eudora Welty, The, 306
Colonel Jack, 107
coloquio de los perros, El ("Colloquy of the Dogs"), 72
commedia, La/La divina commedia (*The Divine Comedy*), 51, 53, 54–55
Complete Poems and Prose, The (Whitman), 183
Complete Stories, The (O'Connor), 320
Comus, 93
Concerning the Jewes, 221
Confidence-Man, The, 187
Confusa, La ("Confusion"), 70
Consolation of Philosophy, 59–60
Contemplations, Les, 157
convivio, Il (*The Banquet*), 53, 54
Corsair, The, 143
Così è (se vi pare), 247–248
Cossacks, The (*Kazaki*), 203–204
Côté de Guermantes, Le (*The Guermantes Way*), 250–251
Countess Cathleen, The, 245
Creditors, The, 227
Crepusculario, 298
Crime and Punishment (*Prestupleniye i nakazaniye*), 196, 197
Cromwell, 156
Cup of Gold, 293
Curtain of Green, A, 306
Cygne, Le ("The Swan"), 195

D

Daisy Miller, 225
Daitaleis (*The Banqueters*), 29–30
Dance of Death, The, 229
Dance of the Forests, A, 323
Daniel Deronda, 191
Dante, 51–55, 59, 81, 119
Death and the King's Horsemen, 324
Death in the Afternoon, 291
Death in Venice, 253
Death of Ivan Ilyich, The (*Smert Ivana Ilicha*), 206
Death of the Hired Man, The, 252
Defence of Poetry, A, 148
Defoe, Daniel, 105–108
Delta Wedding, 306
De monarchia (*On Monarchy*), 54
Descartes, René, 113, 302
Desire Under the Elms, 280
De sui ipsius et multorum ignorantia, 57
Devotions upon Emergent Occasions, 92
De vulgari eloquentia (*Concerning Vernacular Eloquence*), 53–54
Diaries of Court Ladies of Old Japan, 46
Diary of a Madman and Other Stories, 259
Diary of a Writer, The, 198
Dickens, Charles, 81, 164–167
Dickinson, Emily, 206–212
Dictionary of the English Language, A, 117, 118
Dido, Queen of Carthage, 79
Dīvān-e Shams ("The Collected Poetry of Shams"), 48
Divine Comedy, The (*La commedia/La divina commedia*), 51, 53, 54–55, 119
divino Narciso, El (*The Divine Narcissus*), 104

Dnevnik pisatelya ("The Diary of a Writer"), 198
Doctor's Dilemma, The, 237
Dodgson, Charles Lutwidge (Lewis Carroll), 212–215
Doktor Faustus, 255–256
Dombey and Son, 166
Don Juan, 144, 145
Donne, John, 89–92, 277
Don Quixote, 67, 70–71, 72
Dostoyevsky, Fyodor, 196–198
Down and Out in Paris and London, 296
Dramatis Personae, 171
Dream of Fair to Middling Women, 302
Dream Play, A, 229
Drum Taps, 182
Dubliners, 268
Du côté de chez Swann (*Swann's Way*), 250
Du Fu, 39–41
Dukkehjem, Et, (*A Doll's House*), 202
Dunyā Allāh (*God's World*), 309
Dyadya Vanya (*Uncle Vanya*), 239

E

Early Poems, 325
East of Eden, 294
East, West, 327
Echo's Bones, 302
Eclogues, 34
Éducation sentimentale, L', 200
Edward II, 80
Edwin Drood, 167
Eight Men, 305
Elder Statesman, The, 277
Eleutheria, 302
Eliot, George (Mary Ann Evans), 188–192
Eliot, T. S., 275–278
Emerson, Ralph Waldo, 158, 175, 177, 181, 207, 208
Emma (Brontë), 174
Emma (Austen), 141–142
Emperor Jones, The, 279–280
Emperor of the Moon, The, 100
Empyrean Path, The, 287
En attendant Godot (*Waiting for Godot*), 300, 302
Enchantress of Florence, The, 327
Endymion, 149
English Bards and Scotch Reviewers, 143
Enrico IV (*Henry IV*), 248
Ensam ("Alone"), 229
epilogo, L', 247
Epipsychidion, 148
Epistolae metricae, 57
Epithalamion, 75
Essais (*Essays*), 64, 65, 66–67
Essays in Divinity, 92
Esther, 99
Etranger (*The Stranger*), *L'*, 310, 311
Eureka, 164
Euripides, 29, 30
Europeans, The, 225
Eveline, 268
Eve of St. Agnes, The, 150, 151
Everything That Rises Must Converge, 320
Exil et le royaume, L' (*Exile and the Kingdom*), 312
Expressionism, 226
Eye of the Story, The, 306

F

Fabian Essays in Socialism, 236
Fable, A, 286
Faerie Queene, The, 73, 74–75
Fair Jilt, The, 100
Fall of Man, 54, 96, 160
Fall of the House of Usher, The, 163
Family Instructor, The, 107
Family Reunion, The, 277
Fanshawe, 158
Fantastic Beasts and Where to Find Them, 329
Farewell to Arms, A, 291
Father, The, 227
Faulkner, William, 266, 283–286
Faust, 119, 124–125, 199
Faustus, 80
Felix Holt, the Radical, 191
Ferdowsī, 42–45
Fielding, Henry, 114–116, 121
Finnegans Wake, 267, 270–271
Fitzgerald, F. Scott, 289
Flags in the Dust, 284
Flaubert, Gustave, 199–200, 249
Fleurs du mal, Les (*The Flowers of Evil*), 192, 195
Flush, 267
Following the Equator, 222
Forc'd Marriage, The, 99
Forgotten Village, 294
For Whom the Bell Tolls, 291
Four Quartets, 275, 277
Frankenstein, 146, 147
From Zia, with Love, 324
Frost, Robert, 251–253
Frost at Midnight, 136, 137
Fruen fra havet (*The Lady from the Sea*), 202
fu Mattia Pascal, Il (*The Late Mattia Pascal*), 247
Further Range, A, 253
Fury, 327

G

Galatea, La (*Galatea: A Pastoral Romance*), 70, 73
Galileo, 93
Genesis of a Novel, The, 256
Gengangere (*Ghosts*), 202
Genji monogatari (*The Tale of Genji*), 45–46
Georgics, 35
Gerontion, 276
Geschichte Gottfriedens von Berlichingen mit der eisernen Hand, dramatisirt ("The History of Gottfried von Berlichingen with the Iron Hand, Dramatized"), 120
Ghare-Bāire (*The Home and the World*), 243
Ghost Sonata, The, 229
Gift, The, 288
Gift Outright, The, 253
Gilded Age, The, 220
Ginsberg, Allen, 316, 317, 318
Gitanjali, Song Offerings, 243
Godwin, Mary Wollstonecraft, 144, 146–147, 148
Goethe, Johann Wolfgang von, 119–125, 190
Gold-Bug, The, 163
Golden Apples, The, 306
Golden Bowl, The, 225, 226
Good Man Is Hard to Find and Other Stories, A, 319–320

Gorā, 243
Götz von Berlichingen, 120
Grapes of Wrath, The, 293–294
Great Expectations, 166, 167
Great God Brown, The, 280
Great Highway, The, 229
Greene, Robert, 84
Grimus, 326
Ground Beneath Her Feet, The, 327
Gulag Archipelago, The, 13, 315, 316
Gulliver's Travels, 108, 110–111
Gustav Vasa, 228
Guy Mannering, 134

H

Habit of Being, The, 320
Ḥadīth al-ṣabāḥ wa-al-masā' (*Morning and Evening Talk*), 309
haiku, 100–101, 318
Hairy Ape, The, 280
Hamlet, 9, 88
Hard Times, 166
Haroun and the Sea of Stories, 326–327
Harry Potter series, 14, 327, 329
Hawthorne, Nathaniel, 158–160, 186, 224
Heart of Midlothian, The, 134
Hedda Gabler, 202
Hemingway, Ernest, 9, 289–292
Henriade, La, 111
Henry IV, 248
Hernani, 156
Hero and Leander, 80
Hesiod, 18
History of a Six Weeks' Tour, 147
History of Britain, 96
History of Tom Jones, a Foundling, The, 115–116
"Hollow of the Three Hills, The," 158
Holy Sinner, The, 256
Hombres necios ("Foolish Men"), 104
Home Burial, 252
Homer, 17–22, 36, 80, 122, 270, 276
Homeridae, 18, 19
Hours of Idleness, 143
Household Words, 166
House of the Seven Gables, The, 158, 159
Hous of Fame, 59
Hugo, Victor, 154–157
Hunchback of Notre-Dame, The, 156
Hunger Artist, A, 273, 274
Hungerkünstler, Ein (*A Hunger Artist*), 273, 274
Hunting of the Snark, The, 215
"Hymn to Intellectual Beauty," 146
"Hymn to The Pillory," 106
Hyperion, 150–151

I

Ibadan: The Penkelemes Years: A Memoir, 1946–1965, 325
Ibsen, Henrik, 200–203, 227
Iceman Cometh, The, 280
Idandre, and Other Poems, 324
Ideal Husband, An, 232
Idiot, The, 197

Igrok (*The Gambler*), 197
Iliad, 17, 19–21, 22, 36, 149
Illuminations, 234
Imaginary Homelands, 326
Immaturity, 236
Importance of Being Ernest, The, 232
Imru' al-Qays, 38–39
In der Strafkolonie (*In the Penal Colony*), 273, 274
In Dubious Battle, 293
Inferno (Dante), 54
Inferno (Strindberg), 228
Innocents Abroad, The, 215, 219
Innommoble, L' (*The Unnamable*), 302
In Our Time, 291
Interpreters, The, 324
In the Penal Colony, 273, 274
In the Zone, 279
Iphigenie auf Tauris (*Iphigenia in Tauris*), 121
Irène, 114
Isabella, 151
Ìsarà: A Voyage Around Essay, 325
Ispoved (*My Confession*), 204
Ivanhoe, 134
Ivanov, 238
Iz tsikla "Slava miru" ("From the Cycle 'Glory to Peace'"), 282–283

J

Jacob's Room, 264
James, Henry, 224–226
Jane Eyre, 171–172, 173–174, 179
Janet's Repentance, 190
Jazz, 322
Jean Santeuil, 249
Jero's Metamorphosis, 324
Jew of Malta, The, 80
Jim Smiley and His Jumping Frog, 218
John Bull's Other Island, 237
Johnson, James, 127–128
Johnson, Samuel, 116–118
Jonson, Ben, 81
Joseph Andrews, 115, 116
Journal, 148
Journal of the Plague Year, A, 107
Journal to Stella, 109
Journey to the Western Islands of Scotland, A, 118
Joyce, James, 266, 267–271, 301
Judgment, The, 273, 274

K

Kafka, Franz, 271–275
Kammarspel ("Chamber Plays"), 229
Kapitanskaya dochka (*The Captain's Daughter*), 154
Kazaki (*The Cossacks*), 203–204
Keats, John, 148–151, 162
Kenilworth, 134–135
Kerouac, Jack, 10, 316–318
Kew Gardens, 263–264
King Baabu, 324
King Lear, 88
King, Queen, Knave, 287
King's Men, 85
Kleine Herr Friedemann, Der, 254
Kongi's Harvest, 324
Kongsemnerne (*The Pretenders*), 201
Kuangren riji ("Diary of a Madman"), 257
Kubla Khan, 136–137

L

Lady of the Lake, The, 132
Lady Susan, 139
Lady Windermere's Fan, 231–232
Lamia, 150, 151
Landarzt, Ein (A Country Doctor), 273
Laon and Cythna; or, The Revolution of the Gold City, 147
Lay of the Last Minstrel, The, 132
Leaves of Grass, 179, 181, 182, 183
Legend of Good Women, The, 60
Legend of Montrose, A, 134
Leiden des jungen Werthers, Die (The Sorrows of Young Werther), 120–121, 124
Les Misérables, 154, 157
Lettres philosophiques, 111–113
Lewes, George Henry, 188–190, 191, 192
Li Bai, 39–40
Liberal, The, 148
Liddell, Alice, 213–214
Life on the Mississippi, 215, 220
Lille Eyolf (Little Eyolf), 202
Lion and the Jewel, The, 323
Liren xing (The Beautiful Woman), 40
Liṣṣ wa-al-kilāb, Al-, (The Thief and the Dogs), 309
Literati of New York City, The, 164
Little Dorrit, 166
Locke, John, 113
Lolita, 287, 288
Long Day's Journey into Night, 279
Long Voyage Home, The, 279
Losing Battles, 306
Love, 322
Love-Letters Between a Nobleman and His Sister, 100
Love Song of J. Alfred Prufrock, The, 275
Lucky Peter's Travels, 227
Lu Hsun: Complete Poems, 259
Luria, 168
Lu Xun (Zhou Shuren), 10, 256–259
Lycidas, 93
Lycidus; or, The Lover in Fashion, 100
Lyrical Ballads, 129, 130–131, 135–136, 137, 275
Lysistrata, 31

M

Madame Bovary, 199–200
Macbeth, 88
Macdonald, George, 213, 214
Madeleine Férat, 222
Madmen and Specialists, 324
Magic Mountain, The, 253, 254–255
Mahfouz, Naguib, 308–310
Major Barbara, 237
Malentendu, Le (Cross Purpose), 311
Mal giocondo, 246
Malone meurt (Malone Dies), 302
Man and Superman, 237
Mānasī, 242
Mandela's Earth and Other Poems, 325
Man Died, The, 325
Mann, Thomas, 253–256
Mansfield Park, 141

Marble Faun, The, 159–160
Mardi, 184
Mark on the Wall, The, 263
Marlowe, Christopher, 78–80
Married, 227
Martin Chuzzlewit, 166
Mashenka (Mary), 287
Mas̄navī-yi Ma'navī ("Spiritual Couplets"), 46–47, 50
Massacre at Paris, The, 80
Mäster Olof, 227
Measure for Measure, 88
Medny vsadnik (The Bronze Horseman), 153–154
Medved (The Bear), 239
Melville, Herman, 9, 159, 163, 183–187, 318
Melymbrosia, 262–263
Men and Women, 170
Mending Wall, 252
Men Without Women, 291
Mercy, A, 322
Mesmeric Revelation, 194
Metamorphosis, 273, 274
Metaphysical Poets, The, 276–277
Mexico City Blues, 318
Michael, 131
Micromégas, 113
Middlemarch, 191
Midnight's Children, 326, 327
Midsummer Night's Dream, A, 87
Mill on the Floss, The, 190
Milton, John, 93–96, 119, 125
Minstrelsy of the Scottish Border, 132
Mīrāmār (Miramar), 309
Miscellaneous Observations on the Tragedy of Macbeth, 117
Misérables, Les, 154, 157
Miss Julie, 227
Moby Dick, 9, 163, 183, 186–187
Modernist movement, 266, 275
Modest Proposal, A, 108, 110
Molière (Jean-Baptiste Poquelin), 96–98
Moll Flanders, 105, 107
Molloy, 302
Monkey's Straw Raincoat and Other Poetry of the Basho School, The, 102
Montaigne, Michel de, 64–67
"Mont Blanc," 146
Moon Is Down, The, 294
Moon of the Caribbees, The, 279
Moor's Last Sigh, The, 327
More Pricks Than Kicks, 301
Morrison, Toni (Chloe Anthony Wofford), 11–12, 321–323
Mosses from an Old Manse, 159
Mountain Interval, 253
Mourning Becomes Electra, 280
Mowing, 252
Mr. Gilfil's Love-Story, 190
Mrs. Dalloway, 260, 264–265
Mrs. Warren's Profession, 236
MS. Found in a Bottle, 162
Mu'allaqāt, 38–39
Much Ado About Nothing, 87
Murasaki Shikibu, 45–46
Murder in the Cathedral, 277
Murders in the Rue Morgue, The, 160, 163
Murphy, 301–302
Mutanabbī, al-, 41–42
My Butterfly: An Elegy, 251
"My Kinsman, Major Molineux" 158

Mystery and Manners, 320
Mythe de Sisyphe, Le (*The Myth of Sisyphus*), 311
Myth, Literature, and the African World, 325

N

Naar vi døde vaagner (*When We Dead Awaken*), 202
Nabokov, Vladimir, 286–289
Nahan (*Call to Arms*), 258
Narrative of Arthur Gordon Pym, The, 163
Nashe, Thomas, 79
Native Son, 12, 303, 305
"Natural History of Massachusetts," 176
Naturalism, 226, 228
Neruda, Pablo (Neftalí Ricardo Reyes Basoalto), 12–13, 297–300
New Hampshire, 253
Nicholas Nickleby, 165
Nietzsche, Friedrich, 198, 254
Night and Day, 263
1984, 198, 295, 297
Nobel Prize for Literature, 11, 235, 237, 240, 243, 246, 253, 275, 277, 278, 280, 283, 286, 289, 292, 293, 297, 300, 303, 308, 310, 312, 314–315, 321, 323, 325
Northanger Abbey, 141, 142
North of Boston, 252, 253
Notre-Dame de Paris, 154, 156
Novelas exemplares (*Exemplary Stories*), 67, 68, 71–72
Numancia, La (*Numantia: A Tragedy*), 70

O

Ocho comedias, y ocho entremeses nuevos, 72
O'Connor, Flannery, 319–320
Odas elementales (*Elemental Odes*), 300
Odin den iz zhizni Ivana Denisovicha (*One Day in the Life of Ivan Denisovich*), 314
Odyssey, 17, 19–20, 21–22, 36, 122, 149, 270
Oedipe, 111
Oedipus at Colonus, 29
Oedipus the King, 28
Of Education, 95
Of Mice and Men, 293
Oku no hosomichi (*The Narrow Road to the Deep North*), 101, 102
Old Curiosity Shop, The, 165
Old Man and the Sea, The, 9, 292
"Old Manse, The," 158
Old Mortality, 134
Old Times on the Mississippi, 217, 220
"Old Woman's Tale, An," 158
Oliver Twist, 165
Omoo, 184
On a Grecian Urn, 150
One Day in the Life of Ivan Denisovich, 13, 314
O'Neill, Eugene, 278–280
One Writer's Beginnings, 308
On First Looking Into Chapman's Homer, 149
On Indolence, 150
On Melancholy, 150
On Shakespeare, 93

On the Constitution of the Church and State, 138
On the Morning of Christ's Nativity, 93
On the Power of Sound, 131
On the Road, 10, 316, 317, 318
Open Sore of a Continent, The, 325
Optimist's Daughter, The, 306
Oresteia, 24, 25
Orlando: A Biography, 265–266
Oroonoko, 100
Orwell, George (Eric Arthur Blair), 198, 295–297
Os Lusíadoas (The Lusiads), 62–64
Osorio, 137
Othello, 88
Our Mutual Friend, 167
Outsider, The, 305
Ovid, 79, 89

P

Pale Fire, 288
panegyrics, 41
Panghuang (Wandering), 258
Paracelsus, 168
Paradise, 322
Paradise Lost, 93, 95–96, 119
Paradise Regained, 93, 96
Paradiso, 54
Paradoxes and Problems, 92
Parc, Thérèse du, 97, 98
Pargiters: A Novel-Essay, The, 266–267
Parlement of Foules, The, 59
Pastiches et mélanges, 250
Pastures of Heaven, The, 293
Pauline: A Fragment of a Confession, 168, 171
Pearl, The, 294
Peer Gynt, 201–202
Penseroso, Il, 93
People of Hemsö, The, 228
Persians, 24
Persuasion, 142
Peste, La (The Plague), 310, 311–312
Petrarch, 55–57, 59
Phantasmagoria and Other Poems, 215
Phèdre, 98–99
Photographs, 306
Pickwick Papers, 165
Picture of Dorian Gray, The, 229, 231
Pierre, 187
Pippa Passes, 168
Pirandello, Luigi, 246–248
Plaideurs, Les, *(The Litigants)*, 98
Plaisirs et les jours, Les (Pleasures and Days), 249
Plan of a Dictionary of the English Language, The, 117
Playing in the Dark: Whiteness and the Literary Imagination, 322
Podorozhnik ("Plantain"), 282
Poe, Edgar Allan, 160–164, 194
Poema bez geroya ("Poem Without a Hero"), 283
Poems (Eliot), 276
Poems (Keats), 149
Poems (Milton), 93
Poems (Nabokov), 287
Poems (Poe), 162
Poems by Currer, Ellis and Acton Bell, 178
Poems, Chiefly in the Scottish Dialect, 127

Poems from Prison, 324, 325
Poems, in Two Volumes, 131
Poems upon Several Occasions, with A Voyage to the Island of Love, 100
Poetical Works (Coleridge), 138
Poetical Works (Shelley), 148
Poetics, 25, 28
Ponder Heart, The, 306
Portable Faulkner, The, 285
Portrait of a Lady, The, 225
Portrait of the Artist as a Young Man, A, 269, 270
Posteritati, 57
Posthumous Poems, 148
Pound, Ezra, 270, 289
Predlozheniye (*The Proposal*), 239
Prefaces Biographical and Critical, to the Works of the English Poets (*The Lives of the Poets*), 118
Prelude, or, Growth of a Poet's Mind, The, 130, 131
Presence of Grace and Other Book Reviews, The, 320
Pride and Prejudice, 141
Primero sueño (*First Dream*), 104
Princess Casamassima, The, 225
Prisonnière, La (*The Captive*), 251
Professions for Women, 266
Professor, The, 173, 174
Prometheus Unbound, 147
protest fiction, 12, 303
Proust, Marcel, 249–251, 301
Prozess, Der (*The Trial*), 271, 274, 275
Prufrock and Other Observations, 276
Pulitzer Prize, 11, 253, 279, 292, 293, 306, 322
Purgatorio, 54
Pushkin, Aleksandr Sergeyevich, 9, 151–154, 198, 289
Pygmalion, 237

Q

Qaṣr al-shawq (*Palace of Desire*), 308–309
Queen Mab, 146
Quentin Durward, 135
Quidditch Through the Ages, 329

R

Racine, Jean, 96–99, 111
Rādūbīs ("Radobis"), 308
Rape of Lucrece, The, 84, 89
Rasselas, 118
Raven, The, 162, 163
Raven and Other Poems, The, 163–164
Ravenna, 231
Real Life of Sebastian Knight, The, 288
Redburn, 184, 186
Redgauntlet, 135
Red Pony, The, 294
Red Room, The, 227
Reflections of an Unpolitical Man, 254
Rekviem ("Requiem"), 283
Remember, 322–323
Reminiscences, 262
Remorse, 137
Renaissance, 17, 54, 55, 73, 75, 119, 122
Requiem for a Nun, 286
Residencia en la tierra (*Residence on Earth*), 298, 299

Responsibilities: Poems and a Play, 245
Respuesta a sor Filotea de la Cruz ("Reply to Sister Filotea of the Cross"), 105
Review (Defoe), 106–107
Revolt of Islam, The, 147
Rhyme? and Reason?, 215
Richard III, 87
Right You Are (If You Think You Are), 248
Rimbaud, Arthur, 233–235
Rime, 56, 57
Rime in morte di Laura ("Poems After Laura's Death"), 57
Rime in vita di Laura ("Poems During Laura's Life"), 57
Rime of the Ancient Mariner, The, 130, 137
Ring and the Book, The, 171
River Intelligence, 217
Road, The, 324
Road to Wigan Pier, The, 296
Robber Bridegroom, The, 306
Robinson Crusoe, 105, 107
Rob Roy, 134
Roderick Hudson, 225
"Roger Malvin's Burial," 158
Roi s'amuse, Le (*The King's Fool*), 156
Romanciers naturalist, Les (*The Naturalist Novelists*), 223
Roman Elegies, 123
Roman expérimental, Le (*The Experimental Novel*), 223
Romeo and Juliet, 88
Romola, 191
Room of One's Own, A, 266
Roughing It, 215, 220
Rougon-Macquart series, 222–223
Rover, The, 100
Rowling, J. K., 13–14, 327–329
Roxana, 108
Rūmī, 9, 46–51
Rushdie, Sir Salman, 325–327
Ruslan i Lyudmila (*Ruslan and Ludmila*), 152

S

Sacred Wood, The, 276
Sad Fortunes of the Reverend Amos Barton, The, 190
Saint-Beuve, Charles-Augustin, 224
Saint Joan, 237
Salammbô, 200
Salomé, 232
Samarkand and Other Markets I Have Known, 325
Samson Agonistes, 93, 96
Sanditon, 142
Sartoris, 284
Satanic Verses, The, 325, 326
Scarlet Letter, The, 158, 159, 160, 186
Scenes of Clerical Life, 190
Schiller, Friedrich, 123
Schloss, Das (*The Castle*), 271, 274
Scott, Sir Walter, 132–135
Seagull, The, 239–240
Sea of Cortez, 294
Season of Anomy, 324
Sei personaggi in cerca d'autore (*Six Characters in Search of an Author*), 246, 248
Semanas del jardín ("Weeks in the Garden"), 72
Seniles, 57

Sense and Sensibility, 141
Sequel to Drum Taps, 182
Seven Against Thebes, 24
Seventh Heaven, The, 309
Shāh-nāmeh ("Book of Kings"), 42, 43–44, 45
Shaḥḥādh, Al-, (The Beggar), 309
Shakespeare, William, 9, 58, 78, 80–89, 93, 117, 118, 119, 125, 137, 227, 279
Shalimar the Clown, 327
Shame, 326
Shamela, 115
Shaw, George Bernard, 235–237, 279, 300
Shelley, Mary Wollstonecraft Godwin, 144, 146–147, 148
Shelley, Percy Bysshe, 144, 145–148, 162
Shepheardes Calender, The, 73–74
Shirley: A Tale, 174
"Shortest-Way With The Dissenters, The," 106
Shuttle in the Crypt, A, 324
Sidney, Sir Philip, 91
Sikes and Nancy, 167
Silas Marner, 191
Silent China: Selected Writings of Lu Xun, 259
Sisters, The, 268
Six Characters in Search of an Author, 246, 248
Sketches by "Boz," 165
Smarh, 199
Sobytiye ("The Event"), 288
Socrates, 18
Sodome et Gomorrhe (*Sodom and Gomorrah*), 251
Soldiers' Pay, 284
Solitude, 215
Solus Rex, 288
Solzhenitsyn, Aleksandr, 13, 312–316
Sonār Tarī (*The Golden Boat*), 242
Song of Solomon, 11, 322
Sophocles, 9, 24, 26–29
Sordello, 168
Sor Juana Ines de la Cruz, 103–105
Sound and the Fury, The, 285
Soyinka, Wole, 323–325
Speak, Memory, 289
Speak On, Memory, 289
Spenser, Edmund, 73–75, 80, 91
Spoils of Poynton, The, 225
S.S. Glencairn, 279
Stein, Gertrude, 289
Steinbeck, John, 293–294
Stella, 122
Step Across This Line, 327
Stephen Hero, 268, 269
"Steppe," 238
Storm Fear, 252
Strange Interlude, 279, 280
Stratfford, 168–170
Strindberg, August, 226–229
Strong Breed, The, 324
Sturm und Drang, 120
Subterraneans, The, 318
Sukkariyyah, Al-, (*Sugar Street*), 309
Sula, 322
Sun Also Rises, The, 291
Sun-down Poem, 182
Svarta Fanor ("Black Banners"), 229
Sweeney Agonistes, 277
Swift, Jonathan, 108–111, 237
Symbolist movement, 196, 233
Sympathy, 176

T

Tagore, Rabindranath, 240–243
Tale of a Tub, A, 108, 109
Tales of My Landlord, 134
Tales of the Grotesque and Arabesque, 163
Tale of Two Cities, A, 166, 167
Tales of Beedle the Bard, The, 329
Talisman, The, 135
Tamburlaine the Great, 79–80
Tamerlane, and Other Poems, 162
Taming of the Shrew, The, 87
Tar Baby, 322
Tempest, The, 88
Temps retrouvé, Le (*Time Regained*), 251
Tentation de Saint Antoine, La, 199
Tenure of Kings and Monarchs, The, 95
Thébaïde ou les frères ennemis, La ("The Thebaide or the Enemy Brothers"), 97
Thérèse Raquin, 222
Thomson, George, 128
Thoreau, Henry David, 158, 175–177, 318
Three Sisters, 240
Three Sunsets and Other Poems, 215
Through the Looking-Glass and What Alice Found There, 212, 214–215
Thulāthiyyah, Al-, (*The Cairo Trilogy*), 308–309
Time and the Place, and Other Stories, The, 309
Tintern Abbey, 130
Titus Andronicus, 87
To a God Unknown, 293
To a Nightingale, 150
To Autumn, 150
To Damascus, 228
Tod in Venedig, Der (*Death in Venice*), 253
To Have and Have Not, 291
Tolstoy, Leo, 9, 81, 196, 203–206
To Psyche, 150
Tortilla Flat, 293
To the Lighthouse, 260, 265, 266
To the Maiden in the East, 176
To the Man Sitting in Darkness, 221
Tour Through the Whole Island of Great Britain, 108
Tower, The, 245
Town & the City, The, 317
Trabaios de Persiles y Sigismunda, historia setentrional, Los ("The Labours of Persiles and Sigismunda: A Northern Story"), 73
Tradition and the Individual Talent, 276
Transatlantic Sketches, 225
Transcendentalism, 158–159, 175, 177, 207
Trato de Argel, El ("The Traffic of Algiers"), 70
Trial, The, 271, 274, 275
Trial from Pickwick, The, 166–167
Trials of Brother Jero, The, 324
Trionfi, 57
Tri sestry (*Three Sisters*), 240
Triumph of Life, The, 148
Troilus and Cressida, 88
Troilus and Criseyde, 60
Trois Contes, 200
True-Born Englishman, The, 106

Tuft of Flowers, The, 252
Turn of the Screw, The, 225
Twain, Mark, 215–222
Twenty Love Poems and a Song of Despair, 298
Twice-Told Tales, 158
Two Gentlemen of Verona, The, 87
Two Paths, 287
Two Stories, 263
Typee, 184, 186

U

Ugodilo zernyshko promezh dvukh zhernovov: ocherki izgnaniia ("The Little Grain Managed to Land Between Two Millstones: Sketches of Exile"), 316
Ulysses, 267, 268, 269, 270, 301
Uncle Tom's Children, 303–305
Uncle Vanya, 239
Une Saison en enfer (*A Season in Hell*), 234–235
United States of Lyncherdom, The, 221
Uno, nessuno e centomila (*One, None, and a Hundred Thousand*), 247
Unterhaltungen deutscher Ausgewanderten ("Conversations of German Émigrés"; *The German Refugees*), 123

V

Vanity of Duluoz, 318
Vanity of Human Wishes, The, 117–118
vecchi e I giovani, I (*The Old and The Young*), 247
Vecher ("Evening"), 281
Vega, Lope de, 76–78
Veinte poemas de amore y una canción desesperada (*Twenty Love Poems and a Song of Despair*), 298
Venus and Adonis, 84, 89
Verlaine, Paul, 233–234
Versuch, die Metamorphose der Pflanzen zu erklären ("Essay in Elucidation of the Metamorphosis of Plants"; *Goethe's Botany*), 122–123
Verses on the Death of Doctor Swift, 110
Verwandlung, Die (*Metamorphosis*), 273, 274
Viage del Parnaso, 72
Victorian age, 164, 168, 172, 188, 225
Villette, 174
Violent Bear It Away, The, 320
Virgil, 17, 33–38, 57, 73
Vishnyovy sad (*The Cherry Orchard*), 240
Vita nuova, La (*The New Life*), 52–53
Viva Zapata!, 294
V kruge pervom (*The First Circle*), 314
Voltaire, 111–114
Voyage, Le, 195
Voyage Out, The, 262–263

W

Waiting for Godot, 300, 302
Walden, 175, 176

Wallace, 125
Waltz Invention, The, 288
Wanderings of Oisin, and Other Poems, The, 244
War and Peace (*Voyna i mir*), 9, 204
Wasps, 30–31
Waste Land, The, 275, 276
Watt, 302
Waverley, 134, 135
Waves, The, 266
Wayward Bus, The, 294
Welles, Orson, 305
Welty, Eudora, 306–308
What Is Art? (*Chto takoye iskusstvo*), 206
What Maisie Knew, 225
What Moves at the Margin: Selected Nonfiction, 322
When Lilacs Last in the Dooryard Bloom'd, 182
Whirling Dervishes, 51
White-Jacket, 184–186
White Man, Listen!, 305
Whitman, Walt, 179–183, 318
Whoroscope, 302
Who's Got Game?: The Ant or the Grasshopper?, 322
Who's Got Game?: The Lion or the Mouse?, 322
Wide Net and Other Stories, The, 306
Widowers' Houses, 236
Wilde, Oscar, 229–233, 300
Wild Swans at Coole, The, 245
Wilhelm Meisters theatralische Sendung (*The Theatrical Mission of Wilhelm Meister*), 121
William Wilson, 163
Winding Stair, The, 245
Wings of the Dove, The 225
Winner Take Nothing, 291
Winter of Our Discontent, The, 294
Winter's Tale, The, 88
"Winter Walk, A," 176
Wise Blood, 319
Witness Tree, A, 253
Wolfe, Thomas, 317
Woman of No Importance, A, 232
Wood Demon, 239
Woolf, Viginia, 260–267
Wordsworth, William, 129–131, 136, 137, 275
Wright, Richard, 12, 303–305
Wuthering Heights, 10, 177, 179

Y

Years, The, 267
Yeats, William Butler, 243–246, 300
Yecao (*Wild Grass*), 258
Yevgeny Onegin, 152
You Must Set Forth at Dawn, 325
You Never Can Tell, 237
"Young Goodman Brown," 158

Z

Zadig, 113
Zapiski iz myortvogo doma (*The House of the Dead*), 197
Zapiski iz podpolya (*Notes from the Underground*), 197
Zauberberg, Der (*The Magic Mountain*), 253, 254–255
Zola, Émile, 222–224
Zweiter Römischer Aufenthalt ("Second Sojourn in Rome"), 124